Sustainability in Project Management

Sustainability in Project Management

Sustainability in Project Management

A Functional Approach

By

Anna Brzozowska, Arnold Pabian, and Barbara Pabian

CRC Press
Taylor & Francis Group
Boca Raton London New York

CRC Press is an imprint of the
Taylor & Francis Group, an **informa** business

First edition published 2021
by CRC Press
6000 Broken Sound Parkway NW, Suite 300, Boca Raton, FL 33487-2742
and by CRC Press
2 Park Square, Milton Park, Abingdon, Oxon, OX14 4RN

CRC Press is an imprint of Taylor & Francis Group, LLC

ISBN: 9780367518745 (hbk)
ISBN: 9780367696085 (pbk)
ISBN: 9781003055570 (ebk)

Typeset in Times
by KnowledgeWorks Global Ltd.

Contents

Introduction

The Earth is becoming less and less hospitable for people. Climate change, environmental pollution, depletion of natural resources, and decline in biodiversity threaten human existence. Our planet is losing its potential, heading toward the limits of nature's tolerance. In the past 50 years, the impact of human enterprise and human numbers on the Earth has been devastating. We are living at a time of peak consumption and peak waste (Thiele 2016: 200–201).

Research shows that mankind currently needs a regenerative capacity of 1.6 Earths to guarantee the supply of goods and services that are consumed on a global scale every year (WWF International, Living Planet Report 2016: 13). Not only the life and health of people, but also their economic activity depends on nature. Production of goods and services would not be possible without it. All economies of the world are based on natural resources. It is estimated that, globally, nature provides mankind with services worth approximately $125 quintillion a year (WWF International, Living Planet Report 2018: 18). However, the potential of these services is limited and constantly decreasing. The Earth is a very small place in the universe. So small that Carl Sagan compared it to a speck of dust suspended in a sunbeam (Rajasekhar, Challa, Vijaylakshmi and Rajyalakshmi 2019: 229). Not only is the Earth a small planet, but it is also an insulated system that is supplied with no external resources, except for solar energy.

Most producers and consumers ignore the dangers of the deteriorating condition of the Earth and its declining potential. They behave as if they lived in a world without limits. They exploit natural resources, consume water and energy, and pollute the environment on a massive scale. Profits and growth remain more important than environmental and social responsibility. This is confirmed by research. Studies show that corporate involvement in the sustainable development goals is still limited. The involvement is largely symbolic and intentional, rather than substantive (van der Waal and Thijssens 2020). Such behavior has a destructive effect on the biosphere, which people cannot fully control or understand. As D. Fogel emphasized, a modern industrial society can fail if it badly manages and overuses resources (Fogel 2016: 6). There is no business to be done on a dead planet (Jeanrenaud, Jeanrenaud and Gosling 2017: 7).

According to the Nobel Prize winner Paul Crutzen, as a result of human domination, urbanization, depletion of fossil fuels, and environmental pollution, we moved from the Holocene epoch to a new geological epoch called Anthropocene. In this epoch, the climate is changing rapidly, the oceans are acidifying, and biomass resources are dwindling. Not long ago there was talk of climate change, but today there is talk of a climate and environmental crisis. (WWF International, Living Planet Report 2016: 10). Environmental problems are accompanied by such social problems as poverty, exploitation, unemployment, crime, drug addiction, alcoholism, and social diseases, including epidemics.

To reduce environmental and social risks, people have been trying to implement the concept of sustainable development for over a quarter of a century. The results of numerous global and local initiatives are still insufficient. As G. Haugan notes, citing Albert Bartlett, adding the word "sustainable" to our vocabulary, to our reports, programs, and papers, to the names of our academic institutes and research programs, and to our community initiatives, is not sufficient to ensure that our society becomes sustainable (Haugan 2014: 9). Sustainability is not keeping pace with the speed and scale of the rise of environmental and social problems. Actions taken for many years in this area have not significantly improved the state of our planet. There are still too many declarations, reports, programs, and documents that use the words "sustainable" and "sustainability," but they translate into little concrete actions aimed to balance the intergenerational needs. Words and declarations are not enough to bring about positive changes. Specific actions are needed to accelerate progress in sustainable development. They are being undertaken around the world, but with different results. One of the most valuable initiatives is the adoption by the European Union in 2015 of a package of legislation on circular economy. A circular economy assumes reduction to a minimum of the impact of manufactured goods on the environment. It is based on selection of materials and methods of design in such a way that they can be reused. Production should use secondary raw materials and products should be repairable and recyclable. Although these propositions are correct, they have been adopted too late and their implementation has been stretched over time and has not yet produced satisfactory results.

According to Arnold Pabian, in order to stop the destructive human activity on Earth it is necessary to move quickly from the state of deep unsustainability to a state of mass sustainability. While in the current situation only very few producers and consumers genuinely respect the principles of sustainability, only very few people will not respect them in the conditions of mass sustainability (Pabian 2017b: 15). To achieve a state of mass sustainability, it is necessary to gradually transform the modern consumer society into a sustainable one. A sustainable society is, to a large extent, the opposite of a consumer society, which consists mainly of consumers and manufacturers who are antisocial and focused exclusively on achieving economic objectives (homo economicus). A sustainable society is based on sustainable production and sustainable consumption. The 3 × R (Reduce, Reuse, and Recycle) principle, which governs such a society, applies not only to the organizations that make up such a society, but also to private life. According to George Varghese and Lakshmi Viswanathan, the keys to a sustainable future are: awareness of the ecological limits, use of human ingenuity to design ways to live within the bounds, adoption of practices that reduce human imprint, and keeping "going green" central to decision-making (Varghese and Viswanathan 2019: 83). According to Leslie Paul Thiele, to live sustainably is to take responsibility for our lives and our communities (Thiele 2016: 201).

Projects and their management are a popular and widespread form of activity worldwide. Current estimates suggest that approximately 65% of all work being done in modern organizations today is project-based (Pinto and Patanakul 2017: 219). A large part of this huge number of projects is a major contributor to the deterioration of the condition of our planet. These are all those projects that, despite their significant contribution to the development of civilization, do not respect the principles of sustainable development. The problem is not just the final results of the projects, which take the form of various kinds of goods that are neither pro-environmental nor pro-social, but also the work involved in their production. One of the reasons for the low involvement of project teams in sustainability issues is their lack of knowledge in this area. According to Sara Marcelino-Sadaba, Luis Felipe Gonzalez-Jaen, and Arnaya Perez-Ezcurdia, organizations are now more and more willing to integrate sustainability into their activities. Project management can help make this process a success but little guidance is available on how to apply sustainability to projects (Marcelino-Sadaba, Gonzalez-Jaen and Perez-Ezcurdia 2015: 1–16). Similar conclusions were reached by Fabien Brones, Marly Monteiro de Carvalho, and Eduardo de Senzi Zancul: the analysis of the literature reveals that project management principles are addressed in a limited manner in specialized articles on eco-design (Brones, Carvalho and Zancul 2014: 106–118). To meet this need, this book contributes to filling the gap indicated by the above scientists. It presents a full and comprehensive approach to sustainability in project activities. This approach consists in introducing the principles of sustainability into all areas of these activities. This concept is called 4 × SUSTAINABILITY IN PROJECT ACTIVITIES (four times sustainability in project activities) which means:

SUSTAINABLE project team
SUSTAINABLE project team's equipment
SUSTAINABLE project execution
SUSTAINABLE projects.

In the proposed concept, the aim of project management is to achieve a situation where sustainable members of the project team, use sustainable resources to carry out the project in a sustainable way, achieving sustainable objectives. In this way, sustainability covers not only the results of project activities but also the execution of projects and the resources required. Sustainable project management defined in this manner is considered from the perspective of the management function, which also goes beyond the approaches found in the literature. The authors, who are involved in project management, usually consider projects divided into smaller or larger number stages, which include project commencement, preparation for implementation, implementation, supervision and control, and project completion. Although this type of sequence of activities can certainly be called organized activity, in many cases it is made too complicated and imprecisely linked to management, and important issues in this field of knowledge are omitted. Our functional approach to the problem of project management is a recognized and still valid concept that organizes management and facilitates the work of various types of managers. Our reference of this approach to project activities consists in identifying management with a number of basic functions performed by project managers, the implementation of which leads to the achievement of the set objectives. In our book, these functions take the form of sustainable planning, sustainable organizing, sustainable leadership/motivating, and sustainable controlling.

The book consists of five chapters. In Chapter 1, we justify tackling the topic of project management from the perspective of sustainability. The rationale behind this is the worsening condition of our planet, which results from increasing environmental and social threats. We start this chapter by listing and briefly characterizing such threats. Their analysis leads to a pessimistic conclusion: the Earth is in a state of deep ecological and social unsustainability. Then we move on to sustainable development, which is to be the lifeline for the Earth that is sinking deeper and deeper into the abyss of unsustainability. We present the origins of its development and important initiatives. These initiatives make a positive contribution to sustainable development, but are not keeping pace with the rate at which environmental and social threats are increasing. Humankind is moving ever faster to the limits of nature's tolerance. Can this process be stopped given the persistent pursuit of endless economic growth on a planet with limited natural resources? We have serious doubts about that. In Chapter 1, we therefore explain what contribution project management can make to sustainable development. Project management contributing to sustainable development is not easy. Numerous barriers make this task difficult, although there are also a number of factors that are conducive to it. It is important to cancel projects that have a destructive impact on the natural and human environment and to replace them with pro-environmental and pro-social projects.

Chapter 2 of the book focuses entirely on sustainable project stakeholders. We identify stakeholders primarily as people. Only people determine whether a project is sustainable or not. A project's contribution to sustainable development depends on people's ecological and social sensitivity, as well as on their competences in sustainability. The project manager and team members have a special role to play in this respect. Improper selection will result in disregard for pro-environmental and pro-social aspects of the project, which will be manifested by lack of actions in this area or by faking them. Bearing in mind the need for proper staffing of the project team, we present in this chapter the profiles of a sustainable manager and sustainable project team members, and suggest some solutions for their recruitment. As sustainable project staff are key to achieving sustainability objectives, more time and attention needs to be devoted to this issue in the project preparation phase.

Chapter 3 explains how to manage a project in a functionally sustainable way. We take as a basis the main management functions, which are its quintessence. These are planning, organizing, leading/motivating, and controlling. Although transfer of these functions to the project execution sphere is a challenge, we go further by linking them to sustainability. We explain how to use these functions to achieve project objectives that contribute to sustainable development. To distinguish them from classic functions, we give them the following names: sustainable planning, sustainable organizing, sustainable leadership/motivating, and sustainable controlling. Application of a functional approach to sustainable project management organizes this area and enables a clear and concrete presentation of the actions that need to be carried out in order to be successful and achieve sustainable objectives.

Chapter 4 contains a list and a brief description of sustainable physical resources that can be used in project management. This chapter was inspired by the fact that the literature on projects and management lacks an exhaustive and coherent list of sustainable goods. We felt it was inappropriate to encourage project executors to use sustainable goods without indicating their nature and types. That is why we decided to characterize them and show what benefits can be gained in the field of sustainable development by using them in project activities. This chapter plays an important role:

it presents a wide range of sustainable goods that project executors can use. In this chapter, we also explain the impact of sustainability solutions on project budgets and costs.

In Chapter 5, we focus on the use of IT systems and the Internet in sustainable project management. One should keep in mind that these are only tools that facilitate the work of project executors and their use should not create any barriers to sustainable development.

We are aware that implementation of the 4 × SUSTAINABILITY IN PROJECT ACTIVITIES in practice is difficult. It requires specialized knowledge and skills, which this book provides. The 4 × SUSTAINABILITY IN PROJECT ACTIVITIES concept that we propose is a standard that gives the right direction and sense to project activities in terms of sustainability. Coming even a little closer to this standard will be a success and will contribute to the improvement of the state of our planet and the societies that inhabit it. Sustainable project management will prevent damage to the environment and to human beings. Prevention is cheaper and more effective than repairing the damage done.

Undoubtedly, sustainability is becoming more and more boldly integrated into project activities. According to Carl Marnewick, project management is a discipline that is starting to focus on sustainability (Marnewick 2017: 1151–1166). This idea is complemented by Gilbert Silvius, who states that sustainability is a new school of thought in project management (Silvius 2017: 1479–1493). Consequently, this school must be developed. Practicing sustainability can be one of the most rewarding things we do – an opportunity for discovery, personal fulfillment, enriched community, and celebration (Thiele 2016: 204).

1 Project Management in the Face of Environmental and Social Threats

1.1 ENVIRONMENTAL AND SOCIAL THREATS IN THE CONTEMPORARY WORLD

Human beings are not only a source of progress, but they also pose a global threat to their own existence and that of future generations. Leslie Paul Thiele points at the increasing rate of these threats: in the past 50 years, population has more than doubled, increasing by 4 billion people. Carbon dioxide emissions have tripled, paper consumption has quadrupled, fertilizer use has quintupled, and the consumption of other natural resources has also increased to patently unsustainable levels. Stocks of natural resources are precipitously falling. Pollution sinks are steadily filling and they are overflowing (Thiele 2016: 200–201). The growing environmental and social threats in the modern world are pushing the limits of nature's tolerance. This has a negative impact on the state of the Earth, which K. Boulding compares to a spaceship. This spaceship is an insulated system supplied with no external resources other than solar energy (Rogall 2010: 134). The increasing threats may cause a failure that the human race is unlikely to survive. The Earth is a closed thermodynamic system that does not grow materially. The damage caused to the Earth by humans is irreversible and acts to their disadvantage. Humans' relationship with nature is asymmetrical: nature can exist without humans, but humans cannot survive without nature. Destruction of the planet also means destruction of people.

Currently, the deterioration of our planet is accelerating. The world is changing at an exponential pace: in the 10 years that are yet to come, more can happen than in the 100 years that have passed (Bendyk 2013: 7). According to Nikos Avlonas and George P. Nassos, the most destructive impact on Earth in the entire history of man has taken place over the last 100–200 years: human life has been on Earth for about 50,000 years. For the first 49,800 years, man has lived in the open fields; in the mountains; in the forests; next to lakes, rivers, and oceans; or in the savannas. In the past 100–200 years, man has lived in cities consisting of brick, concrete, steel, and glass. Genealogically, this is not normal (Avlonas and Nassos 2014: 249). This destructive impact deepens, leading to an escalation of environmental and social threats.

Numerous environmental and social threats and their destructive impact on the state of the Earth are noticed by many authors dealing with sustainability. Michael Lenox and Aaron Chatterji addressed this problem in the following manner: The Earth is in trouble. The existential threat posed by a changing and environmental "unsustainability" is leading to dire predictions about the future of its land, its sea, and its people. The threat will likely unfold slowly, but once it grains momentum, it might be impossible to stop. The impact could be enormous, as significant as war or plague; in fact, wars and plagues may be direct outcomes of climate change and environmental degradation (Lenox and Chatterji 2018: 4). No less pessimistic picture of reality is expressed in the opinion of Jerry A. Carbo, Viet T. Dao, Steven J. Haase, M. Blake Hargrove, and Ian M. Langella "From an ecological standpoint, the current business methods of marketing, extraction, production, and disposal push us away from a sustainable planet and towards a catastrophic level of destruction. Business practices are currently leading to an environment that is not conducive to human life in the long run and ecological problems that are leading to sicknesses and deaths in the short run" (Carbo, Dao, Haase Hargrove and Langella 2018: 9). Frank-Martin Belz and Ken Peattie describe the hazards as follows: we inhabit a planet that must accommodate 75 million new citizens every year, that suffers enduring problems linked to poverty and inequality, and that faces growing concerns about the future impact of climate change and the likelihood of related crises in food, water, health, and ecology. Addressing these challenges requires action to achieve substantive reforms and ultimately to achieve a fundamental transformation within many spheres of human activity (Belz and Peattie 2010: 13).

At the root of humans' predatory activities lies misplaced anthropocentrism, according to which humans are the center and objective of the universe and the masters of nature who have the right to make all kinds of changes in it that are beneficial to them. This attribution of a superior value to humans marginalizes the natural world, giving nature a secondary, instrumental function, and making it totally subordinate to mankind. This extreme attitude has proved to be a threat to the environment and the social order in the long term. Given the increasing threats, the concept of balanced biocentrism is more progressive, as it cares about and protects nature and preserves the diversity of life on our planet. According to biocentrism, animals, plants, and ecosystems should be treated according to similar moral standards as humans. This is because the entire economy depends on the richness of nature and people's well-being depends on a stable climate, healthy soils and forests, and the richness of oceans and rivers.

We are now living in the time of the so-called "Great Acceleration," which is an unprecedented phenomenon in the 4.5 billion years long history of our planet. During this time, humans have led the Earth to the brink of exhaustion (WWF International, Living Planet Report 2018: 6). The changes that have taken place over the last 50 years have unbalanced the Earth's ecosystem. The more important ones are shown in the following box.

CHANGES WITH A NEGATIVE IMPACT ON THE EARTH'S ECOSYSTEM OCCURRING DURING THE LAST 50 YEARS

The population has doubled.
The volume of the world economy has quadrupled.
The volume of trade increased tenfold.

Plant production tripled and raw wood harvesting increased by 45%.
Humans have transformed 75% of the Earth's surface.
Earth's productivity has decreased in 23% of the global land area.
85% of wetlands have been lost.
The increase in the level of the oceans has reached the rate of +3 mm per year.
The average annual temperature increase has reached +0.2 degrees Celsius.
By 2016, 559 out of 6,190 domesticated breeds of farm animals had been extinct.
The range of flood and hurricane hazards currently covers 300 million people.

Source: Own work based on https://eizba.pl/raport-green-generation-2020-green-e-commerce/.

Erling Holden, Kristin Linnerud, David Banister, Valeria Jana Schwanitz, and August Wierling list the following types of planetary boundaries (Holden, Linnerud, Banister, Schwanitz and Wierling 2018: 81–82):

- climate change;
- loss of biosphere integrity (biodiversity loss and extinctions);
- nitrogen and phodsphorus flows to the biosphere and ocean (nitrogen and phosphorus);
- land-system change;
- atmospheric aerosol loading;
- stratospheric ozone depletion;
- ocean acidification;
- global freshwater use and the global hydrological cycle;
- chemical pollution and the release of novel entities.

According to W. Steffen et al., the first four of these boundaries have already been crossed (Steffen et al. 2015: 736–746). Sally Jeanrenaud and Jean-Paul Jeanrenaud link environmental and social threats to the challenges to sustainable development and specify (Jeanrenaud, Jeanrenaud and Gosling 2017: 9–10, 18–19):

a. key environmental challenges: climate, water, biodiversity, resource depletion, and waste
b. key social challenges: population dynamics, poverty and inequality, exploitation, and well-being

Citing the general classifications of environmental and social threats does not provide sufficient motivation to engage in sustainable development, including in the course of project management. Therefore, these threats are discussed in more detail later in this chapter.

ENVIRONMENTAL THREATS IN THE CONTEMPORARY WORLD

Exhaustion of non-renewable natural resources
Atmospheric pollution
Soil pollution
Water pollution
Greenhouse effect
Reduced biodiversity
Decreasing forest area
Landfilling, illegal landfills
Environmental disasters
Neglected industrial areas and devastated post-mining areas
Poaching and trade in endangered animal and plant species
Development of tourism and collection of natural souvenirs

Source: Own work.

Exhaustion of Non-Renewable Natural Resources

According to the research, the reserves of such elements as iron, lead, copper, and gold are only sufficient for a dozen to several dozen years. Easily accessible and cheaply exploited oilfields will run out in about 20–30 years. Even now, extraction of various types of minerals is becoming more and more difficult, expensive, and energy-intensive. The existing deposits are characterized by a decreasing content of the elements sought, which results in an increase in the areas intended for extraction. In some countries, mining concessions cover a fifth or even a third of the country's territory (e.g. Peru, Honduras) (http://surowce.igo.org.pl/o-surowcach/surowce-na-wyczerpaniu/). Extraction and consumption of natural resources is accelerating. Earth Overshoot Day, which is the day on which the world consumes its annual resources, is rapidly moving in an unfavorable direction. In 1970, the day was on 29 December, while in 2018 it was 5 months earlier, on 1 August. This means that the Earth's inhabitants used up the resources theoretically sufficient for a year in just 7 months (https://businessinsider.com.pl/technologie/nauka/koncza-sie-zasoby-naturalne-ziemi-ostrzega-bank-hsbc/s1w7cxj;http://surowce.igo.org.pl/o-surowcach/zasoby-odnawialne-i-nieodnawialne).

Atmospheric Pollution

Atmospheric pollution is caused by burning fossil fuels, such as coal and oil, methane and freon emissions, forest burning and fires, and automobiles. The main sources of emissions are car exhaust gases, cement and metallurgical dust, power engineering, local boiler plants, domestic furnaces, and fly ash. The upper layers of the atmosphere are polluted by chlorofluorocarbons, which contribute to ozone layer depletion and an increase in the penetration of harmful ultraviolet radiation (https://science.sciencemag.org/content/347/6223/1259855). According to World Health Organization (WHO) reports, 7 million people in the world die prematurely due to air pollution every year. In recent years, as much as 90% of all people have breathed contaminated air (https://www.kopalnia.pl/kopalnia-wiedzy/jakosc-powietrza-na-swiecie-i-w-europie-gdzie-znajdziesz-najczystrze-powietrze-fkq3).

Soil Pollution

A manifestation of soil pollution is its acidification or alkalization, as well as accumulation of pesticides, nitrites, and organophosphorus compounds. This is due to the use of mineral fertilizers, especially nitrogen and potassium fertilizers in agriculture, and to the emission of large quantities of gases into the atmosphere (sulfur dioxide, nitrogen oxides, and carbon dioxide). They reach the soils in the form of acid rain and so-called dry precipitation. More than three quarters of the Earth's total land area has already been degraded and this figure could increase to as much as 90% by 2050. An area the size of half the surface of the European Union is degraded annually. Increasingly growing cities, deforestation, and uncontrolled agricultural development are contributing to this problem. Cultivated fields and pastures currently occupy more than one third of the Earth's land surface. It is the agricultural sector that will suffer the most from the progressive degradation of land as global harvests are projected to decrease by around 10% by 2050. The global consequences are expected to be even greater. Shrinking resources of "good" lands will force migration or forced displacement of as many as approximately 700 million people globally (http://naukawpolsce.pap.pl/aktualnosci/news%2C30020%2Cnawet-90-proc-powierzchni-ladowej-ziemi-moze-ulec-degradacji-do-2050-roku).

Water Pollution

Water and land transport, use of pesticides and fertilizers in agriculture, discharge of sewage, municipal, industrial and even radioactive waste into the seas, rivers, and lakes, as well as excess heat cause adverse changes in the physical, chemical, and bacteriological properties of water. These harmful factors limit or prevent the use of water for drinking and commercial purposes. In many places, eutrophication of aquatic environments occurs (the effect of penetration of phosphorus and nitrogen compounds, called biogens). Biogens are essential for proper functioning and growth of plants and animals; however, in excessive quantities, they are harmful and cause growth of cyanobacteria and algae, reduce photosynthesis, and create so-called dead zones in seas. Resources of clean drinking water in many parts of the world are shrinking. It is expected that by 2025, as many as two out of three people will live in areas affected by serious water shortages (http://surowce.igo.org.pl/o-surowcach/zasoby-odnawialne-i-nieodnawialne/).

Greenhouse Effect

The greenhouse effect is the increase in the temperature of the planet due to the presence of greenhouse gases in its atmosphere. One of those gases is carbon dioxide. There is already 40% more carbon dioxide accumulated in the Earth's atmosphere than in the industrial age and its quantity continues to increase. The greenhouse effect is also caused by methane as a byproduct of agriculture and by fluorocarbons, which are a part of industrial gases. Since the beginning of the previous century, the temperature of the atmosphere has increased by 0.89 degrees Celsius. Temperature increases lead to climate change, including extreme weather events such as very high or low air temperatures, heavy rainfall, heavy snowfall, hurricanes, and dense fogs. These phenomena in turn cause droughts, fires, floods, and other damages. A warmer climate is also conducive to the growth of pests and the spread of new diseases among humans and animals. The greenhouse effect accelerates the melting of glaciers, leading to rising sea and ocean levels. The Arctic ice cap has been melting at the speed of 3.8% per decade since 1979. It is predicted that due to the melting of glaciers, there will be an increase in the sea and ocean level in the range of 26–81 cm by the end of this century (Bendyk 2013: 11, 12). This threatens island countries, as well as the lower coastal areas of the mainland. The largest emitters of greenhouse gases in the world are China, the USA, and the European Union. In the European Union, the following sectors are responsible for greenhouse gas emissions: energy generation (80.7%), agriculture (8.72%), industrial processes and product consumption (7.82%), and waste management (2.75%) (https://www.europarl.europa.eu/news/pl/headlines/society/20180301STO98928/infografika-emisje-gazow-cieplarnianych-w-unii-europejskiej).

Reduced Biodiversity

Reduced biodiversity means extinction of hundreds of plant and animal species, loss of biological diversity, and disappearance of ecosystems. Between 1970 and 2014, the global vertebrate population decreased on average by 60% and the size of freshwater species population decreased by 83% (https://www.green-projects.pl/najwieksze-zagrozenia-dla-srodowiska-plastik-zmiany-klimatu-bioroznorodnosc/). In Europe, 335 species of vertebrates, 38% of European bird species, 45% of butterfly species, and 800 plant species are threatened with extinction (http://jestemnaptak.pl/artykul/utrata-bioroznorodnosci).

Decreasing Forest Area

Currently, the total area of forests in the world is equal to approximately 3,999,134,000 hectares. There is 0.62 ha of forest per one inhabitant of the Earth. Human activity and other factors cause the area of the planet's forests to shrink. Annual forest felling reduces their resources by about 3,713,681,000 m^3 (https://www.bdl.lasy.gov.pl/portal/lasy-na-swiecie). Research shows that 3.6 million hectares of rainforest disappeared in 2018. Most of these forests were cleared in Brazil (1.35 million hectares) (https://forsal.pl/artykuly/1409732,tempo-wycinki-lasow-deszczowych-na-swiecie-raport.html).

Losses associated with the loss of forests are estimated at 2,000–5,000 billion dollars per year, or 7% of the global GDP (https://ziemianarozdrozu.pl/encyklopedia/49/niszczenie-lasow-tropikalnych). The loss of forest area is the consequence of tree felling for manufacturing and heating purposes, land acquisition in connection with industrialization and urbanization, and fires. An example is the fires that broke out in South America in July 2019, destroying large areas of the Amazon rainforest which is the "Earth's green lungs." It produces a significant proportion of the oxygen that is necessary for life on our planet. It is also the world's largest and most species-rich forest area with millions of animal and plant species.

Landfilling, Illegal Landfills

Waste is a serious environmental problem. Products are thrown away, not necessarily because they are worn out, but because they do not have the right color or style in fashion. Products are also disposed of because they cannot be repaired or because the cost of repair often exceeds the cost of purchasing a new product (Ekstrom 2015: 1). The harmfulness of waste depends on its type. For example, most mobile phones contain mercury, lead, cadmium, nickel, chromium, and bromine compounds. If these substances get into the human body, they cause a lot of damage. Mercury damages the nervous system and the kidneys, lead damages the brain, and cadmium damages the liver. The effects of other substances are equally dangerous to the body. One of the most dangerous wastes is plastic. Every year, 100 kg of plastic garbage is produced per every inhabitant of Europe and North America. About 100 million tons of plastic garbage floats on the surface of the oceans. Some of them decompose very slowly, turning into fine dust that enters the digestive systems of fish and other marine animals. It is estimated that about 1 million animals die in the oceans every year because of plastic. The world's largest landfill site was created by sea currents. The drifting Great Pacific Garbage Patch has the area of about 1.6 million square kilometers. This garbage was produced by people and nature has only caused it to gather in one place. On land, too, people huge landfills. An example is the Apex Regional landfill in Las Vegas, with the area of 890 hectares, supplied with 9,000 tons of municipal waste per day (https://polskatimes.pl/te-wysypiska-smieci-sa-tak-wielkie-ze-zmiescilaby-sie-w-nich-polska-5-razy/ar/c11-13850860). Every year, more than 500 billion plastic film packaging is disposed of in landfills around the world (https://www.wfosgw.poznan.pl/kalendarz-ekologiczny/). Plastic film packaging goes not only to landfills, seas, and oceans, but also to other water bodies. They block the flow in rivers, canals, and water mains. Nature is unable to cope with the increasing amount of plastic garbage, because its resistance to the decomposition process is extremely high: degradation of a typical disposable plastic bag takes up to several hundred years, while its average use time is only 25 minutes. Waste spoils landscapes and, as mentioned earlier, is a deadly threat to animals. Animals enter into abandoned bottles and other packaging and often are unable get out. They also eat some waste, which makes them sick. People even litter the outer space. Particularly dangerous in the outer space are waste fractions with size less than or equal to 1 cm. They move at the speed of several kilometers per second and can damage space stations.

Environmental Disasters

Environmental disasters cause unfavorable changes in the natural environment. They destroy flora and fauna, making their survival impossible. Events of this type occur every year. For example, in 2018 there was a leakage of sulfur dioxide into the atmosphere from chemical plants in Armyansk on the Crimean Peninsula, which caused acid rain that destroyed many living organisms. There was also an oil spill into the Magdalena River in Colombia (the content of 600–24,000 barrels of oil was released the water causing the death of many thousands of animals and poisoning hundreds of people). Also, a Sanchi tanker sank in the East China Sea, with almost 1 million barrels of condensed oil on board. The year 2019 was no better than the preceding year. The sinking Grande America carrier vessel in the Bay of Biscay leaked fuel and hundreds of tons of environmentally harmful substances. Similarly, at least 60 tons of heavy fuel oil leaked when the Salomon Trader bulk carrier was pushed aground by a tropical cyclone. In Brazil, in the Minas Gerais region, the dam of a local iron mine burst. The resulting giant river of mud killed hundreds of people and destroyed buildings and nature (https://wlaczoszczedzanie.pl/ekozagrozenia/katastrofy-ekologiczne/najwieksze-katastrofy-ekologiczne-na-swiecie/).

Neglected Industrial Areas and Devastated Post-Mining Areas

Neglected industrial areas are various types of buildings, warehouses, furnaces, silos, roads, and yards that have lost their original functions. Unprotected industrial buildings and landscapes, exposed to different temperatures, rain, snow, and wind, disturb the functional, aesthetic, urban-planning, and architectural spatial order of their surroundings. Devastated post-mining areas are created as a result of mining activities. They comprise excavations, dumping grounds, and bings that change the original form of the ground, cause the destruction of soil layers, and ground and underground ecosystems, and disturb hydrological conditions.

Poaching and Trade in Endangered Animal and Plant Species

Land poaching (capture and killing of mammals and birds), water poaching (capture and killing of fish and other marine organisms), and forest damage (theft of timber, illegal logging, and devastation of flora and fauna) cause a decline of populations of endangered animal and plant species. This harmful activity involves large-scale smuggling and trade in endangered animal and plant species.

Development of Tourism and Collection of Natural Souvenirs

Mass tourism has certain dysfunctions that contribute to environmental devastation. Increased traffic on tourist trails and in resorts located in attractive natural areas involves disturbing the peace of animals, destroying vegetation, and littering. Another negative phenomenon accompanying tourism is the depletion of natural resources caused by collecting so-called natural souvenirs from local nature. During their domestic and foreign trips, tourists collect and bring to their place of residence sand, gravel, stones, shells, fragments of volcanic rocks, fragments of plants, small animals, plants, and other parts of nature, treating them as souvenirs from their travels. Like tourism, collecting natural souvenir is a mass phenomenon and leads to devastation of the natural environment (Pabian, Pabian and Brzeziński 2020).

SOCIAL THREATS IN THE CONTEMPORARY WORLD

Social diseases
Exploitation
Poverty and deprivation
Unemployment
Consumerism
International population migrations

Source: Own work.

Social Diseases

Social diseases are a consequence of the development of civilization and, therefore, they are also called diseases of civilization. They are divided into direct (which can be prevented by maintaining proper lifestyle and hygiene) and indirect (which people have no influence on). Direct social diseases are the result of lack of physical activity, poorly balanced diet (rich in sugars, animal fats, salt, highly processed products, and stimulants), as well as stress, addiction, or workaholism. Indirect social illnesses develop as a result of harmful factors such as smog, soil and water pollution, noise, ionizing radiation, and other pathogenic agents. The most common social diseases are: obesity, diabetes, diarrhea, constipation, stomach and duodenal ulcers, heartburn, hemorrhoids, allergies, respiratory tract diseases, cancer, and mental illnesses. This list should be expanded by addictions, such as alcoholism, drug addiction, anorexia, and bulimia, as well as depression, affective diseases, personality disorders, and neuroses. All these diseases are spreading globally. Although they are not contagious, they lead to disability and in over 80% to premature death (https://www.medonet.pl/zdrowie,choroby-cywilizacyjne—przyczyny-i-leczenie,artykul,1735188.html). Hundreds of millions of people suffer from social diseases globally. Diabetes is a good example. Currently, about 422 million people in the world have diabetes. It is estimated that this number will more than double in the next 20 years. A majority, i.e. 90%, of diabetics, suffer from type 2 diabetes, which is mainly due to an unbalanced diet and low physical activity (Koprowska 2019: 134). The care and treatment of ill people requires a huge amount of work on the part of family members and the health care system, as well as huge funds from public and private sources.

Exploitation

Exploitation takes different forms. There are 21 million victims of forced labor worldwide resulting from human trafficking, slavery, bonded labor, and prostitution. They generate USD 150 billion in illegal profits (Jeanrenaud, Jeanrenaud and Gosling 2017: 19). Forcing children to work is also a form of exploitation. According to the International Labor Organization (ILO), 168 million children worldwide are engaged as child laborers and more than half of these are engaged in hazardous work (…). According to the Department of Labor, there are nearly 140 products from 75 countries listed as products produced by child labor. These products are used throughout the globe including in developed countries (Carbo, Dao, Haase, Hargrove and Langella 2018: 68).

Poverty and Deprivation

The number of people who live below the international poverty line (less than $1.9 per day) worldwide has reached 783 million. The areas of greatest poverty are located in South Asia and sub-Saharan Africa. The consequences of poverty include hunger, malnutrition, limited access to education and other services, and often also social discrimination and exclusion (http://www.un.org.pl/cel1#). Poverty significantly affects children. According to UNICEF data, by 2030, as many as 167 million children will live in poverty (https://businessinsider.com.pl/finanse/raport-unicef-na-temat-ubostwa-wsrod-dzieci/rnrbm9c).

Unemployment

The ILO estimates that 188 million of the 5.7 billion people in the world who are of working age (over 15 years old) will be unemployed by 2020. A further 165 million can only count on a few hours' employment per week, which will not provide them with a decent standard of living as a result of too low wages (https://www.money.pl/gospodarka/mop-25-mln-bezrobotnych-wiecej-na-swiecie-szokujace-6470438699955841a.html). The unemployment rate in various countries of the world ranges from over 30% to a fraction of a percent. Namibia, Bosnia and Herzegovina, and Angola face very high unemployment rates that exceed 30% (https://pl.tradingeconomics.com/country-list/unemployment-rate). Unemployment has negative social, psychological, and economic consequences. The social and psychological consequences affect the unemployed people. Lack of livelihood, loss of work skills, deterioration of health, excess of free time, and tendency to engage in pathological behavior are examples of social problems faced by the unemployed members of the society. Unemployment has a negative impact on the psyche of people who cannot find work. This is reflected in such conditions as stress, depression, helplessness, loss of self-esteem, and inclination to commit suicide. Unemployment also affects the economy. Its economic consequences include: reduced tax and social security revenues, development of the shadow economy, and reduction of total demand for goods and services (https://mfiles.pl/pl/index.php/Skutki_bezrobocia, accessed on 13 March 2020).

Consumerism

Consumerism involves a lifestyle in which happiness is achieved by purchasing all kinds of products and services without moderation. As these purchases far exceed the needs of individuals, a part of them are never used. At the heart of consumerism is the conviction that possession of objects reflects social status and improves the quality of life. Consumerism often takes the form of shopaholism, i.e., an obsession with shopping. This is not only a social problem that requires treatment after consultation with a psychologist or a psychiatrist, but also an environmental problem. In order to meet the needs resulting from over-consumption, it is necessary to produce much more goods and thus use more raw materials, energy, water, and other inputs. For example, the production of a desktop computer and a monitor requires, on average, 1,500 liters of water, 5,300 kilowatt-hours of energy, 240 kilograms of fossil fuels, and 22 kg of chemicals. In total, this amounts to 1.8 tons of raw materials (http://surowce.igo.org.pl/o-surowcach/surowce-na-wyczerpaniu/). Also, more waste and rubbish is produced and have to be disposed of.

International Population Migrations

International migration, especially immigration involving the movement of people from one country to another in order to settle or stay for a long time, is a serious problem in the 21st century. The European Union is an excellent example. As of 1 January 2018, the population of immigrants in the European Union totaled 22.3 million people (4.4% of the 512.4 million of its residents). In 2017, 2.4 million immigrants from third world countries arrived in the European Union. In relation to the population, the highest immigration rate in at that time was in Malta (46 immigrants per 1,000 residents) and Luxembourg (41 immigrants per 1,000 residents) (https://ec.europa.eu/eurostat/statistics-explained/pdfscache/14236.pdf). The main reasons for emigration are to ensure safety and improve the material situation. International population migration poses many problems. Formalization of resettlement, feeding the arriving population, housing, social assistance, work, language learning, and cultural assimilation are all issues that require the involvement of thousands of people and substantial funding in the host countries.

Implementation of related projects and management of these activities may contribute to elimination or reduction of the environmental and social risks listed in this chapter. It is argued that projects play a crucial role in realizing sustainability in organizations and in society, and that project and program managers are significantly placed to make contributions to sustainable management practices (Silvius, Kampinga, Paniagus and Mooi 2017: 1133–1150). Implementing projects in accordance with the principles of sustainable development means responsibly shaping the biosphere and the anthroposphere, thus ensuring social stability, economic well-being, and welfare of individuals.

1.2 SUSTAINABLE DEVELOPMENT AND ITS CHALLENGES

The history of modern environmental movement began over 50 years ago. It was about 50 years ago when we started to read books and articles about the environment, with *Silent Spring* by Rachel Carson (1962), being one of the first important books. Many other outstanding books about the environment have been written since, such as *The Ecology of Commerce* by Paul Hawken (1993) and *Natural Capitalism* by Hawken, Lovins and Lovins (2008) (Avlonas and Nassos 2014: 3). During this period of over 50 years, many different types of conferences, conventions, and summits on sustainable development have been held around the world. They were aimed not only at working out the theoretical foundations of sustainable development, but above all at implementing pro-environmental and pro-social programs on a global scale. The conferences, conventions, and summits were attended by heads of state, foreign delegations, representatives of business and various non-profit organizations, environmentalists, and scientists. The result is a wide variety of documents, declarations, and programs designed to eliminate or stop the growing environmental and social risks. Although these objectives have not been fully achieved, the advisability of these meetings cannot be questioned. They have certainly promoted the idea of sustainable development worldwide and have initiated many international and local activities aimed at protecting the environment and respecting human rights and dignity.

The first part of this section briefly presents the history of sustainable development, the important findings, and the initiatives in this area. The second part of the section focuses on the term "sustainability" and explains its essence.

Origins and Brief History of Sustainable Development

The era of sustainable development started in the 1960s. However, its origins can be traced back to the 18th century when, in 1713, Hans Carl von Carlowitz in his treatise *Die Syvicultura Oeconomica oder Haußwirthliche Nachricht und Naturmäßige Anweisung zur Wilden Baum-Zucht* formulated the concept of forest durability. He drew attention to the necessity of such use of the forest areas that would prevent their over-exploitation. He called for renewal of forests destroyed by excessive felling to supply the industry, for felling only as many trees as can grow back in a given location and securing tree seeds for use in forest plantations. At the beginning of the 19th century, this original concept of sustainability was promoted by all German forestry universities. As German forestry was widely recognized all over the world at that time, the concept was taken up by the academic community in many other countries (Łepko 2017: 45).

At the end of the 20th century, as a result of the outbreak of the so-called ecological revolution, not only the need to protect the nature endangered by the effects of industrialization was noticed. The concept of sustainable development began to extend to the social, economic, and environmental aspects of the functioning of societies and organizations. The interest in this issue was fostered by the spread of the cognition method based on a systemic and holistic approach (which assumed that the reality consists of interrelated elements) and by the gradual dissemination of pro-health and pro-environmental ethics in consumer behavior.

In 1968, the Intergovernmental Conference of Experts on the Scientific Basis for Rational Use and Conservation of the Resources of the Biosphere (Paris, France, 4–13 September) launched the Man and Biosphere program, which aimed to create sustainable relationships between people and the global ecological system. The World Network of Biosphere Reserves was created, which today comprises 701 sites in 124 countries.

The breakthrough was the Stockholm UN conference held in 1972, whose motto was "Only one Earth." During the conference, the model of sustainable development was first defined in a declaration of a UN Convention. This concept has been used in the context of the prospects for the existence and development of the human species on planet Earth. In the same year, the report of the Roman Club by Donell H. Meadows, Dennis L. Meadows, Jørgen Randers, and William W. Behrens, titled "Limits to Growth," was published. It contains an analysis of the future of humanity in view of the predicted increase in the number of inhabitants of the Earth and the depletion of natural resources. Eventually, the sustainable development model was further refined in 1987 in the report "Our Common Future" by The World Commission on Environment and Development, also known as the Brundtland Commission due to the name of Gro Harlem Brundtland, a Norwegian politician who formed and subsequently chaired this commission on behalf of the UN Secretary-General. According to the definition that was adopted, the goal of sustainable development is to fulfill the developmental aspirations of the present generation, in a way that enables fulfillment of the same aspirations by the next generations. This definition is based on two basic concepts: "needs" (especially of poor countries) and "limitations" (environmental capacity). The main message of the "Our Common Future" report is as follows: management should use methods and rates that preserve the planet's well-being and meet the present needs without depriving future generations of the ability to meet their needs. The level of civilization can be maintained provided that proper management is applied in the areas of economy, environment, and social well-being. Threats that may have an adverse impact on the development of civilization were also identified. These include the loss of areas suitable for agricultural production (as a result of soil erosion and desertification), shrinkage of forest resources (as a result of excessive felling), atmospheric pollution (as a result of excessive burning of fossil fuels, leading to the greenhouse effect and acid rain), and dependence of industry on natural resources. The new paradigm of sustainable development links economics and ecology to social challenges, progress, efficiency, and the possibility of further economic development with the preservation and protection of the goods that make it possible. At the same time, as the latest scientific research shows, social sustainability is less explored than the economic and environmental pillars of sustainability (Amrutha and Geetha 2020).

In 1992, during the Earth Summit in Rio de Janeiro (United Nations Conference on Environment and Development), the Rio Declaration on Environment and Development was announced, which contained 27 principles concerning protection of the environment and rational use of the Earth's resources. The Declaration emphasized that people are the most important component in the process of

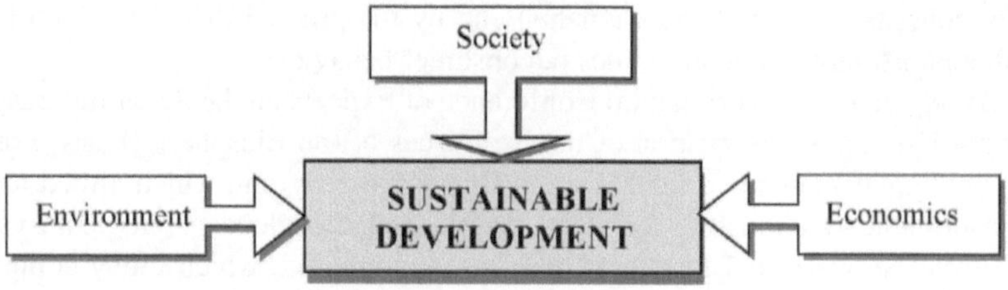

FIGURE 1.1 The concept of sustainable development. (Own work.)

sustainable development. They have the right to healthy and creative lives in harmony with nature. People also bear responsibility. Humans are responsible for ensuring that their activities not only do not damage the environment, but also fairly combine the developmental and environmental needs of the present and future generations. An important factor for achieving sustainable development is participation of women in environmental and developmental management, as well as the exploitation of the potential (creativity, ideals, and courage) of young people. There is an urgent need to take action to eradicate poverty in order to reduce differences in the standard of living. International cooperation should be conducted in a spirit of global partnership in order to preserve, protect, and restore the health and integrity of the Earth's ecosystem. An important part of such cooperation is scientific exchange and improvement of the process of development, adaptation, dissemination, and transfer of technology. Countries should raise awareness and increase public participation in solving environmental problems by creating broad access to information. These actions must be supported by international law that takes into account liability and compensation for adverse effects of environmental damage. In the event of any disaster or hazard that may have a sudden and harmful impact on the environment, a system of mutual notification is important. Developing countries, particularly the ones that are the least developed and the most vulnerable, should be given special privileges. All environmental disputes must be resolved peacefully and by appropriate means, in accordance with the Charter of the United Nations.

The principles contained in the Rio de Janeiro Declaration are the first extended definition of sustainable development, which is now synonymous in the literature with sustainability, durable development, mild development, smart development, self-sustaining development, restrained development, and environmentally friendly development. The deteriorating condition of our planet has become a stimulus to replace the current paradigm of unlimited growth with a new paradigm of sustainability. The document that contains practical methods and conditions for implementing the principles of the Rio Declaration on Environment and Development is the "Agenda 21," which is more than 500 pages long and consists of 40 chapters.

In 2000, at a United Nations summit, leaders of 189 countries adopted the United Nations Millennium Declaration with eight Millennium Development Goals (MDGs), which are listed in the following box.

THE MDG GOALS

1. Eradicate extreme poverty and hunger
2. Achieve universal primary education
3. Promote gender equality and empower women
4. Reduce child mortality
5. Improve maternal health
6. Combat HIV/AIDS, malaria and other diseases
7. Ensure environmental sustainability
8. Develop a global partnership for development

Source: Own work.

The Earth Summit held in Johannesburg in 2002, on the tenth anniversary of the Earth Summit in Rio de Janeiro (Rio+10), initiated a discussion on how to achieve the objectives of sustainable development, i.e., to put its principles into practice. A decade of environmental and global education for sustainable development was organized on behalf of the UN in 2005.

In June 2012, another Earth Summit (Rio+20) was held in Rio de Janeiro. It focused on seven areas that are a priority for the international community: jobs, energy, urban development, food security and sustainable agriculture, water and ocean protection, and response to natural disasters. At that time, UN member states decided to launch a process to develop a set of new Sustainable Development Goals (SDGs) as a continuation of the MDGs. The SDGs take into account the economic, social, and environmental aspects of sustainable development, including eradication of poverty, environmental sustainability, and sustainable consumption and production. The SDGs formulation process was a part of the work on the global post-2015 Development Agenda. In September 2015, in New York City, the leaders of 193 UN member states adopted the document titled "Transforming our world: the 2030 Agenda for Sustainable Development" by Resolution of the General Assembly of the United Nations. The document contains the 17 SDGs presented in the following box.

TRANSFORMING OUR WORLD: THE 2030 AGENDA FOR SUSTAINABLE DEVELOPMENT DOCUMENT CONTAINING 17 SUSTAINABLE DEVELOPMENT GOALS

Goal 1: End poverty in all its forms everywhere
Goal 2: End hunger, achieve food security and improved nutrition and promote sustainable agriculture
Goal 3: Ensure healthy lives and promote well-being for all at all ages
Goal 4: Ensure inclusive and equitable quality education and promote lifelong learning opportunities for all

Goal 5: Achieve gender equality and empower all women and girls
Goal 6: Ensure availability and sustainable management of water and sanitation for all
Goal 7: Ensure access to affordable, reliable, sustainable, and modern energy for all
Goal 8: Promote sustained, inclusive and sustainable economic growth, full and productive employment and decent work for all
Goal 9: Build resilient infrastructure, promote inclusive and sustainable industrialization, and foster innovation
Goal 10: Reduce inequality within and among countries
Goal 11: Make cities and human settlements inclusive, safe, resilient and sustainable
Goal 12: Ensure sustainable consumption and production patterns
Goal 13: Take urgent action to combat climate change and its impacts
Goal 14: Conserve and sustainably use the oceans, seas and marine resources for sustainable development
Goal 15: Protect, restore and promote sustainable use of terrestrial ecosystems, sustainably manage forests, combat desertification, and halt and reverse land degradation and halt biodiversity loss
Goal 16: Promote peaceful and inclusive societies for sustainable development, provide access to justice for all and build effective, accountable and inclusive institutions at all levels
Goal 17: Strengthen the means of implementation and revitalize the global partnership for sustainable development

Source: Own work.

An important initiative in the field of sustainable development was the adoption by the European Union in 2015 of a package of legislation on the circular economy. A circular economy is a concept that assumes reduction to a minimum of the impact of manufactured products on the environment. It is based on a selection of materials that can be reused. Production processes should use secondary raw materials and products should be repairable and recyclable. It is also important to change consumer habits by promoting more frequent use of second-hand, recycled products, as well as rental of products. As a part of this initiative, the following objectives, among others, should be achieved by 2035:

- recycling of 65% of municipal waste;
- recycling of 79% of packaging waste; and
- reduction of landfilling of waste to 10% with a total ban on landfilling of secondary raw materials.

Actions aimed at sustainability are systematically undertaken and implemented at the global, national, regional, and local level. Countries report their progress through

Voluntary National Reviews (Bickler, Morton and Menne 2020: 180–184). An example is Poland, a country where the government adopted on 14 February 2017 the *Strategy for responsible development.* The strategy identifies over 700 actions aimed at increasing the income of Polish citizens and strengthening the social, economic, environmental, and territorial cohesion. It also defines the objectives and priorities for Poland's development until 2020. The strategy takes into account a perspective for the next ten years, until 2030, which is intended to contribute to a high level of sustainable development.

According to Anjala Karol and C. Mashood, sustainable development is an integrated approach for the socio-economic modernization and advancement of a society by both efficient utilization and minimal depletion of natural resources. It is a development that causes minimum negative externalities to the environment (Karol and Mashood 2019: 266). The area of sustainable development is made up of needs, justice, and limits (Figure 1.2). In this space, human needs should be satisfied in observance of social justice and respect for environmental limits.

Sustainability, according to Diane Martin and John Schouten, is the ability of a system to maintain or renew itself perpetually. All of the Earth's natural systems function this way. Take, for instance, the cycle of photosynthesis and respiration. Everything in the cycle is renewable, and the cycle is, therefore, sustainable (Martin and Schouten 2014: 10). Hopkins quotes the following slogan, which reflects well the essence of sustainable development: *Enough, For All, For Ever.* "For All" evokes both social equity and consideration for the non-human inhabitants of shared ecosystems. "For Ever" signals respect for natural resource limitations as well as the pursuit of intergenerational justice (Jeanrenaud, Jeanrenaud and Gosling 2017: 5).

As Erling Holden, Kristin Linnerud, David Banister, Valeria Jana Schwanitz, and August Wierling note, sustainable development is called many things, including

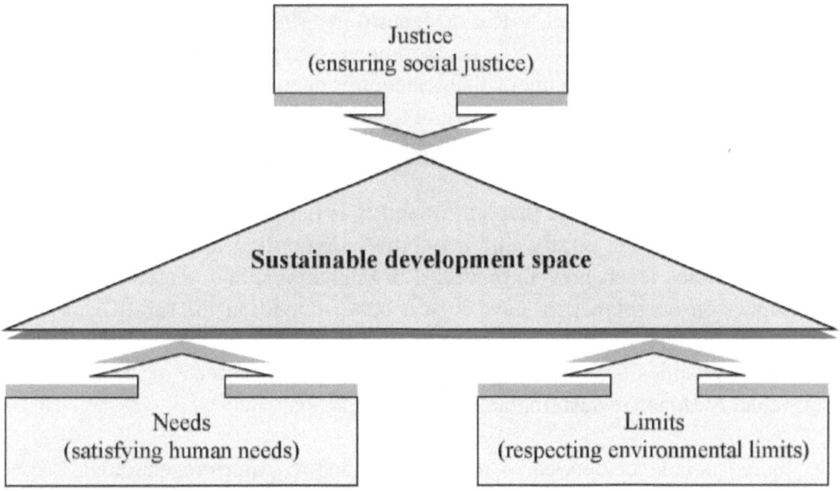

FIGURE 1.2 The sustainable development space. (Own work based on Holden, Linnerud, Banister, Schwanitz and Wierling 2018: 18.)

"a process of human activity," "a social movement," "a practice," "a discourse," and "a narrative." However, sustainable development is primarily a process of change (Holden, Linnerud, Banister, Schwanitz and Wierling 2018: 20).

What is important in thinking about sustainable development is expressed in the pursuit of responsible and thoughtful undertakings in various areas of human activity in the society – economy – environment configuration, related to improving the quality of life and protecting the Earth not only for the present, but also for future generations. The needs of current societies must be met without reducing the chances of future generations. Sustainable development means adoption of appropriate proportions between economic, social (human), and natural capital. As a result of the undertaken activities the ecological awareness of societies, the level of business responsibility for the environment, and interest in responsible consumption are increased. Govindan K., Madan Shankar K., and Kannan D. draw attention to an important aspect of sustainable development: various SDGs that have been achieved with current economic business models initiated the new socio-economic system known as the "sharing economy." This collaborative economy system shares resources among communities and further assists to reduce both negative environmental and societal impacts and to reduce costs (Govindan, Shankar and Kannan 2020).

The Concept of Sustainability

The term sustainability comes from ecological sciences where it means the ability of all or part of a biotic environment to extend its form in the future (Ariansen 1999: 84).

The concept of sustainability was further promoted in 1987 through The World Commission on Environment and Development Report known as the Brundtland's Report. This report uses the term "sustainable development," which has been widely used around the world with reference to various types of environmental and social initiatives. The Earth Summit in Rio de Janeiro in 1992 clarified the understanding of "sustainability" and "sustainable development" in Agenda 21, assuming that it is social and economic development that meets the needs of contemporary societies without compromising the ability of future generations to satisfy their needs. The development of civilization understood in this way finds a balance between ecological, social, and economic goals.

R. Brinkmann emphasizes that sustainability is based on three pillars called 3E. These are environment, equity, and economics. According to this researcher, sustainability studies teach how individuals, organizations, and societies can reduce their impact on our planet to leave it in a better condition for future generations (Brinkmann 2016: 1–2).

D. Fogel specifies the following conditions that must be met for an action to be sustainable. Actions are sustainable if (Fogel 2016: 7):

- there is a balance between resources used and resources regenerated;
- resources are as clean or cleaner at end of use as at beginning;
- the viability, integrity, and diversity of natural systems are restored and maintained;

- they lead to enhanced local and regional self-reliance;
- they help create and maintain community and a culture of place; and
- each generation preserves the legacies of future generations.

G. Haugan claims that the term sustainability is not used consistently and has different meanings for different people and organizations. He discusses various definitions and uses of this term. A brief overview of his definitions is given in Table 1.1.

TABLE 1.1
Definitions of Sustainability Quoted by G. Haugan

Type	Name	Description
1	Basic definition	Sustainability is the ability or capability to continue to exist. Sustain (sustained, sustaining, sustains, or sustainable) is to keep in existence, maintain. Other meanings of the word include: provide for, keep from falling or sinking, to bear up under, withstand, corroborate, or confirm.
2	Forestry definition	Sustainability means a balance between consumption of resources and their reproduction or substitution to ensure their protection. Originally, this was a foresters' doctrine aimed at protecting forest resources: managing forests sustainably to preserve them for future generations.
3	Systems definition	Sustainability is defined as the equivalent of an equilibrium or a state of balance or equality between opposing forces. A resource or commons is in equilibrium if the inputs and outputs are in balance.
4	MIT Sloan School of Management definition	Systems – including natural and human ones – need to be regenerative and balanced in order to last. It means all kinds of systems: economic, environmental, societal, and personal. How can we design and build a world in which the Earth thrives and people can pursue flourishing lives?
5	Environmental sustainability	Sustainability used as a synonym for green or ecology implying that some action or product does hurt the physical environment or it hurts it less than a competitor. An unsustainable situation occurs when any of nature's resources is used up faster than it can be replenished.
6	Ecological footprint	The Global Footprint Network (GFN) defines sustainability as the condition when the ecological footprint as calculated by the GFN methodology, is equal to or less than "one Earth." The ecological footprint value tracks humanity's demands on the biosphere by comparing humanity's consumption against the Earth's regenerative capacity or biocapacity.
7	Generational sustainability	Sustainability means a set of actions to be taken by present persons that will not diminish the prospects of future persons to enjoy levels of consumption, wealth, utility, or welfare comparable to those enjoyed by present persons.
8	Sustainability as a process destination	Sustainability as a process that involves the development of all aspects of human life affecting sustenance. It means resolving the conflict between the various competing goals and involves the simultaneous pursuit of economic prosperity, environmental quality, and social equity. Sometimes known as the "triple bottom line."

Source: Own work based on Haugan 2014: 9–19.

G. Haugan also quotes a definition of global sustainability. Global sustainability is the attainment of enduring economic, social, and environmental well-being of all elements of society (Haugan 2014: 18). Mikael Ottosson and Adders Parment refer to a soft and hard interpretation of the term sustainable development. A soft interpretation of the term – "weak sustainability" – entails us having to allow certain resources to be substituted for others. Hard interpretation of the term – "strong sustainability" – rejects the line of reasoning that allows different parts of the sustainability term to be substituted or balanced against one another (Ottosson and Parment 2015: 14). At the most fundamental level, "sustainability" means the ability of an organization to last and flourish over a long period of time without harming the environment and people.

Some scholars claim that there is a difference between the concepts of sustainable development and sustainability, i.e., sustainable development ultimately gives priority to development and that sustainability primarily is about the environment or that sustainability refers to a goal whereas sustainable development refers to the process that leads us to sustainability. According to Erling Holden, Kristin Linnerud, David Banister, Valeria Jana Schwanitz, and August Wierling, the two concepts entail the same ideas and thus they use them interchangeably (Holden, Linnerud, Banister, Schwanitz and Wierling 2018: 11). The authors of this book share the view of the above authors and use the terms sustainable development and sustainability interchangeably.

Annachiara Longoni emphasizes that sustainability is becoming a key business imperative. For the sake of their long-term success, companies have increasingly recognized the need to ensure the future of both humans and the Earth (Longoni 2014: V). A similar opinion is expressed by Barry Emery: issues of ethics, social responsibility, and sustainability in business have moved from marginal to mainstream (Emery 2012: 11).

In business, implementation of the concept of sustainability is contrary to the desire to maximize revenue and profit. Therefore, business is still looking for its own interpretation of the term sustainability. Instead of following only one path: economic or environmental development, business people choose a third path based on a "win-win" strategy. They recognize that a balance can be struck between economic (material), environmental (natural), and social (human) objectives. Sustainability in business means creating the conditions for a long-term market presence and a renewable business, which is not possible without harmonizing economic, ecological, and social goals.

The term "corporate sustainability" is used in the business environment to refer to management of organizations. Corporate sustainability involves the development of organizations by balancing economic, social, and environmental effects of their operation. According to this concept, an organization meets the current needs of its stakeholders and does not reduce its ability to meet those needs in the future. Moreover, its environmental and social activity is intended to contribute to achieving a competitive advantage in the market.

Another popular concept related to sustainability in business is "corporate social responsibility (CSR)." It means that an organization undertakes environmental and social activities that are voluntary and go beyond legal requirements. An organization attaches great importance to responsible and ethical conduct with respect to the environment.

The concept called "triple bottom line" should also be mentioned. It assumes that organizations try to minimize the risks arising from their activities and strive to create economic, social, and environmental values. The triple bottom line comprises people, the planet, and profit. Companies focus on economic goals – profit maximization is to secure their survival and development. Their second objective is to focus on people, in particular on their employees, in accordance with the principles of CSR. The third area of activity is achievement of environmental objectives. Sustainability in business means a proactive approach to achieving long-term profitability with respect for the environment, human rights, and human dignity.

Let us relate the term sustainability to project activities. We introduce sustainability to projects themselves, as well as to activities constituting their execution. In the case of projects, this means their content, i.e. the products, services, and campaigns that are the object of a project. Project executors should strive to make every part of a project environmentally friendly and pro-social. However, we do not find this approach to be sufficient. We believe that the principles of sustainability should also be observed during project execution. This is reflected in our concept which we call 4 × SUSTAINABILITY IN PROJECT ACTIVITIES. It means that sustainable personnel, using sustainable material resources, executes the project in a sustainable manner.

4 × SUSTAINABILITY IN PROJECT ACTIVITIES

SUSTAINABLE project team
SUSTAINABLE project team's equipment
SUSTAINABLE project execution
SUSTAINABLE projects

Source: Own work.

Thanks to such a comprehensive approach, the whole project activity, including its effects, contributes to sustainable development. The 4 × SUSTAINABILITY IN PROJECT ACTIVITIES concept will be discussed in detail in Chapter 3 and in further chapters of this book.

1.3 PROJECT MANAGEMENT AGAINST THE CHALLENGES OF SUSTAINABLE DEVELOPMENT

Project management can make a significant contribution to sustainable development provided that sustainability is present both in projects and in activities of project teams. Execution of sustainable projects, although essential for creating sustainable societies, encounters many barriers. However, there are far fewer factors that are conducive to execution of such projects. This predominance of barriers over stimulators has a negative impact on the pace of sustainable development, which does not keep pace with the increase in environmental and social risks. In this chapter, we discuss the key benefits of execution of sustainable projects, as well as the factors that facilitate or hinder this process. We consider the problem of the presence of sustainability in projects and project organizations and present solution in this area that make the greatest contributions to sustainable development.

Project Management in the Process of Creating Sustainable Societies

Projects contribute to accelerated civilizational development. As a result of their execution, new solutions in various areas of human activity are created, also ones of a breakthrough nature. 3D printers, 3D TVs, e-book readers, i-Pods, tablets, smartphones, and hybrid cars are only examples of solutions affecting our lives in the 21st century. However, the civilizational development so desired by man has a serious flaw: it is a source of environmental and social risks. Thus, if projects contribute to accelerated civilizational development and such development creates risks, then project activities must significantly contribute to making those risks worse. The more unsustainable the projects, the more this negative phenomenon is growing. However, environmental and social risks can be reduced or even eliminated by increasing the share of sustainable projects in the total number of such undertakings. The most beneficial from the perspective of sustainable development is to allow only those projects that are beneficial to the environment and the society.

> Sustainable projects contribute to the development of civilization without harming people and the environment.
>
> *Source*: Own work.

The growing environmental and social risks are forcing us to change the direction of our development. The development to date has led to the emergence of consumer societies. Consumerism has taken hold of man and is constantly growing. Today, producers and consumers behave as if they lived in a world without limits. The limits of nature's tolerance, as results from our deliberations, do exist: the Earth is an insulated system with no external resources, except for solar energy. In order to protect it, action must be taken to transform modern consumer societies into sustainable ones. A sustainable society is to a large extent the opposite of a consumer society that consists mainly of antisocial consumers and producers who satisfy exclusively their own needs. A sustainable society, as shown in Figure 1.3, is based on sustainable consumption and sustainable production. Sustainable consumption is created by sustainable consumers. Sustainable production is the work of sustainable producers.

Moturu Venkata Rajasekhar, Krishnaveer Abhishek Khalla, Dharmavaram Vijaylakshmi, and Nittala Rajyalakshmi call the transition from unsustainable to a sustainable society sustainable development (Figure 1.4) (Rajasekhar, Challa, Vijaylakshmi and Rajyalakshmi 2019: 237).

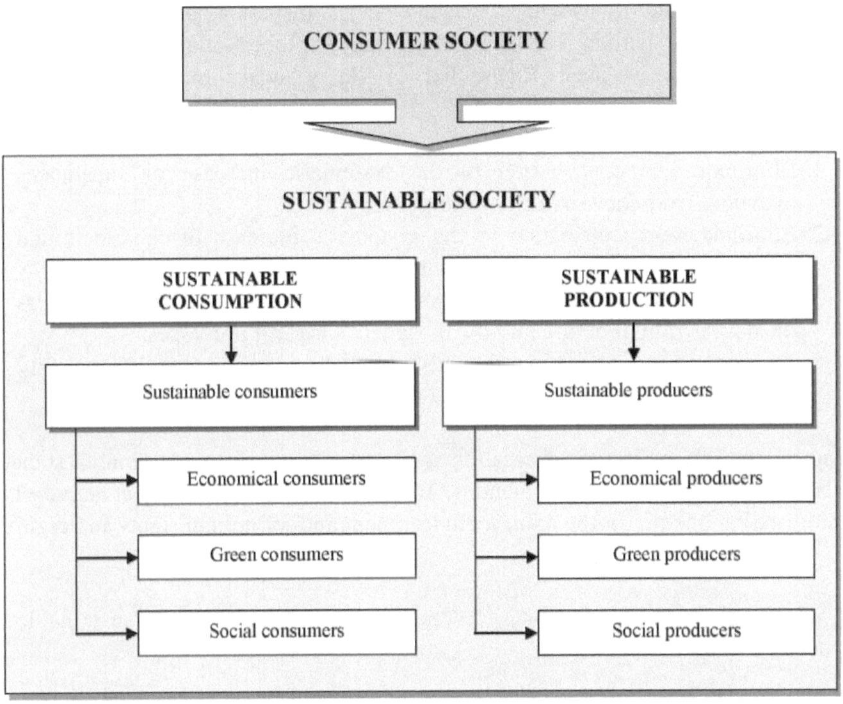

FIGURE 1.3 Sustainable society of the future. (Own work based on Pabian 2015a: 185; Pabian 2013a: 199.)

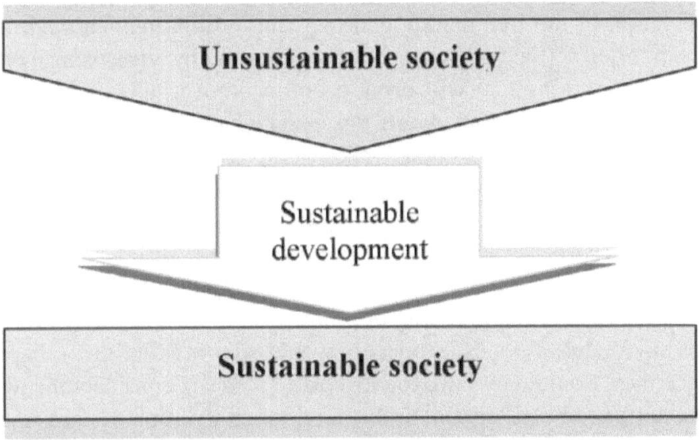

FIGURE 1.4 Sustainable development. (Own work based on Rajasekhar, Challa, Vijaylakshmi and Rajyalakshmi 2019: 237.)

Moturu Venkata Rajasekhar, Krishnaveer Abhishek Khalla, Dharmavaram Vijaylakshmi, and Nittala Rajyalakshmi, citing K. Robert, claim that to create a sustainable society, we must (Rajasekhar, Challa, Vijaylakshmi and Rajyalakshmi 2019: 239):

1. Eliminate our contribution to the systematic increase of substances extracted from the Earth's crust to the biosphere.
2. Eliminate our contribution to the systematic increase of chemicals and compounds produced by society within the biosphere.
3. Eliminate our contribution to the systematic physical degradation as well as the destruction of nature and the biosphere's natural processes.
4. Eliminate our contribution to conditions that undermine people's capacity to meet their own basic needs.

Projects should contribute to creation and development of a sustainable society. Every manifestation of environmentally friendly and pro-social project activity is a manifestation of care for the natural environment and for human rights and dignity.

Sustainable projects contribute to creation and development of a sustainable society.

Source: Own work.

As we mentioned, the accelerated development of civilization is accompanied by excessive consumption and its constant stimulation. According to Husniy Mohammed Al Ali, Mian M. Ajmal, Angappa Gunasekaran, and Petri T. Helo, this is a barrier to achieving environmental objectives. Consumerism is a consequence of the commercial operation of the free market and mercantile thinking. Through marketing activities, supported by the reality created by media and by advertising, one can now promote almost anything that will bring profit. Moreover, as research shows, in a world dominated by media and advertising, people have low awareness of environmental advertising compared to other types of advertising. Although social advertisements appear in the media, e.g. calling for reduced consumption of energy, they are relatively few compared to advertisements whose aim is to increase sales of traditional goods (Al Ali, Ajmal, Gunasekaran and Helo 2019: 84–97).

Consumption, not production, is the main source of problems, because only demand gives sense to manufacturing of products and provision of services. If people did not buy material goods, producers would stop making them, because with zero revenue they would only have to pay costs. L. Sklair considers the ideology of mass consumption to be the central problem of our civilization. He sees the cause of excessive consumption as the transition from utilitarianism to hedonism and from satisfaction to insatiable pleasure. C. Campbell tries to figure out how people manage to develop a regular and endless program of desire for new goods and services. According to K. Rassula and S. Hollander, it is external and internal factors that create the conditions for a consumer society, triggering the desire to own more and more goods and services (Dam and Apeldoorn 2008: 262). Mass consumption is a consequence of the behavior of millions of individuals – customers who no longer associate going to a store with just shopping. M. Solomon emphasizes: people around the world are beginning to get used to the materialistic lifestyle and the values of well-known brands that constitute a symbol of prosperity. Shopping is no longer a tedious task that consists in finding the necessary products, but becomes a form of leisure activity. Possession of commonly desired products is becoming a way of expressing one's status, although it often requires many sacrifices (Solomon 2006: 605). New consumer styles are characterized by the following features (Rogall 2010: 71):

1. striving to stand out from others through status symbols;
2. interest of most people in consumer goods owned by neighbors and friends (a phenomenon known as keeping up with the Jones);
3. desire to have the latest in technology;
4. progressive individualization; and
5. laziness.

In practice, it is often the case that alien styles of consumption are taken over and creolized, i.e. combined with local values.

Most projects contribute to an increase in consumption. The resulting new products, services, and technologies attract the attention of individual and institutional buyers. This leads to purchases, the number of which increases as the attractiveness of the new goods increases. Marketing, in particular the so-called promotional mix, has a very significant impact on the growth of consumption. It is a combination of specific instruments of impact on the environment through communication, which allows organizations to achieve their marketing goals (Pabian 2008: 29). The basic components of promotional mix are: advertising, direct marketing, sales promotion, public relations, personal selling, and digital marketing/social media (Andrews and Shimp 2018: 10). A lot of books have been published worldwide that instruct producers and sellers how to use promotional mix instruments to increase sales and thus consumption of manufactured goods. Their authors include George E. Belch and Michael A. Belch (Belch and Belch 2018); Robyn Blakeman (Blakeman 2018); Jerome M. Juska (Juska 2018); Micael Dahlen, Fredrik Lange, and Terry Smith (Dahlen, Lange and Smith 2010); William F. Arens, Michael F. Weigold, and Christian Arens (Arens, Weigold and Arens 2009).

Growing consumption is not conducive to sustainable development. Production of new goods and services requires consumption of huge amounts of raw materials, energy, water, and other goods, which are beginning to be scarce on Earth. Consequently, one of the important objectives of project activity should be to stabilize and even reduce consumption. The goal is to create goods that are genuinely needed by people and limiting promotional activities that are not always fair. An example is *greenwashing* and *astroturfing*. *Greenwashing* is an unethical behavior that consists in a mix of false or confusing information in promotional messages about the environmental performance of offered products or services and activities of companies, which are aimed at increasing sales and improving the image. D. Martin and J. Schouten quote the following seven sins of *greenwashing*: the sin of hidden trade-off, the sin of no proof, the sin of vagueness, the sin of worshiping false labels, the sin of irrelevance, the sin of lesser of two evils, and the sin of fibbing (Martin and Schouten 2012: 195). Astroturfing, on the other hand, is manifested in organization of seemingly spontaneous campaigns and spreading positive opinions about pseudo-environmentally friendly and pseudo-pro-social products or services. Thanks to the Internet, their range can be practically unlimited.

Sustainable projects have a positive impact on the structure of consumption. They result in sustainable products and services that are offered for sale. In this way, their share in the structure of goods purchased in the market and consumed is increased.

Source: Own work.

The greatest barrier to sustainable development is humans themselves. Many people do nothing to protect the environment and are not socially active because they hope that this will not be noticed and punished (free-rider problem), they care less about the common good than about private property (tragedy of the commons), and it is difficult for them to do anything for the community if it leads to their loss (prisoner's dilemma) (Pabian 2012a: 127). Most people do not see the environmental and social risks because the perception system with which nature has equipped them has a number of limitations resulting from the construction of the human body. They cannot control these risks either. Egocentrism, conservatism, technocentrism, anthropocentrism, and materialism are widespread value systems that do not promote sustainability. According to F. Belz and K. Peattie, promoting sustainable development requires profound changes in people's behavior and ways of thinking. They should take the following directions (Belz and Peattie 2010: 84):

a. from egocentric (me first) to altruistic (others first);
b. from conservative to open to change;
c. from indulgent to frugal;
d. from materialist to post-materialist;
e. from technocentric (technology rules) to ecocentric (nature knows best); and
f. from anthropocentric (human centered) to biocentric (all species matter).

The prerequisite for engaging in sustainable development is that human beings should give up their selfishness in exchange for actions that benefit others, acknowledge the superiority of nature over technological achievements, attribute a similar value, and thus also rights, not only to humans but also to the other species living on Earth, give up the pursuit of material goods, understand the changes taking place, and accept progressive solutions.

> Sustainable projects require a change of attitude: getting rid of selfishness by stakeholders in favor of actions that benefit people and the environment.
>
> *Source*: Own work.

Of course, not all people in the world are selfish and distance themselves from sustainable development. It is comforting that for many of them sustainability is a priority, which is reflected not only in their views but also in their actions. An evidence of people's growing involvement in environmental protection and social issues is organizations operating worldwide with hundreds of thousands of activists. Examples of this type of organization are given in Table 1.2.

TABLE 1.2
Examples of International Environmental Organizations and Agencies Working in the Area of Environmental Education, Sustainable Development, Biodiversity, and Environmental Protection

Organization Name	Description
Greenpeace International	An international non-governmental organization founded in 1971 which works to protect the environment. The organization has branches in 55 countries around the world and is financed entirely by individual donors. It does not accept money from companies or governments to guarantee its independence.
World Wide Fund for Nature (WWF)	An international non-governmental environmental organization established in 1961. The WWF's mission is to stop the degradation of the Earth's environment and create a future in which people will live in harmony with nature. During more than 50 years of its existence, the WWF has initiated, conducted, and helped implement several thousand nature-conservation projects around the world.
Citizens' Climate Lobby (CCL)	An international non-governmental organization established in 2007. The main objectives of the organization are to reduce greenhouse gas emissions and promote the transition to an economy based on renewable energy sources through a free-market approach: a financially neutral fee and a carbon dividend, and to stop subsidizing fossil fuel extraction companies.
United Nations Environment Program (UNEP)	The UN Agenda established by the UN General Assembly Resolution 2997 of 16 December 1972 to conduct UN environmental protection activities and to continuously monitor the state of environment worldwide.
People for the Ethical Treatment of Animals (PETA)	The world's largest animal-rights organization. By exposing animal abuse cases, educating the public, and encouraging lifestyle changes, the organization seeks to improve the lives of animals. It is supported by over 5 million people. The organization is known for publishing shocking footage of abuse of animals.

(*Continued*)

TABLE 1.2 (*Continued*)
Examples of International Environmental Organizations and Agencies Working in the Area of Environmental Education, Sustainable Development, Biodiversity, and Environmental Protection

Organization Name	Description
International Union for Conservation of Nature (IUCN)	An organization active in the field of nature conservation founded in 1948. Its mission is to help societies around the world to protect the integrity and diversity of nature and to achieve environmentally sustainable use of natural resources. The organization brings together 83 countries, over 1,000 governmental and non-governmental agencies, and 11,000 experts and scientists.
Friends of the Earth International	A federation of independent environmental organizations operating around the world. It has about 1.5 million members in 70 countries who campaign on contemporary environmental and social issues while working towards local and global sustainable development.
ClientEarth	A non-governmental organization operating in the field of environmental law. It has offices in London, Brussels, and Warsaw. ClientEarth operates in the field of law, science, and public policy and works out legal solutions to key environmental problems. The organization operates in the area of legislation and proper implementation of international and national laws, and monitors compliance with laws. ClientEarth publishes opinions, analyses, and reports, and runs and supports social campaigns.
The Ocean Cleanup	The main goals of The Ocean Cleanup are to draw attention to the pollution of oceans with trash and to create facilities to help clean the oceans.
Global Ecovillage Network (GEN)	An association of people and communities (eco-villages) that promotes "sustainable plus" life by restoring the condition of the soil and giving more to the natural environment than is taken from it. Members of the network share ideas, information, and technology, thus forming cultural and educational exchange.
Consumers International	An independent international organization dedicated to the protection of consumer rights. Its members are more than 200 consumer organizations from more than 100 countries around the world. The organization works with its partners on issues that have an impact on protection of consumer rights not only at the national level but also, above all, internationally.
International Cooperation and Enforcement Network (ICPEN)	An organization consisting of consumer-protection authorities from 36 countries worldwide. Its objectives are to exchange information on market practices with a cross-border dimension that may have a negative impact on consumers' interests and to promote cooperation between the authorities responsible for implementing consumer legislation.

Source: Own work based on https://wlaczoszczedzanie.pl/ekolinki/miedzynarodowe-organizacje-ekologiczne/

Another positive initiative of people and organizations involved in sustainable development is to establish various types of days and holidays to draw the public's attention to environmental and social problems and to stimulate them to work towards sustainability. These include global and local initiatives established within individual countries. The following box shows the key types of days and holidays that promote sustainable development worldwide.

FROM THE CALENDAR OF GLOBAL AND INTERNATIONAL SUSTAINABLE DEVELOPMENT INITIATIVES

World Wetland Day (2 February)
World Wildlife Day (3 March)
International Anti-Dam Day (14 March)
World Oceans Day (17 March)
International Forest Day (21 March)
World Water Day (22 March)
International Bird Day (1 April)
World Health Day (7 April)
Earth Day (22 April)
International Day for Biological Diversity (22 May)
World No Tobacco Day (31 May)
World Environment Day (5 June)
World Oceans Day (8 June)
World Day to Combat Desertification (17 June)
International Day for the Preservation of the Ozone Layer (16 September)
European Mobility Week (16–22 September)
Day of Wild Fauna, Flora and Natural Habitats (19 September)
World Cleanup Day (21–23 September)
Car-Free Day (22 September)
World Habitat Day (3 October)
World Animal Day (4–11 October)

Source: Own work based on https://www.wfosgw.poznan.pl/kalendarz-ekologiczny/

The strong involvement of societies in sustainable development is also evidenced by the various protests organized to defend nature and human rights and dignity. The participants of the protests demand that the climate disaster be averted and social problems be solved. An example of such an international protest was the Youth Climate Strike on 15 March 2019. More than 120 towns and cities protested against global warming and the damage caused by human activities. Meegan Jones points out an important aspect of organization of various types of sustainable events: "Those who stage these events have a social and environmental responsibility to reduce their impact. If all event organizers, from the largest commercial shows to small community fairs, kept sustainability at the core of their planning, the cumulative outcome would be impressive" (Jones 2010: V).

A factor that has been conducive to the implementation of sustainability principles is the IT revolution. Jerry A. Carbo, Viet T. Dao, Steven J. Haase, M. Blake Hargrove, and Ian M. Langella show the usefulness of information technology (IT) in activities that contribute to sustainability. Information systems (IT) are made up of the following components: people (users and specialists), software (programs), hardware (machines and computers), networks (communication networks), data (data and knowledge base), and procedures (IT-driven business processes) (Carbo, Dao, Haase, Hargrove and Langella 2018: 138). An important role in this system is played by the Internet. The Internet has created possibilities to exchange information and maintain contacts in cyberspace that were unknown in the past. Visualization of the content transmitted over the Internet enables virtual learning of a diverse world and mutual exchange of ideas to a huge number of people. According to Kirsten Kinzer, public participation is particularly important in implementing sustainable development plans. What matters is cooperation and collaboration, which are facilitated by the Internet (Kinzer 2018: 719–728). The Internet improves cooperation during execution of projects. This is particularly important when stakeholders, including project team members, are separated by large distances. The Internet offers unlimited possibilities in sharing information during the project preparation and execution phases. It is also a source of knowledge and exchange of experience concerning projects that have already been completed. The Internet plays another important role. It enables the use the potential of the crowd to create ideas for new projects, as well as to evaluate and verify existing ideas.

Sustainable projects are easier to prepare, execute, and implement using the Internet.

Source: Own work.

The number of factors that hinder sustainable development, and thus sustainable projects, is far greater than that of stimulators. In this area, of great importance are the national culture, the structure of production in individual countries, the economic situation of countries, the pro-environmental and pro-social law and its restrictiveness, and education in the field of sustainable development. We will briefly discuss these factors.

Culture is a collection of values, beliefs, behaviors, customs, and attitudes that distinguish one society from another (Griffin and Pustay 2010: 108). Culture has the following characteristics: it is learned, shared, transgenerational, symbolic, patterned, and adoptive (Doh and Luthans 2018: 124). Because each country has its own culture, societies in different countries respond differently to sustainability ideas and solutions. In various countries, sustainable development encounters more or fewer cultural barriers. Certain cultural characteristics favor the implementation of its principles, while other characteristics inhibit this process. Here are some examples. Research by B. Husted has shown that rich countries with a low degree of distance to power, a low level of preference for male characteristics, and a high preference for individualism are more likely to support environmental sustainability. Egalitarianism, feminism, and individualism facilitate the implementation of the values of sustainability in nations with such characteristics (Husted 2005: 349–371). Also, such aspects of cultures as being future-oriented, innovation-orientated, and human-orientated are allies of sustainability. People's belief in the possibility to shape the future becomes an important stimulus to take action aimed to eliminate environmental and social risks. Innovation is a source of progress in the area of sustainability. It leads to creation of modern environmentally friendly and pro-social products, services, and technologies. Sustainability is also facilitated by people-oriented cultures. This is because being people-oriented is based on the belief that humans are the greatest value that should be protected now and in the future by eliminating all kinds of threats, including those of an environmental and social nature (Pabian and Pabian 2012: 7).

The culture of the country of origin of project stakeholders has an impact on the sustainability of projects.

Source: Own work.

Involvement of governments and societies in sustainable development depends to a large extent on the structure of the country's industry, in particular on the share of non-sustainable production sectors in the overall economy. We will explain this using the example of hard coal mining in Poland, which is one of such sectors. In 2018, Polish mines extracted 63.4 million tons of hard coal. They employ about 83,000 workers (https://forsal.pl/artykuly/1407981.zatrudnienie-w-gornictwie-rosnie-choc-wydobycie-spada.html). Both hard coal mining and employment in the Polish mining industry have been declining for many years, which is a positive trend in terms of sustainability. However, a rapid and complete dismantling of this sector is practically impossible. This is because this would involve closing down the mines, which involves mass layoffs of employees and sale of assets. Environmental goals cannot be achieved by exacerbating social problems. The process of closing down coal mining must therefore be extended over a period of time in which miners will be provided with jobs in other sectors of the economy and in which it can be ensured that energy is obtained from sources alternative to coal. In unsustainable sectors of the economy, such as hard coal mining, an unwillingness to take pro-environmental actions is observed. Workers fear that such actions will negatively affect the development of their sectors, resulting in job losses. Therefore, they may be opposed to the idea of sustainable development. Consequently, the more unsustainable sectors in the structure of a country's economy, the less interest in sustainable development among decision-makers and thus the less interest in executing sustainable projects.

Non-sustainable sectors of the economy, although they are in great need of sustainable projects, can hinder their development.

Source: Own work.

Another factor influencing sustainable development is the economic situation of business entities and citizens in individual countries. In countries with a high per capita GDP (over USD 40,000–50,000), people enjoy high incomes and can afford to buy environmentally friendly products and services, even though their prices are higher than those of standard goods. Residents of third world countries, where the GDP per capita is on the level of several hundred dollars, cannot afford this kind of expenditure. The same is true for companies. Companies with small revenues and financial problems will not invest in environmentally friendly and pro-social projects unless they are forced to do so by the applicable legislation.

In wealthy societies, it is easier to initiate and finance sustainable projects.

Source: Own work.

The law in force in individual countries has a significant impact on the type and scope of pro-environmental and pro-social projects that are executed. The law on sustainable development can be very liberal or very strict. Its prohibitions and prescriptions can be enforced in a strict or lenient way. All this influences the activity of people and companies in the area of sustainable development. The more sustainability regulations there are and the more stringent and rigorously enforced they are, the more sustainable projects are initiated. People and companies engage in pro-environmental and pro-social activities for fear of legal sanctions.

Strict enforcement of legislation on sustainability encourages initiation and execution of sustainable projects

Source: Own work.

Education in the field of sustainable development is one of the most important factors that influence achievement of pro-environmental and pro-social goals. Such education should not only be present in curricula at every level of education (kindergarten, primary, secondary, and higher education, or post-graduate education and doctoral studies), but should also continue for the rest of people's life in accordance with the principles of Lifelong Learning. A properly educated society will be more willing to engage in sustainable development and thus to initiate and execute sustainable projects. As shown by studies concerning students and teachers, a positive attitude towards sustainable development is particularly demonstrated by those who have been trained in this field (Ayesha, Yousuf, Muhammad and Ali 2020: 250).

> Education in the field of sustainable development enriches the knowledge about the environmental and social risks, and the ways to prevent them, and shapes pro-environmental and pro-social attitudes, which encourage initiation and execution of sustainable projects.
>
> *Source*: Own work.

Research carried out worldwide in various sectors of the economy has revealed many factors that negatively or positively affect sustainable development, and thus the initiation and execution of projects in this area. We will review them briefly later in this chapter.

Christopher Wright and Daniel Nyberg discovered that companies announce programs aimed to reduce energy consumption and greenhouse gas emissions and, as time goes by, they return to the "business as usual" approach. In their opinion, climate change initiatives go through the following three phases (Wright and Nyberg 2019: 20):

1. Phase I – Management presents the problem of climate change in internal and external forums as an urgent social and business issue and indicates how their company can contribute to solving it.
2. Phase II – Managers try to translate their declarations into practical actions.
3. Phase III – The company slows down the initiative and prioritizes financial considerations instead, thus reaching the "business as usual" state (such situations may coincide with a period of weaker corporate performance or changes in top positions).

Research carried out by Robert G. Eccles and Svetlana Klimenko has shown that business leaders face a serious barrier to sustainable development activities, which is shareholder resistance. Business leaders believe that efforts to promote sustainable development are contrary to the expectations of shareholders, which does not encourage managers' activity in this area. However, the situation is improving over time. Interviews with 70 senior managers from 43 global investment firms show that environmental, social, and governance (ESG) issues are currently their key concern. Moreover, corporations will soon start to be accounted for by their shareholders for their activities in the ESG area. In 2006, when the UN "Principles of Responsible Investing" were announced, 63 investment firms (asset owners, asset portfolio managers, and service providers) managing $6.5 trillion of assets signed a commitment to include ESG in their investment decisions. By April 2018, the number of signatories of this commitment increased to 1,715 and the value of the assets they manage – to 81.7 trillion dollars (Eccles and Klimenko 2020: 128).

Research conducted in Poland in the brewing industry has shown that internal rather than external barriers are a greater obstacle to implementation of sustainable development/social responsibility strategies. The most important internal barriers are: the human factor, namely employees' mentality (73.8% of the respondents), the costs of implementation of investment projects (60.5%), lack of employees' commitment (52.7%), reluctance and resistance to new solutions (45.7%), technical and technological deficiencies (inadequate equipment and technologies) (44.9%), inappropriate system of communication between departments and employees (39.5%), lack of ideas for development (29.3%), reporting costs (20.3%), and no obstacles (1.6%). The following factors were indicated as the most important external barriers: lack of interest (cooperation) on the part of stakeholders (47.70% of respondents), laws (45.30%), competitive pressure in the sector (43.80%), lack of demand for products (drop in profits, 43.00%), taxes, customs (36.7%), political conditions (27.7%), lack of access to new technologies (25.4%), climate conditions, weather changes (15.6%), takeovers of e.g. of suppliers (12.9%), and lack of obstacles (5.1%) (Jaźwińska 2016: 159–161).

Dimple Bhandari, Rajesh Kr Singh, and Suresh K. Garg emphasize that organizations face a number of barriers while implementing cleaner technologies. On the basis of literature reviews and experts' opinions, four categories of barriers, namely technical information barriers, operational and strategic barriers, financial and economic barriers, and human barriers are identified. As it turned out, financial and economic barriers have become the biggest obstacle to the implementation of cleaner technologies (Bhandari, Kr Singh and Garg 2019: 156–167).

Research in the energy sector has shown that most organizations have difficulties in implementing sustainable changes. The main factor facilitating such changes is effective and transparent communication. The main barriers to sustainable energy are fear and flexibility (Al Ali, Ajmal, Gunasekaran and Helo 2019: 84–97).

On the basis of their research, Walter Leal Filho, Antonis Skouloudis, Luciana Londero Brandli, Amanda Lange, Salvia Lucas Veiga, and Avila Lez Rayman-Bacchus have identified barriers to sustainable procurement practices in higher education. They specified the following types of barriers: tending toward a narrow operational more than a strategic focus, organizational inertia, resource constraints, and lack of implementation guidelines. The authors emphasize that developing and implementing sustainable procurement policies and practices require a reflexive approach (Filho, Skouloudis, Brandli, Lange, Veiga and Rayman-Bacchus 2019: 1267–1280).

Sustainability in Projects and Activities of Project Teams

Sustainability can be present in project activities in two main areas. The first is the object of the project, i.e., products, services, and campaigns created as a result of project activities. For example, the aim of the project is to develop the concept of concept and design a new product. This product can be designed as sustainable, partially sustainable, or unsustainable. Sustainable products created as a result of project activities are described in Chapter 4.

TABLE 1.3
Presence of Sustainability in Project Activities

	Object of the Project		
Project Organization	**Sustainable**	**Partly Sustainable**	**Unsustainable**
Sustainable organization	1	2	3
Partly sustainable organization	4	5	6
Unsustainable organization	7	8	9

Source: Own work.

The second area that can be covered by sustainability is project organization. A project organization is a project team consisting of a manager and his or her subordinates, whose task is to execute the project. For such a project to be created, members of the project team need physical resources in the form of materials, equipment, and means of transport. In addition, the project team must have access to some premises. These may be the offices where it will conduct its business. All these resources, both human and physical, can be unsustainable, partially sustainable, or sustainable. The profiles of a sustainable project manager and members of his or her team are presented in Chapter 2. Sustainable physical resources are discussed in Chapter 4. Having people and physical resources is not enough to complete a project. The project team must start operating, i.e., working on the project. This work can be done in a sustainable, partially sustainable, or unsustainable way. Chapter 3 explains what sustainable project activities are.

As follows from the above statements, sustainability can be present in different areas of project activity. Table 1.3 shows nine possible cases.

From the point of view of sustainability, the least favorable option is represented by field 9. In this case, sustainability is not present in any project activity. Both the object of the project and the project organization are not sustainable and do not contribute in any way to sustainable development. The most desirable, model solution to be pursued by project initiators and executors is shown in field 1. A sustainable project organization carries out a project that results in products, services, and campaigns that are also sustainable. This concept is presented in more detail in Table 1.4.

As Table 1.4 shows, a sustainable project organization is made up of sustainable human and physical resources. Work on a project is also carried out in a sustainable manner. Between the least and the most advantageous solution, from the standpoint of sustainability, there are intermediate options (fields 2–8). They reflect situations where sustainability is present in at least one of the areas under consideration, which are the project organization and the object of the project.

As one can easily guess, field 1 in Table 1.3 corresponds to our 4 × SUSTAINABILITY IN PROJECT ACTIVITIES concept. This is, as we have already mentioned, a standard that is hard to achieve but that should be pursued. Project teams, however, do not face the "all or nothing" dilemma, which in our case means "to completely conform to this standard or to completely ignore sustainability

TABLE 1.4
Concept of Sustainable Project Organization

Inputs	Sustainable Project Organization				Outputs
Sustainable goods needed to execute the project	Sustainable project team members	Sustainable construction infrastructure used by the project team	Sustainable furnishing of the premises where the project activity is carried out	Sustainable equipment used in project activities	Sustainable products and services as a result of project activities
Sustainable Project Activity (Work on the Project)					

Source: Own work based on Pabian 2017b: 12.

in projects." As shown in Table 1.3, they have various other possibilities of introducing sustainability into projects and their execution (fields 2–8). The options, symbolized by fields 2–8, contain more or less sustainability, which means that any project can make even a small contribution to sustainable development.

Management plays a priority role in projects and project activities that take sustainability into account. Whether and to what extent sustainability is present in a project and in a project organization depends on the decisions made in the management process. The issue of sustainable project management is discussed in detail in Chapter 3 of this book.

2 Project Stakeholders in the Sustainability Concept

2.1 ECOLOGICAL AND SOCIAL RESPONSIBILITY OF STAKEHOLDERS

Project stakeholders are usually a very diverse group of people in terms of views and attitudes. The term project stakeholder means people who have any connection to a project, including people who support, have an interest in, and benefit from the project. From the point of view of sustainability, it would be best for all stakeholders to demonstrate pro-environmental and pro-social attitudes. In such case, the project would certainly contribute to sustainable development. In practice, in most cases it is not possible to achieve this ideal state. In order to achieve pro-environmental and pro-social objectives, it is therefore necessary to focus on the group of stakeholders who are the originators of the project, approve and finance it, and take part in its execution. We call them key stakeholders. Their attitude to sustainability and their experience in this area determine whether the project will contribute to sustainable development and whether it will be executed in accordance with its principles. Key stakeholders are listed below.

Applicant

Applicant is the person (or persons) who came up with the idea for the project. Whether and to what extent the project will serve people and the environment well depend on the environmental and social sensitivity of the applicant and his or her commitment to sustainability.

Persons Approving the Project and Its Finances

The project will not be implemented in a company or other organization unless it is approved by its senior management and unless funds are allocated for it. Top managers who prefer short-term profits and have an indifferent or negative attitude to sustainability are not willing to support sustainable projects, let alone finance them. In practice, the following excuses can be found: we do not need such a project, we cannot afford to finance it, we will deal with it at a different time, we have more urgent and more important tasks now, we lack the right staff, and we lack deeper knowledge about sustainability. It is therefore quite necessary for top managers to have a high environmental and social sensitivity. In such a case, the senior management will not only see and appreciate the sustainable value of the project, but will also approve it and include it in their financial plans. It can even suggest its own innovative solutions to be added to the project concepts.

Project Manager

Project manager is the person who makes the most important decisions and manages the project activities. This person also has a significant influence on the selection of project team members. The project manager should have a genuine interest in achieving the pro-environmental and pro-social objectives of the project. In this case, sustainability is reflected in the choice of people and physical resources, as well as in the project activities and their results. One should keep in mind that even charismatic managers can have problems with initiating and executing sustainable projects. Michael Lenox and Aaron Chatterji emphasize that a charismatic executive who is passionate about sustainability needs to convince many others and secure commitment of their time and resources. Personal charisma ultimately does not create value on its own and businesses need to create and capture value to survive (Lenox and Chatterji 2018: 76).

Project Team Members

Project team members are a group of people carrying out the work that makes up the project under the supervision of the project manager. Their environmental and social sensitivity may have a very positive impact on the execution of the project. This sensitivity strengthens their motivation to achieve sustainability goals. It also triggers creativity in the search for pro-environmental and pro-social solutions.

Sustainable key stakeholders are an important condition for initiating and executing a sustainable project. They are listed in Figure 2.1. The profiles of a sustainable project manager and sustainable members of a project team are presented in Sections 2.2 and 2.3 of this chapter.

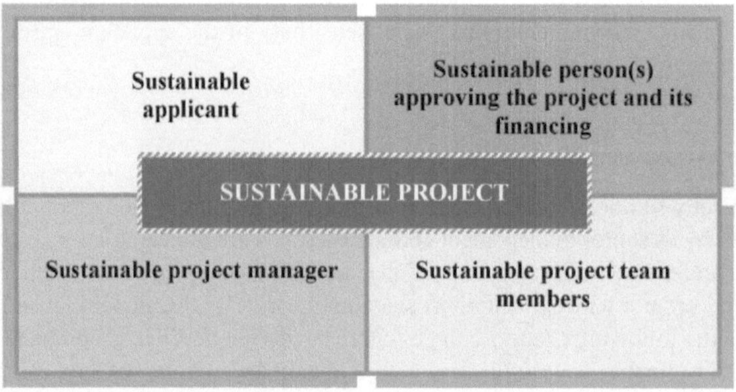

FIGURE 2.1 Sustainability of key stakeholders as a prerequisite for initiating and executing a sustainable project. (Own work).

Key stakeholders should be considered to be individuals, not just organizations or some groups of people. This is important because it enables a reasonably precise determination of the stakeholder's relationship to sustainability and his or her involvement in such activities. The use of the phrase "the stakeholder is the company AMH" explains nothing, even if the company is to some extent environmentally friendly or pro-social. The people employed by the company may relate to sustainability issues in various ways. If such a company assigns an employee who is not fully convinced of the idea of sustainability to deal with the project, the environmental and social goals will be marginalized in the project. Thus, from the point of view of sustainability, it is the individual people involved in the preparation and execution of a project who should be assessed, not the organizations on the list of stakeholders that these individuals represent.

The nature is also considered to be one of the stakeholders (Karol and Mashood 2019: 266). The relationship between every project and the environment is obvious. Every project has a specific impact on the environment, and the environment influences its execution and results. However, the environment does not have its own mind and does not show needs in the human meaning of this term. Therefore, the interests of the environment are represented by those stakeholders who are environmentally sensitive and want to contribute to its improvement.

The key stakeholders of a project are therefore a specific group of people who can be assigned to the categories we propose in Figure 2.2.

Activists – people who not only have a very high ecological and social sensitivity, but are also actively involved in "fixing the modern world": they initiate and participate in various sustainability campaigns, their lifestyle is based on the principles of sustainability, and they promote the idea of sustainability in their circles.

Supporters – people who support sustainable development, but only occasionally and with little involvement in matters related to it. From time to time, they buy healthy food, sometimes they support social movements with small amounts of money, and they make an effort to sort their household waste. If they minimize water

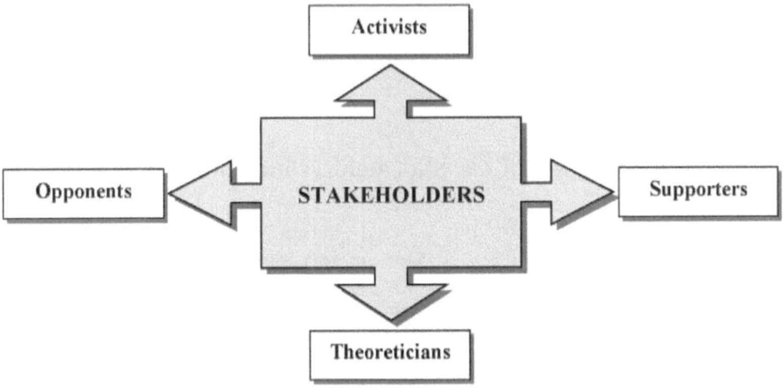

FIGURE 2.2 Groups of stakeholders with different attitudes toward sustainability. (Own work).

and electricity consumption in their homes and apartments, this is due to financial motives (lower consumption and bills) rather than the idea of sustainability.

Theoreticians – people who consider the ideas of sustainability to be right, but do not engage personally in their implementation. They do not want to limit themselves in satisfying their needs. They explain their passiveness in various ways, e.g. they think that their micro pro-environmental and pro-social activities can in no way influence the fate of the world and will not be appreciated by anyone.

Opponents – people who oppose the idea of sustainability. They identify this movement with a harmful ideology that inhibits economic development and threatens their interests. Opponents often are business owners or employees of companies operating in unsustainable sectors of the economy. They fear that sustainable development will lead to the closure of these sectors and thus to the destruction of their businesses and jobs.

Project execution involves keeping a register of stakeholders. When entering the key stakeholders in such a register, one must indicate the groups (activists, supporters, theorists, or opponents) that the persons belong to. For this purpose, an additional column may be provided in the Register with the name "stakeholder attitude to sustainability" or the group's name may be placed next to the name and function of the stakeholder. An example of such a listing is shown in Table 2.1.

From the point of view of sustainability, the more key stakeholders are included in the groups of "activists" and "supporters," the more likely the project is to be executed. If a majority of the stakeholders in the register are sustainability opponents, there is little hope for support for the project and its successful implementation.

Project proponents also play an important supporting role in preparation and execution of sustainable projects. **A project proponent** is a person of high professional status who recognizes the value of the project and is fully convinced that it must be executed. Therefore, he or she supports the project by communicating with other stakeholders both at official meetings and during informal meetings. In order for a project proponent to properly fulfill his or her role in the area of sustainability, he or she should have knowledge in this area, the ability to convince people that he or she is right, and the belief that the project will bring significant benefits to the environment and the society. The basis of the project proponent's activity is knowledge

TABLE 2.1
An Extract from a Register of Key Stakeholders Including Their Attitudes to Sustainability

Category	Type	First and Last Name, function, and Organization	Attitude to Sustainability
Internal stakeholders	Company management	J. Wolter, Managing Director	Supporter
		K. Abort, Deputy Production Director	Activist
		G. Malynski, Deputy Finance Director	Theoretician

Source: Own work.

about sustainability, especially information on environmental and social risks, their sources, the scale of occurrence, and the ways to prevent them. This type of information enables the project proponents to use concrete arguments during discussions with other stakeholders so as to encourage them to incorporate sustainability principles into the project.

A very important group of stakeholders are **customers**, i.e., individuals or groups of people who will use the products or services resulting from the project. In the planning phase, the target buyers and users of these goods should be clearly identified. These are persons or organizations who need these goods in order to satisfy specific needs. In the case of sustainable projects, the concept of which we present in this book, we do not require customers to demonstrate pro-environmental and pro-social attitudes. There are three really important issues here: whether the goods created by the projects meet the customers' needs, whether the goods are environmentally friendly and pro-social, and whether there is market demand for them. If these conditions are met, the degree of sustainability of the buyers does not play such an important role. One must keep in mind that environmentally friendly and pro-social products are purchased by both sustainable and unsustainable customers. Sustainable customers are motivated in their purchase decisions by sustainable development, while unsustainable customers are motivated only by economic considerations. A sustainable customer buys a sustainable washing machine because it uses less electricity and water, which contributes to environmental protection, while an unsustainable customer buys it only because of the financial benefits he or she will gain by paying less for electricity and water. In both cases, the use of a sustainable product contributes to environmental protection.

It should be added that although customers do not have any influence on the execution of a project (they do not approve it, finance it, or control its course), it is always necessary to recognize their needs and requirements. Products and services created as a result of a project can only be successful in the market if the customers who use them are satisfied or even delighted with them.

When considering the project stakeholders, shareholders should not be overlooked. Shareholders play one of the most influencing roles in any firm and market. They persuade all aspects of green strategy including the purchase of a green product, the packaging of the product, the product nature, advertisement, promotion and also in programs related to green awareness (Acharya and Gupta 2019: 13).

2.2 PROFILE OF A SUSTAINABLE PROJECT MANAGER

Sustainable organizations require sustainable leadership (Carbo, Dao, Haase, Hargrove and Langella 2018: 155). To save the Earth, we will need expert managers to recognize great ideas, turn them into products, and figure out how to sell to the mass market (Lenox and Chatterji 2018: 61). Thus, if the project team is to be a sustainable organization, it should be led by a sustainable manager. Leadership can be defined in a simple way. Warren Bennis, considered to be a pioneer and leader in the field of leadership says, "Leadership is the capacity to translate vision into reality." Bill Gates, founder of Microsoft, describes leaders as "those who empower others." Peter Drucker, a management guru, offers the following definition "The only definition of a leader is someone who has followers" (Carbo, Dao, Haase, Hargrove and Langella 2018: 155–156). Jerry A. Carbo, Viet T. Dao, Steven J. Haase, M. Blake Hargrove, and Ian M. Langella define leadership as influencing followers to accomplish objectives (Carbo, Dao, Haase, Hargrove and Langella 2018: 156).

The project manager makes the most important decisions and manages the project activities. Smooth implementation of sustainability principles in the course of this activity depends largely on the characteristics, willingness, and commitment of the project manager. The project manager makes and approves the most important decisions about the project activities in the short and long term. It is up to him or her to decide whether or not socio-ecological tasks are included in this activity. The project manager gives these tasks priority or marginalizes them, strongly enforces them, or gives the impression of being committed to sustainable development. The scope and pace of implementation of the sustainability principles in project activity is therefore largely determined by the characteristics and activity of the project manager.

As M. Epstein and A. Buhovac emphasize, research clearly shows that effective implementation of a sustainability strategy is possible only with the commitment of top management (Epstein and Buhovac 2014: 47). In many cases, effective implementation of a sustainability strategy is impossible because managers do not have the appropriate knowledge and are not committed to the process. R. Eccles and G. Serafeim consider lack of competence as one of the main barriers to the development of sustainability strategies. According to the researchers, new strategies that are related to environmental and social challenges often require new qualifications (Eccles and Serafeim 2013: 48). Therefore, the basic condition for a genuine and effective involvement of a project manager in sustainability issues is his or her knowledge in this area and socio-ecological sensitivity. The model solution is to entrust the function of a project manager to sustainable managers or sustainability-oriented managers. We will call them sustainable project managers. They have the following characteristics (Cohen 2011: 1–21, 132–158):

- they want to be responsible for the health of the Earth;
- they work for future generations to make them able not only to survive but also to burgeon;
- they focus on the future;
- they pursue economic, environmental, and social objectives;
- they are focused on sustainability in production and consumption, which is more important to them than growth;
- they control the impact of their actions on people and the environment;
- they minimize the negative impact of their actions on the planet; and
- they develop products, services, and technologies in accordance with sustainable development principles.

A slightly different approach is proposed by Jerry A. Carbo, Viet T. Dao, Steven J. Haase, M. Blake Hargrove, and Ian M. Langella. In their opinion, socially sustainable leadership has the following characteristics (Carbo, Dao, Haase, Hargrove and Langella 2018: 158):

1. Compassion (the ability to recognize the needs of others and the ability to openly love and respect one's followers).
2. Honesty (honest leaders tell the truth and do not deceive others).
3. Fairness (socially sustainable leadership demands a sense of fairness and a deep concern for justice).
4. Commitment (leaders must have fortitude, willpower, and hope to sustain their commitment).
5. Prudence (prudent leaders think before they act; they have the ability to gather, assess, and process information).

A project manager should therefore be a sustainable manager with a strong focus on the attitudes and activities listed above. A sustainable project manager is a management specialist who also has knowledge and skills in the field of sustainable development. Table 2.2 shows the characteristics and main areas of activity of such a manager in the area of sustainability in detail.

Sustainable project managers understand and accept sustainable development. They have extensive knowledge of environmental and social risks present on a local and global scale and ways to reduce them. They also know whether and what environmental and social problems may result from the execution of the project and how to eliminate them.

Sustainable project managers are characterized by high social and environmental sensitivity. They feel responsible for the state of the planet on which they live and on which the projects under their leadership are executed. They want to work for future generations so that they can both survive and burgeon. They not only focus on the present and the near future, but also seek to anticipate the social and environmental consequences of their decisions in the long run.

TABLE 2.2
Characteristics and Main Areas of Project Manager's Activity in the Area of Sustainability

Sustainable Project Manager				
Sustainable project manager's characteristics conducive to commitment to sustainable development				
Knowledge in the area of sustainability	Socio-environmental sensitivity	Innovation in sustainability	Openness to sustainability solutions	Ability to convince and encourage implementation of sustainability principles
Main areas of activity of a sustainable project manager in the field of sustainability taking into account ethical principles				
Development of project team members in the area of sustainability				
Performance of the project management functions according to the principles of sustainability: planning, organization, leadership/motivation, and control				

Source: Own work based on: Pabian 2015b: 7.

Another important characteristic of sustainable project managers is their innovative capacity. As R. Lussier emphasizes, innovation means implementing new ideas. These usually concern new things (product innovation) or new ways of doing things (process innovation). New ideas are the result of creativity, so it is creativity that leads to innovation (Lussier 2009: 95–96). There is a close link between projects and innovation, which results in unique products. Projects are defined as temporary endeavors undertaken to create a unique product, service, or result (Pinto and Patanakul 2017: 219).

Innovative solutions in the field of sustainability may concern both products and services created as a result of project execution as well as its individual phases. Sustainable project managers suggest to designers solutions that eliminate or significantly reduce the social and environmental harmfulness of products and services resulting from project activities. By managing their projects, they implement innovative, pro-environmental, and pro-social solutions concerning the work performed by the members of project teams and the resources they require.

Openness to change and willingness to make changes are other attributes of sustainable project managers. Ch. Achua and R. Lussier recognize these characteristics as some of the key elements of leadership (Achua and Lussier 2010: 6–8). Based on the analysis of data as well as on their own experience, project managers see the accumulation of local and global social and environmental problems. They recognize this growing trend as an unfavorable development that should be countered by sustainability initiatives. They are open to such initiatives and very satisfied if project team members recommend pro-environmental and pro-social solutions. They consider and implement them carefully if they contribute even minimally to an improvement of the environment or solve any social problems. They search for innovators, appoint innovation leaders, and trigger the innovative potential of their project teams.

An important characteristic of sustainable project managers is their ability to convince and encourage implementation of sustainability principles. This skill can be useful both during the preparatory activities and the project execution phase. It is particularly important to convince the persons who approve and finance projects as to the need to undertake pro-environmental and pro-social initiatives. This is a difficult task because, as A. Ghillyer notes, most companies focus on short-term profits – such pressure affects the social behavior of organizations. The management may be willing to lose a part of these profits in order to achieve social goals (Ghillyer 2009: 421). The ability to convince and argue certainly helps sustainable project managers to persuade the management of the companies in which the projects are carried out to set pro-environmental and pro-social goals. It is equally important to convince project team members of the need to undertake sustainability initiatives in the course of project execution. Sustainable project managers want their team members to understand the issues of sustainable development and to take action to achieve its goals with confidence.

Convincing others to undertake pro-environmental and pro-social initiatives is more effective if sustainable project managers provide concrete evidence that this will benefit the environment, the society, and the company. Here are some arguments for creating sustainable products. Research results show that many consumers are willing to pay more for a product that supports environmental and social goals. The percentage share of such consumers in selected European Union countries is the following: Germany – 35%, Italy – 34%, France – 30%, Holland – 30%, Belgium – 29%, Great

Britain – 28%, and Poland – 13%. For some non-European countries, this share is much higher, e.g. China – 80%, India – 71%, and USA – 39% (Mirońska and Zaborek 2014). The markets for products that support sustainable development are showing an upward trend. In the European Union, the average annual increase in sales of environmentally friendly products is 20%, while in Poland it is about 30%. More than a half of the people worldwide (54%) declare that such terms as green, environmentally friendly, fair trade, and sustainable development are important (Sieńkowska 2013).

Let us go to the main areas of activity of a sustainable project manager in the area of sustainability listed in Table 2.2. The most important area of this activity is performance of project management functions in accordance with the principles of sustainability. It consists in planning, organizing, motivating, and controlling, the aim of which is to achieve not only economic goals but also sustainable planning, sustainable organizing, sustainable leadership/motivating, and sustainable controlling goals. These are discussed in detail in Chapter 3.

When performing the management functions, a sustainable project manager should take care of the continuous development of his or her project team in the field of sustainable development. This can be done in two ways: by recruiting team members with the appropriate sustainability qualifications, and by developing the social and environmental attitudes and behaviors of the already employed staff. Here is an example concerning recruitment: when the CLP Holdings Limited (Hong Kong) realized that it had to diversify its energy sources (including hydroelectric, wind, and solar power in addition to fossil fuels), it recruited dozens of engineers qualified in these technologies. The new competent staff helped the CLP to increase the percentage share of electricity from renewable sources from less than 1% in 2004 to 18% in 2011 (Eccles and Serafeim 2013: 48).

Employment of competent staff to execute a project must be carried out in parallel with education and improvement programs for those team members who do not have knowledge of or experience in sustainable development. It may happen that the project team has to include a specialist with unique professional skills for whom sustainability is a completely alien and unknown area of knowledge. Many organizations develop their staff in the area of sustainability. For example Nissan, a leading auto manufacturer, has trained 99% of its company staff in environmental issues to foster understanding and sustainability awareness (Epstein and Buhovac 2014: 54). A sustainable project manager can offer various forms of education and training in the area of sustainability to his or her team members, from post-graduate studies, through training courses, to coaching.

The following issues are particularly relevant for training and other educational programs:

a. What knowledge and skills in the field of sustainability have the members of the project team acquired and have the planned changes in their attitudes occurred?
b. Do the team members use the acquired knowledge and skills to carry out the project?
c. Are the benefits achieved commensurate with the costs incurred for training and other educational programs?

It is important that the development of the members of a sustainability project team also takes place in direct contact with the project manager. G. Jones and J. George emphasize that the role of managers is not limited to making decisions, they also act as coaches and facilitators in relation to their subordinates (Jones and George 2011: 247).

All project managers encounter different ethical issues in the course of their activities. If they prioritize achievement of project goals, then ethics will certainly become of secondary importance. Unethical behavior can take place virtually at all stages of project execution. Withholding important information about the project from superiors and co-workers, overstating wages, falsifying data in reports, and attempts to bribe are examples of extremely irresponsible and unethical behavior. Unethical behavior can also take place in the area of sustainability. For example, it is unethical to pretend to be pro-environmental and pro-social, to swap sustainable resources for non-sustainable ones during execution of projects, and to hire acquaintances without any knowledge and experience in the field of sustainability. Fortunately, only a small percentage of adults seem unethical by nature. Recent research reported in an article published by the Deloitte Idea Labs asserts that a small percentage of adults appear to be inherently unethical (Douglas and Wykowski 2017: 260).

Ethics should form the basis of the functioning of every project team. It is manifested in the following areas:

a. the attitude of the organization in which the project is executed toward the members of the project team;
b. the attitude of the project team to that organization;
c. the attitude of the project team to the external stakeholders; and
d. the relationship between members of the project team.

Maryyam Kouchaki and Isaac H. Smith suggest that people who want to act ethically should take a three-stage approach. First, they should prepare in advance for moral challenges. Second, they should make good decisions in times of trial. Third, they have to take time to reflect and constantly draw conclusions from ethical successes and failures. It is worth being ethical because unethical behavior causes stress. Ethical stress results in employee fatigue, reduced job satisfaction, lower motivation, and increased turnover. Thus, Maryyam Kouchaki and Isaac H. Smith encourage people to follow the guidelines of deontology (the science of moral duties). They conclude their deliberations with the following statement: "success without honor is worse than deception," which certainly applies to executors of all kinds of projects (Kouchaki and Smith 2020: 138, 141).

A sustainable project manager should be an authentic leader. According to Richard L. Daft and Dorothy Marcic, to be authentic means being real, staying true to one's values and beliefs, and acting based on one's true self rather than emulating what others do. Authentic leaders inspire trust and commitment because they respect diverse viewpoints, encourage collaboration, and help others learn, grow, and develop as leaders (Daft and Marcic 2013: 458). Authentic leaders have the following key characteristics (Daft and Marcic 2013: 459–460):

1. Authentic leaders pursue their purpose with passion.
2. Authentic leaders practice solid values.
3. Authentic leaders lead with their hearts as well as their heads.
4. Authentic leaders establish connected relationship.
5. Authentic leaders demonstrate self-discipline.

A sustainable project manager should also be a transformational leader. Transformational leaders are distinguished by their special ability to bring about innovation and change by recognizing followers' needs and concerns, providing meaning, challenging people to look at old problems in new ways, and acting as role models for the new values and behaviors (Daft and Benson 2016: 430).

Perhaps the greatest challenge for a sustainable project manager is to become a charismatic leader. The qualities of charismatic leaders are the following (Achua and Lussier 2010: 297):

a. vision;
b. superb communication skills;
c. self-confidence and moral conviction;
d. ability to inspire trust;
e. high risk orientation;
f. high energy and action orientation;
g. relational power base;
h. minimum internal conflict;
i. ability to empower others; and
j. self-promoting personality.

Every manager has interpersonal, informational, and decisional roles in his or her organization (Ghillyer 2009: 8–9). This also applies to the sustainable project manager whose organization is the project team. No less important are skills. In addition to conceptual skills, project managers should have human relations skills and technical skills. Human relations skills are those that managers need to understand and work well with people. Technical skills are the specific abilities that people use to perform their jobs (Ghillyer 2009: 10).

Project managers are selected in the initial phase of project work, namely before the preparation of the project charter. As the persons responsible for the entire project work, they must be able to participate in its preparation. Information about the project charter can be found in Chapter 3.

Project managers play a key role in making project activities pro-environmental and pro-social. However, without project teams competent in sustainability to manage, it is difficult, if not impossible, for project managers to achieve sustainability goals. In section 2.3, we explain how to create a sustainable project team.

THE PROFILE OF A SUSTAINABLE PROJECT MANAGER

Has high social and ecological sensitivity.
Has extensive knowledge about sustainability and constantly improves it.
Feels responsible for the health of the Earth.
Wants to work for future generations so that they can survive and burgeon.
Focuses on the future.
Considers sustainability to be more important than short-term profits and growth.
Controls the environmental and social impact of project activities.
Has a vision of sustainability and implements it by managing the project.
Minimizes the negative impact of project activities on the environment.
Is enterprising and action-oriented.
Is innovative – constantly looks for and implements new sustainability solutions.
Is open to all environmentally friendly and pro-social solutions.
Can convince and motivate others to implement sustainability principles.
Has excellent communication skills.
Takes care of the development of project team members in the area of sustainability.
Is honest and ethical.

Source: Own work.

2.3 MEMBERS OF THE SUSTAINABILITY PROJECT TEAM AND THEIR RECRUITMENT

The need to employ sustainability experts in organizations and project teams is becoming increasingly important in the global business world. M. Epstein and A. Buhovac emphasize that organizations need educated and trained people who are sensitive to sustainability issues; financial and human resources have a significant impact on the ability to implement sustainability programs (Epstein and Buhovac 2014: 33).

A sustainable project manager, in order to effectively achieve the ecological and social goals set in a project, should have a special human resource in the form of sustainable members of the project team. A sustainable member of a project team is a synthesis of three personalities: an economic worker, an ecological worker, and a social worker. These types of people, concerned about the growing environmental and social problems, contribute to sustainable development both in the workplace and in their private lives. They show concern for the state of the Earth and for their immediate surroundings. They work for future generations to make them able not only to survive but also to burgeon. They initiate and actively contribute to the environmental and social goals of their project team.

A sustainable member of a project team should have the same four out of the five sustainability characteristics that we have assigned to a project manager. They include:

- socio-environmental sensitivity;
- knowledge in the area of sustainability;
- innovation; and
- openness to solutions in this area.

However, the main areas of activity in the area of sustainability for a project manager and project team members are different due to their different roles in the project organization. A sustainable project manager manages the project team and thus plans, organizes, motivates, and controls in accordance with the principles of sustainability as well as develops his or her subordinates. His job is to influence the people who are members of the project team. He or she sets out tasks for them and checks whether and how they have been completed. The work of project team members is of an executive nature. They do their jobs using various devices (computers, photocopiers, telephones, and others) and mainly influence physical things. An example of a physical thing is a piece of paper on which a project schedule is written or a prototype of a device being tested. The pro-environmental and pro-social activity of a project team member is therefore manifested in the following activities:

a. designing solutions that do not harm people or the natural environment;
b. performing work in a pro-environmental and pro-social manner;
c. participating in a pro-environmental and pro-social shaping of their workplace and its surroundings; and
d. participating in social projects.

To explain the essence of the above activities, let us use the following example: one of the members of a project team is preparing guidelines for office equipment. In this work, he uses a computer and a photocopier. If this person includes environmentally friendly furniture in the guidelines, this solution will contribute to environmental protection (a). If he uses a computer and a photocopier in an energy-efficient way when preparing guidelines, and also uses environmentally friendly paper and double-sided printing, his work will also contribute to sustainable development (b). The initiative to replace standard lightbulbs in his office with energy-efficient ones will also be environmentally friendly (c). During his employment in a project team, this employee may also support various social campaigns (d). As the example shows, practically every aspect of the activities of a sustainable member of a project team is characterized by a pro-environmental and pro-social attitude.

THE PROFILE OF A SUSTAINABLE MEMBER OF THE PROJECT TEAM

Has knowledge about sustainable development.
Wants to contribute to elimination of environmental and social risks.
Fully accepts the environmental and social objectives of the project team and actively participates in their achievement.

Reports the need for pro-environmental and pro-social equipment for his or her workplace.
Performs his or her work in accordance with sustainability principles.
Take into account the principles of sustainability in his or her projects.
Notify the project manager of new sustainability initiatives.
Participates in social campaigns.
Is honest and ethical.

Creating a project team consisting of sustainable members is a big challenge for the project manager and the organization where the project is being executed. Richard Templar appeals to managers: you have to be good at finding the right people to fill the right jobs (Templar 2015: 32–33). Finding the right people to work in a project team is a difficult task. Richard L. Daft and Dorothy Marcic say: even when unemployment rates are high, companies often have trouble finding people with the skills the organization needs. A survey by Manpower Inc. of 33,000 employers in 23 countries found that 40% reported having difficulty finding and hiring the desired talent (Daft and Marcic 2013: 324).

Recruitment of sustainable members of the project team is about finding people who are not only professionals, but also have knowledge of and experience in sustainability. This requires sustainability requirements to be taken into account at every stage of the recruitment process. The most important phases of the recruitment process that take this condition into account are presented later in this section.

Recruitment of project team members should be preceded by preparatory activities consisting in:

a. drawing up a list of tasks to be performed in order to execute the project;
b. determining the number of team members who are required to perform these tasks;
c. assigning tasks to individual team members; and
d. preparing a list of required qualifications for each team member.

At this stage of preparation for the recruitment process, instead of names, the following phrases are used: team member 1, team member 2, team member 3, etc. This is because these are separate positions in the project team that have not yet been filled with specific people. During the preparatory phase, a document must be drawn up, the structure of which is shown in Table 2.3.

In the project team member requisition form, not only their qualifications and professional experience (column 3), but also their aptitudes desirable from the point of view of sustainability (column 4) should be specified. The requisition form drawn up in this way clearly imposes the obligation to recruit to the project team people who are not only specialists in their field but are also actively involved in sustainable development.

TABLE 2.3
Requisition for Project Team Members with a List of the Required Qualifications and the Desired Environmental and Social Aptitudes

Project Team Members	Tasks/Work to be Performed on the Project	Required Qualifications and Professional Experience	Desirable Pro-environmental and Pro-social Characteristics and Attitudes
C1			
C2			
C3			
C4			

Source: Own work.

Project team members can be recruited in following two ways:

1. the top management of the organization and the project manager indicate specific people and offer them participation in the project, or
2. information about the recruitment to the project team is made public inside the organization or also in its surroundings. In response to this information, candidates for members of the project team come forward and the best qualified persons are selected from among them.

Recruitment of project team members requires submission of appropriate documents, including those confirming professional qualifications and sustainability aptitudes and achievements. Examples of documents that prove involvement in sustainable development are certificates of completion of environmental protection courses and certificates of participation in social campaigns.

After pre-selection of the candidates to work on the project team on the basis of the submitted documents, interviews are held with the candidates. If a candidate's supporting documents do not mention the candidate's views and commitment to sustainable development, questions on this matter must be asked during the interview. Examples of such questions are given in the following box.

EXAMPLES OF SUSTAINABILITY QUESTIONS TO BE ASKED WHEN INTERVIEWING CANDIDATES (RECRUITMENT TO A PROJECT TEAM)

1. What do you think is the importance of care for the natural environment and what should it consist in?
2. How do you contribute to environmental protection in your work and private life?

3. Is it possible to protect the natural environment by working on the project team that you want to be a part of and how can it be done?
4. What social problems are you most concerned about and why?
5. Should one actively engage in solving ecological and social problems?
6. What should such activity consist in?
7. Do you have any experience in this area?
8. How can project team members contribute to solving environmental and social problems?
9. Have you taken part in any social campaigns?
10. What was your participation in such campaigns?

During the recruitment phase, attention must also be paid to the ethical attitudes of the candidates. Only people who adhere to ethical standards should be hired in a project team. A positive ethical evaluation of a candidate in the recruitment process does not guarantee that he or she will carry out the project in accordance with ethical principles. It may happen that in the recruitment process, the candidate only appears to have positive ethical attitudes. Consequently, the best test of ethical conduct is actual work on a project. A good test of ethical conduct is the candidate's activity during the probation period, if such a period is provided for in the employment contract with the new member of the project team. An employee with a strong tendency for unethical behavior must be fired from the team. This is because he or she will expose the team to problems, negatively affect its image, and set a bad example his or her colleagues.

The staff recruiting members of the project teams can examine the ethical attitudes of candidates in different ways: ask them questions about ethical issues, test them in this area, and learn about their behavior in previous jobs. The recruiting staff should also be prepared for the unusual situation where it is not them but the candidate who initiates an interview on ethical values and asks questions. As a member of the recruitment team, are you prepared to answer the following questions asked by the candidate?

1. What ethical dilemmas can I encounter while working on the project team?
2. What actions are taken to promote ethical practices in the project team's activities?
3. Is there any formal document that regulates the ethical issues related to the activities of project teams in your company?
4. Is it acceptable for ethical conduct to cause a significant delay in project execution?
5. Is it acceptable for ethical conduct to cause an increase in the cost of project execution?
6. How should I react when I receive an order from my superior that violates ethical principles?

The persons recruiting members to work on the project team can use various types of tools that make it easier to organize information about the candidates, to compare candidates, and to select them. An example of such a tool is a selection grid containing the first and last names of the candidates and a list of criteria to be evaluated on a scoring scale. These criteria concern both, the professional qualifications of the candidates (educational background, professional experience, communication skills, etc.) and their attitudes and commitment to sustainable development (social and environmental sensitivity, social and environmental qualifications, social and environmental activities, etc.). It is important to give high priority to sustainability criteria and to evaluate candidates carefully on their basis. The selection grid is the basis for selecting the best candidates to work on a project team. These are all persons who have received the highest ratings in terms of the criteria contained therein.

In the recruitment process, candidates may be subjected to tests that make it possible not only to assess their professional skills, but also to assess their sensitivity and their social and environmental skills. The boxes below contain examples of the behavior to be assessed during two different sustainability tests.

SUSTAINABILITY TEST 1

Selection and Ordering of Computer Hardware

Behavior to be assessed: Does the candidate choose green computer hardware or conventional hardware? Is he or she interested in the impact of the hardware considered on human health and the natural environment (asks the sellers about those matters, reads descriptions of the hardware)? Does he or she choose hardware with low energy consumption? Does he or she choose electric energy saving functions? Does he or she pay attention in environmental aspects to the weight and size of the hardware? Does he or she choose hardware made of recycled materials? Does he or she choose hardware tested for chemical emissions? Does he or she check the durability of the hardware? Does he or she check ecological certificates? Does he or she order hardware from socially and environmentally responsible vendors?

Source: Own work.

SUSTAINABILITY TEST 2

Use of Office Equipment

Behavior to be assessed: Does the candidate switch the equipment on only for the duration of use or is it switched on unnecessarily (consumes energy while waiting to be used)? Does he or she use the equipment in a manner that is safe to people and the natural environment (uses it in accordance with the manual and the occupational health and safety regulations)? Does he or she safely use the materials needed for operation of the equipment? Does he or she sort the waste produced as a result of use of the equipment? Does he or she follow the rules concerning return and disposal of those equipment components that become worn during use and are regularly changed (e.g. toners in photocopiers and computer printers)? Does the candidate intend to use the equipment for a long time, e.g. for several years, or does he or she plan to replace it with a new one? What are the reasons for such replacement? Is it environmentally sound?

Source: Own work.

As a result of the recruitment process, the project team is joined by people who not only have high professional qualifications, but also demonstrate social and environmental sensitivity and activity.

Recruitment to project teams must be entrusted to people with the appropriate sustainability background. If a sustainable project manager conducts the recruitment process, the problem is basically solved. Such a manager has the appropriate knowledge and experience to assess whether or not a candidate for a project team member is sensitive and active in terms of sustainability. It is worth noting at this point that participation of a project manager in the process of recruitment of project team members is actually necessary. A project manager must select people who recognize his or her leadership and are able to work efficiently in the project team. It is not acceptable to create a project team consisting of people in conflict with each other and who reject the authority of their manager.

From the point of view of sustainability, an unfavorable situation occurs when the top management, with no knowledge of or experience in sustainability, of an organization in which the project is to be carried out determines the composition of the project team and appoints its manager. In this case, the members of the project team are unlikely to have any qualifications in sustainability. This can be prevented by involving a sustainability specialist from the company's own or surrounding environment in the recruitment process, possibly by outsourcing recruitment to external agencies.

A project team consisting of a sustainable project manager and sustainable members can start the project by performing the activities presented in Chapter 3.

RECRUITMENT OF SUSTAINABLE MEMBERS OF THE PROJECT TEAM

Preparation for the Recruitment

Draw up a list of tasks (work) to be performed in order to execute the project.

Determine the number of team members who are required to perform these tasks.

Assign tasks to individual team members.

Prepare a list of the required qualifications for each team member taking into account sustainability requirements.

Conduct the Recruitment

Announce the recruitment to the project team or extend the offer to specific specialists.

Analyze the documents submitted by the candidates. Carefully analyze their aptitudes and sustainability achievements.

Pre-select the candidates on the basis of the submitted documents.

Leave the documents of the best candidates who meet the sustainability criteria.

Interview the candidates. Ask questions about the candidates' knowledge and commitment to sustainable development.

Test your candidates for sustainability attitudes.

Select the best candidates.

Formalize their employment in the project team.

Source: Own work.

3 A Functional Approach to Sustainable Project Management

3.1 PROJECT MANAGEMENT AS A SEQUENCE OF FUNCTIONS AND ACTIVITIES

Every project team, regardless of its size, is an organization. It consists of a smaller or larger number of persons who act under the leadership of a manager. A project team has specific objectives, which it achieves by using tangible and intangible resources. Thanks to the division of labor, individual tasks are performed in a professional manner by various types of specialists. Considering project activity in terms of management and its functions is therefore fully justified and even necessary for proper project execution.

Management, commonly referred to as the pursuit of objectives through the organization and coordination of people, remains a core feature, and function, of modern society (Wilkinson, Armstrong and Lounsbury 2017: 1). Management is the process of deciding the best way to use an organization's resources to produce goods or provide services (Ghillyer 2009: 4). Management is about making people achieve the organization's goals with specific resources. Thus, in the case of projects, management is to cause the members of the project team to use the resources allocated to them to achieve their objectives. What does this causing consist in and who does it? Causing is an activity that consists in planning, organizing, leading, and controlling. Although this division of the management functions is widespread worldwide, one must keep in mind that their names and numbers may vary slightly. This is evidenced by the following exemplary list of authors who in their books describe management through the lens of the functions specified in brackets: R. Daft and D. Marcic (planning, organizing, leading, and controlling) (Daft and Marcic 2013: 9, 158–600); S. Certo and T. Certo (planning, organizing, influencing, and controlling) (Certo and Certo 2009: 121–123, 179–570); and A. Ghillyer (planning, organizing, staffing, leading, and controlling) (Ghillyer 2009: 7, 109–364). Given the project management functions, project management can therefore be defined as an activity that consists in planning, organizing, leading, and controlling that result in the project team achieving the project objectives.

In this book, we do not deal with classical project management, but with management in the sustainability concept. Sustainable management is a new and emerging area of knowledge that is a part of sustainable science. S. Cohen said that sustainability management is in its infancy. Today, it will not be able to predict its pace, shape or trajectory. According to this author, sustainability management is the practice of economic production and consumption that minimizes environmental impact and maximizes resource conservation and reuse. At the heart of sustainability, management is a concern for the future (Cohen 2011: 146). B. Bossink defines sustainable management in terms of eco-innovations as the development of new initiatives in an organization to sustain, improve, and renew the environmental, social, and societal quality of its business processes and the products and services these business processes produce (Bossink 2012: 1). A. Pabian defines sustainable management as a process where objectives are achieved by organizations in observance of the principles of sustainable development. In functional terms, sustainable management is planning, organizing, leading, and controlling that results in creation, functioning, and development of a sustainable organization, i.e., an entity that contributes to balancing of intergenerational needs (Pabian 2013b: 5). Let us relate this concept to project management.

Sustainable project management is an activity that consists in planning, organizing, leading, and controlling, carried out in accordance with the principles of sustainability, as a result of which the project team achieves project goals.

Source: Own work.

In our approach to project management, sustainability permeates all areas of project activity and complies with the 4 × SUSTAINABILITY IN PROJECT ACTIVITIES principle.

Sustainable project management results in creation of a sustainable project organization (project team) and then in execution of a project by the organization that takes into account pro-environmental and pro-social objectives. A sustainable project organization consists of sustainable employees who use sustainable physical resources to execute the project in a sustainable manner.

Source: Own work.

In the 4 × SUSTAINABILITY IN PROJECT ACTIVITIES concept, we combine sustainability not only with the goods that result from execution of projects, but also relate it to the people who execute projects, the resources they use, and the work they do. This comprehensive approach is intended to encourage project teams to seek solutions that contribute to sustainable development in all areas and phases of their activities. Sustainability added to the term project management is reflected in its functions. These functions are:

1. Sustainable planning is about defining the objectives of a project taking into account the principles of sustainability and deciding how best to achieve them.

2. Sustainable organizing of project activities means allocating resources, grouping activities of a similar nature, and appointing people to carry them out in compliance with the principles of sustainability.
3. Sustainable leadership/motivating focuses on influencing the members of the project team and the collaborators in such a way that they work according to the goals and in observance of the principles of sustainability.
4. Sustainable controlling means comparing the actual level of completion of project tasks in the area of sustainability with standards and then taking corrective action if necessary.

Sustainable project management is directed toward three types of objectives: economic, ecological, and social. Although in many cases, environmental and social objectives are interdependent, e.g. polluted air (environmental problem) causes people to become ill (social problem), there are also situations where there is little or no connection at all between these objectives. Examples include poverty, exploitation, and drug addiction. This justifies considering environmental and social objectives separately, rather than merging them into a single objective.

In order to properly define environmental and social objectives, sustainable project management requires a review of the damage that a project can cause to the environment and to people. The idea is to identify it, determine its sources, estimate its size, and seek ways to eliminate or significantly reduce it. Sustainable project management is based on the 3C principle:

1. Commitment – engaging all members of the project team and other project shareholders in pro-environmental and pro-social activities;
2. Continuity – causing pro-environmental and pro-social activities to be present in all phases of project execution; and
3. Continuous improvement – continuous search for and implementation of solutions that limit the negative impact of the project on the natural environment and humans.

An important issue in project management is project centralization or decentralization. Centralization means that decision authority is located near the top of the organization. With decentralization, decision authority is pushed downward to lower organization levels (Daft and Marcic 2013: 242). The problem of centralization and decentralization applies to both large and small project teams. In the case of centralized management, the majority of or all decision-making powers are vested in the project manager. The manager makes decisions and delegates tasks to the project team members also in the area of sustainability. Decentralization, on the other hand, involves delegating a substantial part of the decision-making powers to the members of the project team. Most decisions are made by them without consulting the manager. The manager stops interfering in all, even the tiniest matters related to project execution. It encourages team members to make decisions, reserving the right to interfere on key issues. Consequently, they also have more freedom in their sustainability efforts. Depending on the extent of the decision-making powers delegated to the team members, there may be a greater or lesser degree of decentralization. Decentralization is justified if the members of the project team are highly qualified and competent in their respective fields of activity, as well as in the field of sustainability. Otherwise, interference can occur due to wrong decisions made by less experienced project staff.

Pro-environmental and pro-social activities can be carried out in both centralized and decentralized management conditions. In the case of centralization, activity of the project team that contributes to sustainable development is guaranteed by:

a. a sustainable project manager whose decisions take into account sustainable development matters;
b. a project plan that contains pro-environmental and pro-social activities that must be carried out.

From the point of view of sustainability, in a centralized project management system, at least one of the above conditions must be met. If the project manager is not sustainable and the plans do not include pro-environmental and pro-social activities, sustainability will not be present in the project activities.

Decentralization of project management is more advantageous. The members of the project team have more decision-making powers, including those concerning their involvement in sustainable development. Decentralization increases motivation to work and triggers creativity. If the members of the project team are environmentally and socially sensitive, creativity is reflected in the search for and implementation of sustainability solutions.

> Decentralization of project management enables better use of the intellectual potential of team members. They have a lot of freedom to come up with and implement creative sustainability solutions.
>
> *Source*: Own work.

Another important issue that affects the project team's involvement in sustainable development is formalization of project activities. Formalization consists in introducing rules and procedures that govern the work and behavior of project team members. Formalization is the greater the more rules and instructions apply and the more detailed and rigorous they are. High formalization of work processes makes it possible to predict its amount and effects. However, in the event of a reformulation, project team members are too constrained in their actions by excessive regulations. This blocks their initiative and creativity. On the other hand, in a situation of insufficient formalization, they have an excessive degree of freedom. This may be conducive to improvisation that is not always favorable to the performance of work. Lower levels of formalization are recommended for highly qualified, experienced, and disciplined personnel.

In the case of high formalization, sustainability is only present in the activities of the project team if it is included in the applicable rules and instructions. Since team members have to follow such rules and instructions, sustainability can be guaranteed only by being included in their content. At the same time, one should keep in mind that the consequence of high formalization is a large number of instructions and documents, mostly in paper form, which is not environmentally friendly. On the other hand, limiting the initiative and creativity of project team members with numerous rules and instructions is not pro-social. It can cause frustration, dissatisfaction, work fatigue, and even diseases.

A high degree of formalization in the case of projects where creative work prevails is not advisable. Less formalization triggers the initiative and creativity of the project team members, also in the area of sustainability. As they have a lot of freedom of action, they can implement their own solutions that contribute to sustainable development.

The more creative the work done by the project team members, the lower the level of formalization should be.

Source: Own work.

Formalization in sustainable project management requires sustainability to be taken into account in existing instructions and procedures.

Source: Own work.

Inclusion of sustainability principles in project management presents new challenges for project managers. The manager is responsible for the environment and must not harm people or the Earth: you mustn't do anything that is going to do harm, cause lasting damage, put anyone at risk of health or life, or cause any land to be utilized in a worse way than it was before you came along. You don't have to be an eco-warrior, but you do have a responsibility not to cause harm or damage. Therefore, Richard Templar asks managers the following question: Can you put your hand on your heart and say your managerial role is "clean"? (Templar 2015: 208).

The manager, when managing the project team, makes decisions that should take into account the needs of sustainable development. According to Jonathan P. Doh and Fred Luthans, the decision-making process consists of nine stages: 1. Problem perception, 2. Problem identification, 3. Problem formulation, 4. Search for alternatives, 5. Evaluation of alternatives, 6. Choice of alternatives, 7. Start of operation, 8. Implementation, and 9. Control (Doh and Luthans 2018: 390). Adaptation to this procedure and careful consideration of the decision problem at all stages facilitate accurate decision-making. Making the right decisions is not easy. Why do managers make bad decisions? Here are some reasons: being influenced by initial impressions, justifying past decisions, seeing what you want to see, perpetuating the status quo, being influenced by emotions, and overconfidence (Daft and March 2013: 217–218).

Project team management is possible thanks to communication. Communication takes place within the project team as well as between the team and its surroundings.

The project manager is the best-informed person on the team. He provides the team members with the information necessary for their day-to-day activities and defends the team's interests. Good managers develop effective communication skills. They use these skills to absorb information, motivate employees, and deal effectively with customers and coworkers (Ghillyer 2009: 56). Written communication and oral communication stand out.

Management is based on authority, responsibility, and delegation. Authority is the formal and legitimate right of a manager to make decisions, issue orders, and allocate resources to achieve organizationally desired outcomes. Responsibility is the duty to perform the task or activity as assigned. Delegation is the process that managers use to transfer authority and responsibility to positions below them in the hierarchy (Daft and Marcic 2013: 237–238). Proper use of authority, responsibility, and delegation in the management of a project team results in a real whole and a productive entity that produces more than the sum of the resources invested in it.

3.2 PROJECT INITIATION IN THE LIGHT OF SUSTAINABILITY

There are many possibilities to initiate projects that take sustainability into account. We divide them into three basic categories as shown in Figure 3.1. Projects in the first category are aimed to counteract environmental and social risks. Projects of the second type are intended to contribute to the creation of sustainable organizations, which are one of the foundations of sustainable development. Projects in the first and second category are carried out in order to promote sustainable development. The third category comprises projects where sustainability should be present, although their initiators did not plan this type of activity beyond the legal requirements. In the following section, we discuss these project categories in detail.

Initiating Ecological and Social Projects

Projects of this type are aimed to eliminate or reduce environmental and social risks. Their classification is given in Table 3.1.

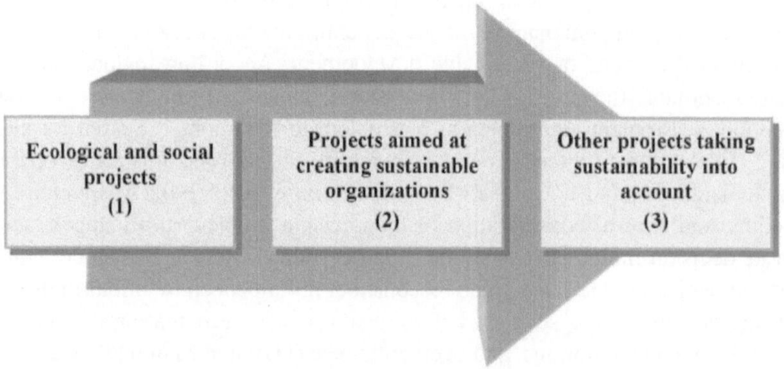

FIGURE 3.1 Types of projects taking sustainability into account. (Own work.)

TABLE 3.1
Types of Projects Aimed at Countering Environmental and Social Risks

Group		Type
Projects countering environmental and social risks	Projects countering environmental risks	Projects preventing the depletion of non-renewable natural resources
		Projects preventing air pollution
		Projects preventing soil contamination
		Projects preventing water pollution
		Projects preventing the greenhouse effect
		Projects preventing loss of biodiversity
		Projects preventing reduction of forest areas
		Projects reducing waste and preventing illegal landfills
		Projects preventing environmental disasters
		Projects preventing emergence of neglected industrial areas and land devastation
		Other projects
	Projects countering social risks	Projects preventing lifestyle diseases
		Projects preventing human exploitation
		Projects preventing poverty and deprivation
		Projects preventing unemployment
		Projects limiting consumerism
		Projects reducing international population migrations
		Other projects

Source: Own work.

The projects listed in Table 3.1 are divided into two categories: those directed outside the organization and those directed inside the organization. Outward projects are not related to the activities of companies, and concern environmental and social problems in the surroundings. Examples of these are: afforestation of land, feeding of animals, elimination of rubbish from rivers and lakes, financial aid to local hospices, and sponsoring of sports teams. Inward projects concern problems occurring inside companies that are related to their operations. Their examples include reducing the amount of production waste, installing filters on factory smokestacks, and creating health programs for own employees.

When initiating the projects listed in Table 3.1, one needs to know and understand the environmental and social needs of one's region and company. Environmental interviews are a helpful tool in identifying these needs. In the case of outward environmental projects, information on the state of the local environment and the possibilities for its improvement is important. In order to initiate inward environmental projects, it is necessary to explain what damage the company causes to the environment, what its source and size are, and how it can be eliminated.

Environmental interviews are also necessary for projects of a social nature. To initiate the right projects, one needs to listen to the needs of the local community and one's own staff. To this end, meetings are organized with the inhabitants of the region and the local authorities, as well as with employees of one's own company.

Maps of environmental and social problems of the local community and one's own organization are useful in initiating the aforementioned projects. They reflect the full spectrum of problems that require resolution. On the basis of these, the most important problems can be selected and remedied using projects.

Initiating Projects Aimed at Creating Sustainable Organizations

Projects aimed at creating sustainable organizations are intended to transform existing unsustainable or not very sustainable businesses, companies, and institutions into sustainable ones. In the model approach, sustainable organizations meet the conditions defined by the 4 × SUSTAINABILITY rule. Such organizations conduct sustainable operations based on sustainable resources. This activity results in sustainable products or services. Such organizations contribute to sustainable development in virtually all areas of their operations. Without this type of organizations, full sustainable development will not be possible. Transformation of current consumer societies into sustainable societies will also fail. The concept of a sustainable organization based on the example of a manufacturing company is shown in Table 3.2.

The choice of a production company to illustrate the key characteristics of a sustainable organization is purposeful and results from the fact that production entities have the greatest share in the devastation of the environment and also contribute to many social problems (e.g. production of unhealthy food, drinks, cigarettes, and alcohol). A sustainable organization in the proposed approach is a model solution that should be pursued by any entity wishing to make a genuine contribution to sustainable development. Its structure can be adapted to any type of organization, including non-productive ones by replacing production with another type of activity. This is what we did in Chapter 1, where we adapted the concept to the needs of a project organization.

TABLE 3.2
Concept of a Sustainable Organization

Sustainable Incoming Goods	**Sustainable Organization**				**Sustainable Outgoing Goods**
Sustainable machinery, equipment, raw materials, etc.	Sustainable workers	Sustainable building infrastructure	Sustainable furnishings	Sustainable machines and production and transport equipment	Sustainable products and services
	Sustainable Operations				

Source: Own work based on Pabian 2017b: 12.

As shown in Table 3.2, a sustainable organization has the following characteristics:

a. its human and physical resources are sustainable;
b. it operates in a sustainable manner;
c. the incoming goods that enabling its operations are sustainable; and
d. the effects of these operations, taking the form of products/services, are sustainable.

The profiles of employees hired in managerial and non-managerial positions in a sustainable organization are analogous to those of a sustainable project manager and his or her team. We described them in Chapter 2. Chapter 4 focuses on sustainable building infrastructure, furnishings, machines and equipment, as well as products, and contains an explanation of their key characteristics and specific examples.

In the proposed model of an organization, sustainability covers all its resources and processes. Therefore, it is comprehensive and complete, unlike other approaches where sustainability is included in a fragmented and selective way. For example, covering only the organization's physical resources with sustainability without considering people and their activities can lead to the following unsustainable actions and behaviors: non-compliance with occupational health and safety regulations, overloading of machinery and equipment, excessive use of materials, exploitation of employees, and unethical behavior.

Having familiarized ourselves with the concept of a sustainable organization, we can move on to projects related to its creation. Such creation can be done in two ways: by transforming existing entities into sustainable organizations or by creating such organizations from scratch. To become sustainable organizations, business entities that are currently unsustainable can initiate projects in the three main areas listed in Table 3.3.

Table 3.4 shows the different activity options for the areas listed in Table 3.3. Option 1 is the most desirable as the organization is active in all three areas. Less activity in favor of sustainable development is reflected in options 2, 3, and 4, which cover two areas. Even less activity in only one area is illustrated by options 5, 6, and 7.

TABLE 3.3
Main Areas of Initiation of Sustainability Projects in a Production Organization

Main Areas of Initiation of Sustainability Projects		
Sourcing goods from sustainable sources	Transforming the business into a sustainable organization	Production of sustainable products/services

Source: Own work.

TABLE 3.4
Sustainability in the Project Initiation Phase (Types of Sustainability Projects)

Options	Sourcing Based on Sustainable Goods	Creating a Sustainable Organization	Production of Sustainable Goods
Option 1	x	x	x
Option 2	x	x	-
Option 3	x	-	x
Option 4	-	x	x
Option 5	x	-	-
Option 6	-	x	-
Option 7	-	-	x

Source: Own work.

The range of activities supporting sustainable development may vary also in individual areas. For example, transformation of a company into a sustainable organization can be focused on only one or all of the resources listed in Table 3.2 or on all of them. Table 3.5 gives examples of projects to be implemented in each of the areas under consideration.

TABLE 3.5
Examples of Projects Contributing to the Creation of a Sustainable Organization

Area of Activity	Examples of Projects
Production of sustainable goods	Designing and launching production of environmentally friendly office furniture
	Designing and launching production of environmentally friendly packaging
	Design and implementation of catering services based on organic food
Creating a sustainable organization	Organization of a series of training courses for employees on sustainability
	Designing and building an environmentally friendly office building
	Designing, buying, and commissioning an environmentally friendly production line
	Replacing company cars with electric ones
	Replacing computer hardware with environmentally friendly models
	Selecting and replacing lighting in production buildings with energy-efficient ones
Sourcing based on sustainable goods	Choosing the assortment and suppliers of environmentally friendly paper for production of books
	Choosing the assortment and suppliers of environmentally friendly paints for construction services
	Choosing the assortment and suppliers of environmentally friendly materials for furniture production

Source: Own work.

Initiation of Other Projects Involving Sustainability

In practice, there are many projects that do not fall into the categories described previously in Section 3.2. The following are examples of projects aimed at achieving economic objectives without environmental and social objectives:

- building new production facilities;
- launching new process lines;
- developing new products and services;
- launching new distribution channels;
- developing new software; and
- placing products on foreign markets.

If such projects include any undertakings related to the protection of the natural or human environment, they result only from the applicable laws. Adherence to such laws is a condition for opening a production plant, launching a production line, launching a product, etc. However, as practice shows, restricting oneself to compliance with environmental and social laws is insufficient from the point of view of sustainable development. That is why it is so important to take additional actions within projects that go beyond the existing environmental and social laws. Figure 3.2 shows two states:

a. the current state where economic objectives prevail and pro-environmental and pro-social activities are kept to a minimum and result from the applicable laws, and
b. the desirable state were environmental and social objectives are as important as economic objectives and where organizations go beyond the existing laws and carry out many additional projects that contribute to sustainable development.

Of course, there are more and more companies in the market whose activities come closer to the desired state. They actively contribute to sustainable development by setting ambitious environmental and social objectives for themselves.

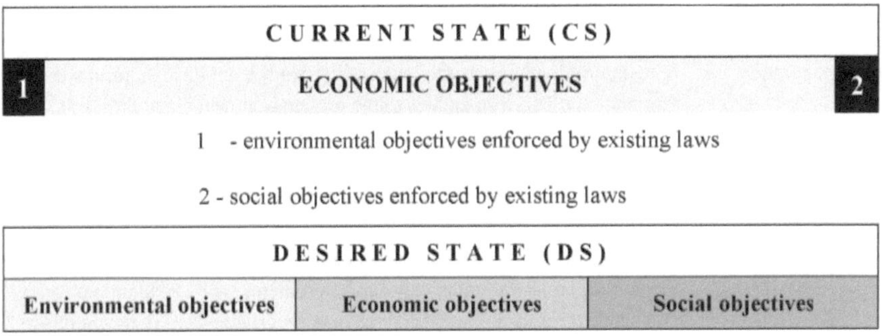

FIGURE 3.2 Share of sustainability in projects. (Own work.)

Therefore, the goal is to move projects from the current state status to the desired state status and thus to develop pro-environmental and pro-social activities in a way that goes far beyond the requirements of the current legislation. Such activities performed within projects can be facilitated by answering the following questions:

a. Can our project cause any damage to the environment and the society and what damage is that?
b. How much damage will it cause and how will it affect our business and further development?
c. What should we do to prevent or minimize this damage?
d. What additional actions can we take to contribute to environmental protection and to solving local social problems?

The search for answers to these questions requires a deeper reflection on the environmental and social effects of projects, as well as a search for solutions that contribute to sustainable development.

Sustainability in the Project Charter

Approval of a project charter implies its final acceptance and entitles the project manager to take further action. The planned sustainability activities should be reflected in the project charter. Table 3.6 shows an example of the structure of a project charter and explains what sustainability issues it should contain.

TABLE 3.6
Sustainability in a Project Charter

Project Charter Broken Down into Sections	Sustainability Issues
Project objectives	Environmental and social objectives may be the main or only one of the project objectives. The objectives should be defined precisely, preferably in figures, and deadlines should be specified, e.g. as a result of installation of environmentally friendly machines, electricity consumption will be reduced by 15%, water consumption will be reduced by 20%, and noise levels will be reduced by 30%. Reducing the noise level will result in at least 10% less worker absenteeism associated with hearing problems.
Project description	The description presents the scope of the project and its main results and limitations. This also applies to the pro-environmental and pro-social initiatives it contains. In the case of planned purchase and installation of environmentally friendly machinery, the names and number of environmentally friendly machines must be entered and a short technical description must be given, including efficiency, production quality, and parameters that contribute to sustainable development. The risks must also be listed. In our example, they can be problems with installation of the machines (e.g. lack of connections in appropriate places in the premises or too much weight that requires reinforcing the floors).

TABLE 3.6 (*Continued*)
Sustainability in a Project Charter

Project Charter Broken Down into Sections	Sustainability Issues
Project requirements	The project requirements applicable to sustainability initiatives vary depending on the type of project. In our example related the purchase and installation of environmentally friendly machines, it is necessary to clarify the mandatory limits for such aspects as energy consumption, water consumption, air pollution, disposal of processing fluids, noise, and vibrations.
Design risk	The magnitude of the project risk depends on various events, the occurrence of which may make it difficult or even impossible to achieve or exceed the planned objectives. A failure to meet the delivery deadline for environmentally friendly machines may be one of the risk factors that interfere with the execution of our sample project.
Timeline of planned activities	The timeline of the activities that make up the project, including ones related to sustainability, can be presented in the form of a description, a table, or a schedule, or using one of the network methods. This issue is discussed in more detail in Section 3.3. In the case of purchase of environmentally friendly machines, deadlines must be planned for preparing and placing an order, delivery, assembly, staff training, and initial start-up.
Financing of the project	In the project budget, sustainability tasks either constitute a separate cost item, e.g. purchase and installation of filters for an industrial stack, or increase the costs of manufacturing or purchase of various goods included in the project, e.g. purchase of environmentally friendly machines instead of cheaper standard equivalents. In the information on project financing, it is necessary to estimate the costs of financing of pro-environmental and pro-social projects and the benefits that can be achieved as a result. The issue of project costs and budget is discussed in more detail in Chapter 4.
Key stakeholders	The issues related to stakeholders are discussed in detail in Chapter 2. From the point of view of sustainability, of particular importance for project implementation is the degree of sustainability of the applicant, the person(s) approving the project and its financing, the project manager, and the members of the project team.
Conditions of project acceptance	The project must be accepted in order to achieve its objectives. This involves performance, in a timely manner and within the budget, of all project activities, including those related to sustainability. The conditions of project acceptance must specify who accepts and formally approves the project.
Project manager	The profile of a sustainable project manager is described in Chapter 2. This part of the project charter must specify the scope of his or her duties, powers, and responsibilities.
Project team and its structure	The profile of sustainable project team members is described in Chapter 2. This section of the charter must list the members of the project team, state their qualifications, and specify their duties, powers, and responsibilities.

Source: Own work.

The project charter contains the arrangements that should be respected during project execution. Therefore, its contents should be thought through and refined. Particular attention should be paid to the project objectives, budget, and deadlines. The objectives should be realistic to achieve, taking into account internal and external conditions. When determining the budget, it is a good idea to protect it against the effects of inflation and other types of unforeseen circumstances. Over time, the prices of the goods to be purchased may increase, which risks exceeding the budgeted amounts. Setting too short deadlines for the execution of project tasks may also have negative consequences. When setting deadlines, different types of internal problems, e.g. illness of a team member, and external problems, e.g. contract termination by the main equipment supplier, must be taken into account. It is therefore a good idea to spend more time on, and pay more attention to, the project charter to avoid many problems during its execution.

3.3 SUSTAINABILITY AND RISK IDENTIFICATION IN THE PROJECT PLANNING PHASE

Planning plays a very important role in the implementation of every project. Managers use planning to identify and select the organization's objectives and directions (Jones and George 2011: 189). The same is true for project teams. Project managers use planning to identify and select objectives and directions for the project team.

Planning strengthens and organizes the activities of the project team that contribute to sustainable development. If such activities are not included in the plans, the project will not contribute to solving environmental and social problems. Inclusion of sustainable development activities in the project plan makes them an integral and permanent part of the project.

The two most important components of the planning process are defining the goals and drawing up plans to achieve them. A goal is a desired future circumstance or condition that the organization attempts to realize. Goals are important because organizations exist for a purpose, and goals define and state that purpose. A plan is a blueprint for goal achievement and specifies the necessary resource allocations, schedules, tasks, and other actions. Goals specify future ends; plans specify today's means (Daft and Benson 2016: 211). Goals establish a uniform direction to the project team and enable effective control of its activity. Based on them, plans are drawn up – they are "maps" according to which the project team follows its goals. Goals and plans are two different things. Skipping the goal-setting phase or associating goals with plans are serious errors in project activity. This can be explained by giving a simple example. Suppose you live in Liverpool, England, and you want to get to Manchester by car. This is your goal. This can be achieved in different ways by choosing different routes. For example, you can choose to drive on the A580 and then the A6, or choose the M62 and then the M602. Choosing a specific road/route from Liverpool to Manchester will be your plan, your road map. As the example shows, every goal can be achieved in different ways, by different routes. Some are shorter and easier to travel, while others are

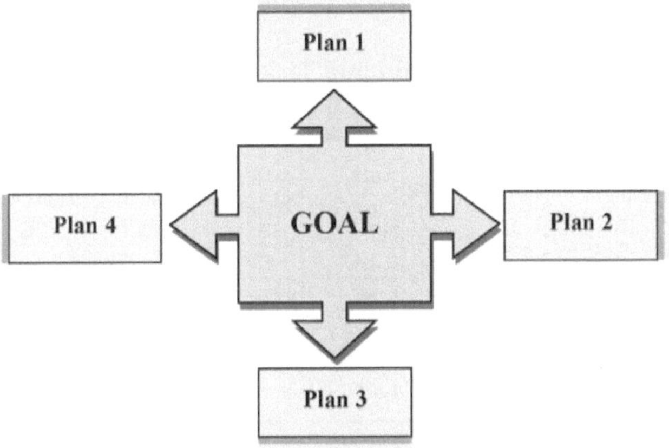

FIGURE 3.3 The goal and various plans (roadmaps) to achieve it. (Own work.)

longer and may require crossing different types of barriers. Thus, each planning phase, both setting the goals and making the plans, is very important and requires concentration and a lot of effort. At the same time, one should keep in mind that proper setting of project goals does not guarantee success at all. It is crucial to plan, i.e., to set up a roadmap that will ensure that the goal is reached quickly and effectively.

Richard L. Daft and Alan Benson emphasize that planning positively affects an organization's performance. This is due to the following reasons (Daft and Benson 2016: 224):

- goals and plans provide a source of motivation and commitment;
- goals and plans guide resource allocation;
- goals and plans are a guide to action; and
- goals and plans set a standard of performance.

In project activities, setting goals and drawing up plans are facilitated by the so-called work breakdown structure. This structure should take into account environmental and social goals. Depending on the type and scope of the project, it may contain fewer or more intermediate elements between the final, planned result of the project activity and its smallest part called a work package. In this book, the intermediate elements are called tasks. Table 3.7 shows an example of decomposition of a project into four tasks, each of which is divided into four work packages.

Table 3.8 contains an example of a detailed project's decomposition into tasks and work packages. As the stakeholders of this project want to contribute to sustainable development, a part of the work packages includes pro-environmental actions (1.5, 1.8, 2.4, 2.5, 2.8, 3.5, and 4.4) and one of them also includes pro-social actions (1.7). The pro-environmental and pro-social activities are in bold in the table. The project

TABLE 3.7
Example of Project Decomposition into Tasks and Work Packages

Main Project Task							
Task 1				Task 2			
Package 1A	Package 1B	Package 1C	Package 1D	Package 2A	Package 2B	Package 2C	Package 2D
Task 3				Task 4			
Package 3A	Package 3B	Package 3C	Package 3D	Package 4A	Package 4B	Package 4C	Package 4D

Source: Own work.

consists in preparing the 50th anniversary of Company XYZ. The anniversary celebration will take place in an auditorium rented by the company and will consist of three parts:

a. the main part, during which, among other things, the company's best employees will be presented with occasional medals and with individual diplomas;
b. the entertainment part; and
c. a banquet to be held in the foyer of the auditorium.

The celebration will be accompanied by a mobile exhibition on the history and achievements of Company XYZ, which will be moved to the company's headquarters and set up in the hall after the event. The plan also includes preparation of a commemorative folder, which will be handed out free of charge to guests arriving at the anniversary celebration.

Both setting the goals and drawing up of the plans require compliance with certain rules. When setting the goals, it is a good idea to follow the SMART principle which contains the following requirements:

1. Specific – each goal should only concern one environmental aspect;
2. Measurable – the goals should be quantified;
3. Achievable – the goals must be possible to achieve;
4. Realistic – the goals should be realistic; and
5. Time-bound – the goals should have a specific timeframe in which they should be achieved.

It is very important to express goals in figures and to specify their deadlines. A goal set in the following manner meets these requirements: "to make 120 medals from an environmentally friendly material by 20 November 2020," as opposed to the phrase "to make commemorative medals from an environmentally friendly material in the

TABLE 3.8
An Example of Decomposition of a Project into Tasks and Work Packages Including Pro-Environmental and Pro-Social Activities

Project

Preparation of the 50th Anniversary of Company XYZ

Task 1	Task 2
Organization of the anniversary celebration	Production of a commemorative medal
Task 3	Task 4
Production of a commemorative folder	Preparation of a commemorative exhibition

Tasks		**Work packages**
Task 1: Organization of the anniversary celebration	1.1	Preparation of the program of the ceremony and its staffing
	1.2	Specification of the date and place of the ceremony
	1.3	Preparation of the guest list
	1.4	Renting the premises
	1.5	Creating scenery **from environmentally friendly materials**
	1.6	Preparation of the entertainment part
	1.7	Preparation of a banquet in the foyer **based on organic food; at the end of the ceremony, handing over the unspoiled, unconsumed food to the poor through the ABC Foundation**
	1.8	Sending invitations printed **on environmentally friendly paper**
Task 2: Production of a commemorative medal	2.1	Selection of persons to be awarded medals (120 persons)
	2.2	Preparation of a preliminary specification for the medal
	2.3	Preparation of the design of the medal and the mold
	2.4	Production of 120 medals **from environmentally friendly materials**
	2.5	Ordering 120 decorative medal boxes **made of environmentally friendly materials**
	2.6	Placing medals in the decorative boxes
	2.7	Preparation of a design for the diploma to be handed with the medal (content and graphic art)
	2.8	Printing of 120 diplomas to be handed with the medals **on environmentally friendly paper**
Task 3: Production of a commemorative folder	3.1	Preparation of a preliminary specification for the folder
	3.2	Preparation of texts to be placed in the folder
	3.3	Preparation of photos to be placed in the folder
	3.4	Preparation of the folder designed based on the prepared texts and photos
	3.5	Printing 300 copies of the folder **on environmentally friendly paper**
Task 4: preparation of a commemorative mobile exhibition	4.1	Preparation of a preliminary specification for the exhibition
	4.2	Preparation of texts to be placed on the boards
	4.3	Preparation of photos to be placed on the boards
	4.4	Preparation of the specification and placing the order for the display equipment made of **environmentally friendly materials**
	4.5	Production and delivery of the display equipment
	4.6	Preparation of the design of the exhibition
	4.7	Installation of the exhibition

Source: Own work.

near future." In the second case, the goal is not defined precisely and therefore is incorrect. Its wording does not include numbers or deadlines. It is rare that a goal cannot be expressed in numbers.

Bart Bossink makes an important point about goals: the project manager and project members' work based on the concept that a goal can raise people's awareness and stimulate their creativity and that many people are determined to find a way to achieve a set target (Bossink 2012: 65).

A properly prepared plan explains the issues detailed in Figure 3.4. Whether it is written on a single A4 sheet of paper or requires hundreds of such sheets of paper and lots of computer memory depends on the type and size of the project. A plan to build a solar power plant is much more extensive than a plan to feed wild animals during the winter. When planning small and simple projects, it is enough to make one plan in which all the issues presented in Figure 3.4 are explained. If the project is complicated and is expected to take many months or years to complete, a detailed presentation of all tasks in one plan is the wrong solution. Such a plan, due to the hundreds and sometimes thousands of tasks and work packages it contains, would be too extensive, complicated, and difficult to use in practice. In such cases, a master plan should first be prepared, listing all the tasks that make up the project, without providing details. Then, on the basis of the master plan, detailed plans are drawn up for each work package. In some cases, it is also necessary to prepare employment plans, machinery work plans, transport unit work plans, and materials consumption plans. When drawing up a master plan and detailed plans, one should avoid creating one very broad and unclear planning document. With detailed plans, it is easier to manage the project team and the subcontractors. Each of them receives a detailed plan that covers only the tasks they have to perform.

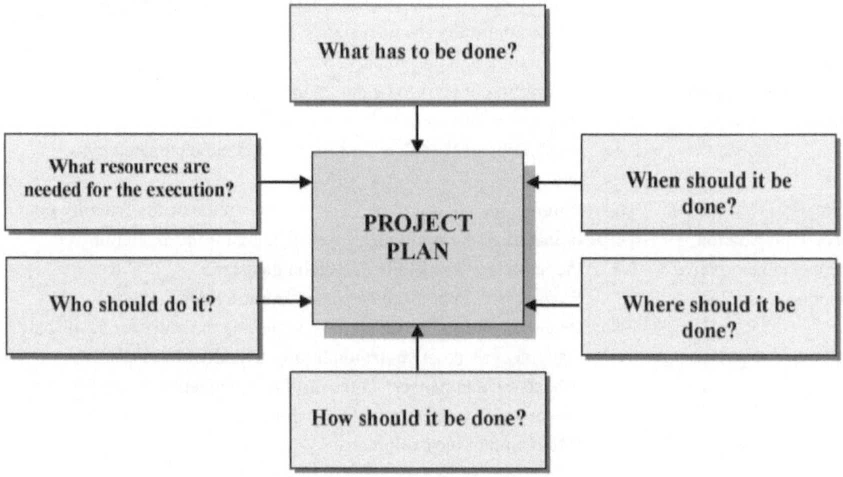

FIGURE 3.4 Arrangements contained in a properly drawn-up plan. (Own work.)

Forms of Presentation of the Timeline of the Planned Activities

It is not enough to have a plan in your head. In most cases, the plan must be presented in electronic form and on paper. Planning involves the problem of reflecting the timeline of actions. We will not discuss this issue extensively, as it is not related to sustainability and is discussed in detail in virtually every book on management and project management. We will only present four possible forms of a written plan, supported by simple examples. These forms are: the descriptive form, the tabular form, a schedule, and the network method. These forms will be used to plan a commemorative mobile exhibition. This is Task 4, which is part of the project entitled "Preparing the 50th Anniversary of Company XYZ" (Table 3.8).

The Descriptive Form of the Timeline of Planned Activities

This is the simplest form of presentation of the timeline of the planned activities. It can be used for the simplest projects with a small number of activities. We discourage the use of the descriptive form because it does not reflect in a transparent way the time relationships between the activities that make up the project. The following box provides an example of the use of the descriptive form to present the timeline of the activities included in Task 4 (preparation of a commemorative mobile exhibition).

PLAN FOR THE PREPARATION OF A COMMEMORATIVE MOBILE EXHIBITION (TASK 4) A DESCRIPTIVE FORM

The mobile exhibition will be prepared by A.K., a member of the design team, who will first prepare the preliminary specification for the exhibition and the texts to be placed on the boards (he has a degree in humanities). He will prepare the preliminary specification on 2–3 March 2020 and the texts on 4–10 March. Then he will commission R.D. (a graphic artist) to collect photographs illustrating the history of the company (work in the archive) and to take a dozen or so photographs showing its contemporary face (the headquarters, the means of transport, and the production building). R.D. will do his work on 11–16 March. After preparing the texts and commissioning the photographs, A.K. will prepare the specification and place an order for the exhibition equipment made of environmentally friendly materials on 11 March. The production and delivery of the exhibition equipment will take place in the period of 12–18 March. After collecting all the photos, R.D. will prepare a design of the exhibition on 17–19 March. The exhibition will be assembled (the boards will be installed on exhibition stands and set up) on March 20 by technical workers G.L. and S.U.

Source: Own work.

Presentation of the Plan in a Tabular Form

A slightly better way of presenting a plan than a description is to prepare it in a tabular form. Table 3.9 shows the plan for the preparation of the commemorative mobile exhibition (Task 4), which was presented in a descriptive form in the previous part of this chapter.

Presentation of the Plan in the Form of a Schedule

Many authors who write about project management issues use the term schedule in an imprecise way. They identify this concept with a timeline of project activities. However, a schedule is a concrete tool used to present the timeline of planned activities by means of horizontal stripes placed on an adopted time scale. It consists of two parts: an analytical summary and a graphic part. The analytical summary is made up of several columns that contain a list of planned activities and basic data related to them. In our sample schedule (Table 3.10), the analytical part consists of four columns that specify the item number, the type of the activity, the duration of the activity, and the persons performing the activity. The analytical part can certainly consist of more columns with more information about the performance of individual actions. The graphic part, on the other hand, is made up of a time scale on which horizontal stripes corresponding to the duration of individual activities are placed. Time scales can be different: monthly, weekly, daily, hourly, or specified in minutes. The appropriate time scale depends on the complexity of the project and the level of detail and type of the schedule. In the case of complex projects continuing for many months, the general

TABLE 3.9
Plan for the Preparation of a Commemorative Mobile Exhibition in a Tabular Form (Task 4)

No.	Activity	To be Done By	Date Subsequent Days of March 2020
1	Preparation of a preliminary specification for the exhibition	A.K.	2–3
2	Preparation of texts to be placed on the boards	A.K.	4–10
3	Preparation of photos to be placed on the boards	R.D.	11–16
4	Preparation of the specification and placing an order for display equipment made of **environmentally friendly materials**	A.K.	11
5	Production and delivery of the display equipment	Company X	12–18
6	Preparation of the design of the exhibition	R.D.	17–19
7	Installation of the exhibition	G.L., S.U.	20

Source: Own work.

TABLE 3.10
Schedule for the Preparation of a Commemorative Mobile Exhibition (Task 4)

No.	Activity	Duration of the Activity in Days	To be Done By	Subsequent Working Days March 2020																
				2	3	4	5	6	9	10	11	12	13	16	17	18	19	20	23	24
1	Preparation of a preliminary specification	2	AK																	
2	Preparation of texts	5	AK																	
3	Preparation of photos	4	RD																	
4	Preparation of the specification and placing an order for display equipment	1	AK																	
5	Production and delivery of the display equipment	5	Company X																	
6	Preparation of the design of the exhibition	3	RD																	
7	Installation of the exhibition	1	GL SU																	

Source: Own work.

plans usually adopt monthly time scales. Detailed plans use scales specified in weeks, days, or even minutes. It all depends on the duration of the work included in the plan.

The advantage of schedules is that they clearly reflect the timeline of activities. Based on the arrangement of the horizontal stripes on the time scale, one can see which activities are performed one after the other and which run parallel or partially overlap.

Presentation of the Plan Using the Network Method

There are many different network methods. Some of them are listed as follows:

- CPM (Critical Path Method)
- PERT (Program Evaluation and Review Technique)
- PM (Precedence Network – Method)
- GASP (Graphical Procedure for Analysis and Synthesis of Programs)
- D-CPM (Decision CPM Network)

TABLE 3.11
Stages for Use of the CPM Method

Stage	What Has to be Done
1	Divide the planned project into simple processes (activities)
2	Specify the duration of the activities
3	Build a network of dependencies (network model)
4	Enter activity times in the network
5	Calculate the network
6	Determine the critical path

Source: Own work.

- DTN (Decision Tree Network)
- LFGN (Linear Flow Graph Network)
- GERT (Graphical Evaluation and Review Technique)
- CYCLONE (Cyclic Operations Network)
- DELTA (Decision, Event, Logic, Time, and Activity Chart)

The key aspects of the use of these network methods are explained using the example of the CPM. It requires execution of the activities listed in Table 3.11.

Use of the CPM method will be illustrated, as in previous cases, using the example of Task 4, the aim of which is to prepare a commemorative mobile exhibition. In Stage 1, this task is divided into activities, which are listed in the first column of Table 3.12. Stage 2 is to determine the times needed to complete these activities. These times are shown in column 3.

TABLE 3.12
Preparation of a Commemorative Mobile Exhibition (Task 4) – List of Activities, Their Numbering, and Their Duration

Activity	Activity Number in the Network Model	Duration of the Activity in Days
Preparation of a preliminary specification	1–2	2
Preparation of texts	2–3	5
Preparation of photos	3–4	4
Preparation of the specification and placing an order for display equipment made of environmentally friendly materials	3–5	1
Production and delivery of the display equipment	5–6	5
Preparation of the design of the exhibition	4–6	3
Installation of the exhibition	6–7	1

Source: Own work.

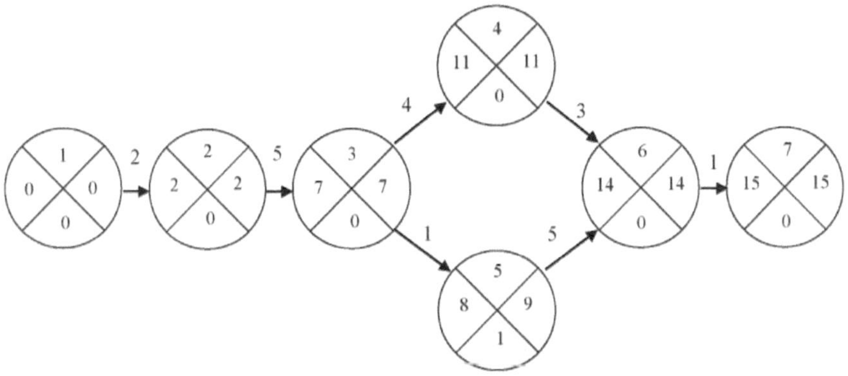

FIGURE 3.5 The network model of the task consisting in preparation of a commemorative exhibition (Task 4). (Own work.)

Stage 3 involves building a network model. A network model consists of arrows and wheels. Arrows denote activities, i.e., actions that continue in time (the length of the arrow does not reflect the duration of the action). Wheels, on the other hand, reflect zero processes – they symbolize the links between the activities in the network model. The network model developed for Task 4 is shown in Figure 3.5. The events are numbered from 1 to 7. Activity numbers consist of two numbers: the number of the event preceding the activity and the number of the event following the activity. The activity numbers are entered in column 2 of Table 3.12.

The network model shown in Figure 3.5 contains the results of the work done in Stages 3, 4, and 5 of its preparation. Above the arrows, the durations of the actions were entered and then the network was calculated as described below.

Meaning of the symbols is shown in Figure 3.6.

m, n – event numbers

T_{mn} - duration of activity m-n
t_{em} - the earliest time of occurrence of event m
t_{en} - the earliest time of occurrence of event n

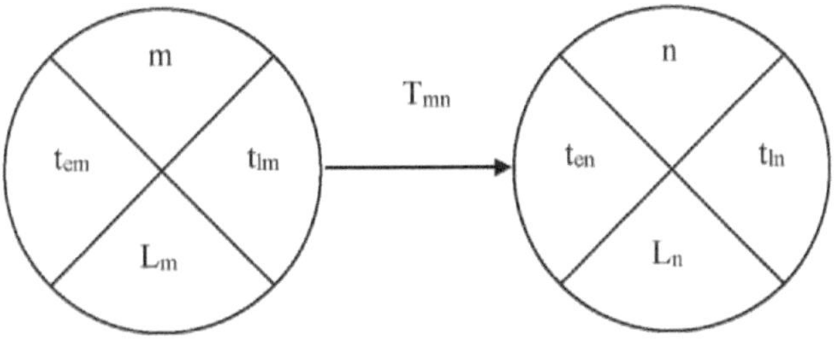

FIGURE 3.6 Calculating the network. (Own work.)

t_{lm} - the latest time of occurrence of event m
t_{ln} - the latest time of occurrence of event n
L_m L_n - the float for events m and n

Calculate the earliest times of the events using the following formula and enter them into the network.

$$t_{en} = \max(t_{em} + T_{mn})$$

Calculate the latest times of the events using the following formula and enter them into the network.

$$t_{lm} = \min(t_{ln} - T_{mn})$$

Calculate the float for the events and enter them into the network.

$$L_m = t_{lm} - t_{em}$$

$$L_n = t_{lm} - t_{en}$$

The calculation of the float is limited to calculation of the total float because this value is needed to determine the critical path.

$$Z_t = t_{ln} - T_{mn} - t_{em}$$

Then proceed to the critical path. The critical path is formed by critical events and critical activities. Critical events are those events for which the float is 0. For critical activities, the value of the total float is zero. In our example, the critical path is formed by the activities and events with the following numbers: 1–2, 2–3, 3–4, 4–6, and 6–7. All the activities and events in the critical path must take place at a strictly planned time. Activities and events outside the critical path may be delayed or accelerated within the limits of the calculated float.

TABLE 3.13
Total Float for the Activities in the Network Model

Activity Number in the Network Model	Total Float
1–2	0
2–3	0
3–4	0
3–5	1
5–6	1
4–6	0
6–7	0

Source: Own work.

PROJECT PLANNING

Set project goals with sustainability in mind.
Check if the goals are realistic to achieve and quantified, and have specific time frames.
Think about how these goals can be achieved – prepare some alternative ways of doing things.
Analyze these activities, taking into account the barriers that prevent them from being completed.
Choose an activity that will enable achieving the project goals in the fastest, easiest, and least costly way.
Prepare a plan for this activity.
Present the plan in a descriptive, tabular form, preferably in the form of a schedule or a network model.
Check if the plan answers the following questions: What needs to be done? When does it need to be done? Where does it need to be done? How does it need to be done? Who has to do it? What resources are needed for it?
Present the plan for approval.

Source: Own work.

Risk Management

Even the best prepared plan does not guarantee that the project will be successful. Richard Templar advises all managers: you must have a plan B and a plan C. You have to plan for disasters. Never assume it's all going right – it isn't. Never assume you will always do OK – you won't. Never assume technology will always work – it isn't. Never assume you've got enough time – you haven't. Never assume they'll turn up on time – they won't. Never assume you won't forget things – you will. Never assume plan A will work – it won't. Never assume plan B will also work – one day that won't either (Templar 2015: 116). Risk management is therefore an important part of project planning activities. It consists in identifying risks, assessing their consequences, and preparing and implementing measures to eliminate or reduce them. Risk management is necessary because there may be problems during the execution of the project which will disrupt the course of work and adversely affect its effects. Project teams that prepare in advance for such eventualities will have a better chance of success. Prevention is much cheaper than dealing with problems that have already occurred. In this section, we focus on risk management in relation to sustainability activities. We explain this problem using the example of the following work package: preparation of a banquet based on organic food, which is part of a project aimed to organize an anniversary celebration.

The publication titled "A Guide to the Project Management Body of Knowledge (PMBOK 6)" indicates two types of risks:

a. negative risks identified as threats with a negative impact on the goals set;
b. positive risks identified as opportunities with a positive impact on the goals.

Thus, a risk in relation to sustainability activities is any event that can prevent achieving or exceeding the goals set in this area.

Risk management involves several steps, which are presented later in this chapter and explained using the example of the aforementioned work package, the aim of which is to prepare a banquet based on organic food. The first three steps are to identify risks. In Stage 4, a plan is drawn up to eliminate the risks or to reduce their harmful effects.

Stage 1

Risk Identification

When identifying risks, one can refer to the past, to those incidents that disrupted the same or similar activities carried out previously, or use one of the heuristic methods (creative thinking methods), e.g. brainstorming. In our example, brainstorming was used. The project manager conducted it in the project team. The members of the team presented potential risks that could disrupt the preparation of the banquet on the basis of organic food. The list of threats created in this way was analyzed and verified. The result is a list of risks, a part of which is contained in Table 3.14.

Stage 2

Risk Level Assessment

Estimation of the probability of risk occurrence can be based on objective data, i.e., information about its occurrence in similar situations in the past, or on personal opinions. The risk level is usually defined as a percentage (0% – risk will not occur; and 100% – risk will definitely occur) or by categories (low, medium, and high risk). In our example, let us assume that we do not have any objective data. Consequently, we will use the opinions of 12 people who have some experience in using the services of catering companies. Prior to collecting opinions, we divide the risk into categories and assign scores to them (Table 3.15), as well as determine the risk levels (Table 3.16).

TABLE 3.14
Risk Factors That Threaten the Preparation of a Banquet Based on Organic Food

Risk Factors
The price of catering based on organic food is high and will exceed the budget allocated for this activity.
Catering companies operating in the region do not have organic food in their offer.
It is not be possible to prepare the banquet exclusively on the basis of organic food (a part of the food served at the banquet will not be organic).

Source: Own work.

TABLE 3.15
Risk Breakdown into Categories

Risk Types	Score
Low	1
Medium	2
High	3
Very high	4

Source: Own work.

TABLE 3.16
Risk Levels

Type	Score
Low	1–1.5
Medium	1.6–2.5
High	2.6–3.5
Very high	3.6–4.0

Source: Own work.

The detailed calculation is based on the example of the first risk factor listed in Table 3.14 (the price of catering based on organic food is high and exceeds the budget allocated to this activity).

As the data in Table 3.17 show, six people described the risk as very high, five people as high, and two as medium. On this basis, we can calculate the average value of the scores, which is 3.25.

$$(5 \times 4 + 5 \times 3 + 2 \times 2):\ 12 = (20 + 15 + 4):\ 12 = 3.25$$

This means, according to Table 3.16, the risk of high prices for organic food catering is high.

TABLE 3.17
Estimation of the Risk of High Price of Organic Food Catering by 12 People

Person	P1	P2	P3	P4	P5	P6	P7	P8	P9	P10	P11	P12
Score	3	4	4	2	4	3	3	4	3	4	2	3

Source: Own work.

Stage 3

Assessment of the Potential Impact of the Risk on the Task

At this stage, it is necessary to indicate the consequences of occurrence of the risk factors. In our example, we consider the factor of occurrence of high organic food catering prices. To determine the consequences of occurrence of this factor, we will again use the opinions of people who have experience in using catering services. The consultation results in the following list of consequences of high organic food catering prices:

- no money to pay for organic food catering;
- insufficient amount of food at the banquet due to the need to reduce the order volume; and
- discontent of the guests attending the banquet due to the insufficient amount of food.

The identification of the risks in the three steps taken so far makes it possible to develop a plan to reduce their potential harmful effects.

Stage 4

Risk Effect Mitigation Strategy

In the case of the identified risks, one of the options for further action detailed below must be chosen.

1. Risk tolerance – accepting the risk and, because of its low harmfulness, not doing anything to reduce it.
2. Transfer – transferring the risk to another organization or through insurance.
3. Counteracting – taking action to reduce the risk to an acceptable level.
4. Postponement – doing nothing at a given time or stopping activities due to the too high risk.

In our example, the risk of a high organic food catering price is high; therefore, a plan was developed to deal with the negative consequences of such a situation (Table 3.18).

TABLE 3.18
Strategy to Reduce the Risk of High Prices of Organic Food Catering

Risk	The Strategy to Reduce the Risk
Of a high price of organic food catering	Study the market for catering services in terms of the assortment and the prices of organic food at an early stage (two months before the start of organization of the banquet). If the prices of organic food catering prove to be too high, which may cause the budget allocated for the banquet to be exceeded, request additional funds for the preparation of the banquet. If additional funds are not allocated, reduce the share of organic food in the menu to a level that can fit within the allocated budget.

Source: Own work.

When executing large and costly projects that continue for many years, it is important to estimate the climate risk. This is due to the fact that climate change can seriously disrupt projects and affect their results. Hurricanes, heat waves and resulting fires, floods, and droughts caused by climate change are able to disrupt any project. They pose a risk to the people and property involved in projects. There is also a risk that, as the climate crisis deepens, countries will introduce increasingly stringent regulations, for which the project initiators and executors should also be prepared.

Linked to climate risk is the so-called "carbon risk," i.e., the impact of government policies aimed to slow down the pace of climate change on business strategies and on return on investment. Countries can introduce increasingly stringent regulations that will force the cost of emissions to rise. This problem can be at least partly solved by calculating the internal price of own emissions of carbon dioxide (Internal Carbon Pricing). Its essence is to determine the value of pollutants emitted by the company on the basis of emission fees set by the regulators or the market prices of emission allowances. Governments of more than 60 regions, countries, and provinces – representing roughly half of the global economy – have introduced carbon emission charges in their climate policies and 180 countries have ratified the Paris Agreement on reduction of CO_2 emissions. One of the forms of emission charges applied by countries is the emission tax. Countries impose a tax on companies calculated per ton of CO_2 emitted into the atmosphere. Another form is the Cap and Trade system. It consists in determining the permissible limit of total amount of CO_2 emissions in a country or region. This amount is then divided into allowances which enable their holders to emit a given number of tons of CO_2. Allowances are normally either auctioned or granted free of charge to participating companies. Allowance holders can also sell and buy them on the secondary allowance market. The price established as a result of these transactions determines the cost of the reduction of pollution by ton. The range of the internal CO_2 emission price globally is huge: from just 1 cent per ton to over 100 dollars. For individual consumers, 10 dollars per ton of CO_2 emission means an increase in the price per gallon (3.79 liters) of gasoline by approximately 10 cents (Aldy 2019: 145–153).

The risks associated with execution of projects result not only from environmental risks, but also from social risks. A very good example of this is the Covid-19 pandemic. The coronavirus was detected in late 2019. In just a few months, the epidemic spread all over the world. Millions of people were infected and hundreds of thousands died (at the time of writing this text, the number of infected people was over 5 million and the number of deaths exceeded 300,000). In the service sector (e.g. tourism, hospitality, catering and restaurants, hairdressing, cosmetics, and others) revenues of companies dropped almost to zero. In other sectors, they decreased significantly as a result of broken supply chains, closed borders, discontinued transport, and a drop in demand for goods and services (e.g. clothing, electronics, cars, furniture, and others). Millions of companies around the world suspended their operations during the pandemic, reduced their scope, or went bankrupt. The number of unemployed increased significantly despite ambitious government plans to reduce the negative impact of the epidemic on the economy. In these conditions, execution of many projects had to be significantly reduced or postponed to another time.

RISK MANAGEMENT STAGES

Risk identification
Risk level assessment
Assessment of the potential impact of the risk on the project tasks
Risk effect mitigation strategy

Source: Own work.

3.4 PRO-ENVIRONMENTAL AND PRO-SOCIAL ORGANIZATION OF PROJECT ACTIVITIES

Organization of project activities is the responsibility of the project team leader. Each member of the team also organizes various activities as a part of the tasks assigned to him or her. In order for this organizational activity to be pro-environmental and pro-social, both the manager and the team members should be sustainable in the aspects we described in Chapter 2. The project team is an organization. Organizations have always played an important role in economies and contributing to the development of civilization. According to Morgen Witzel, organization – that is, a group of people brought together for a common purpose – is an essential feature of human civilization (Witzel 2017: 205). Companies should integrate social, environmental and economic concerns into all areas of the organizations (Epstein and Buhovac 2014: 95).

Areas of Sustainable Organization of Project Activities

Sustainable organization of project activities is divided into the three basic areas of activity shown in Figure 3.7.

As can be seen from Figure 3.7, organization in the sustainability concept is a structured sequence of events. First, the organizational structure of the project

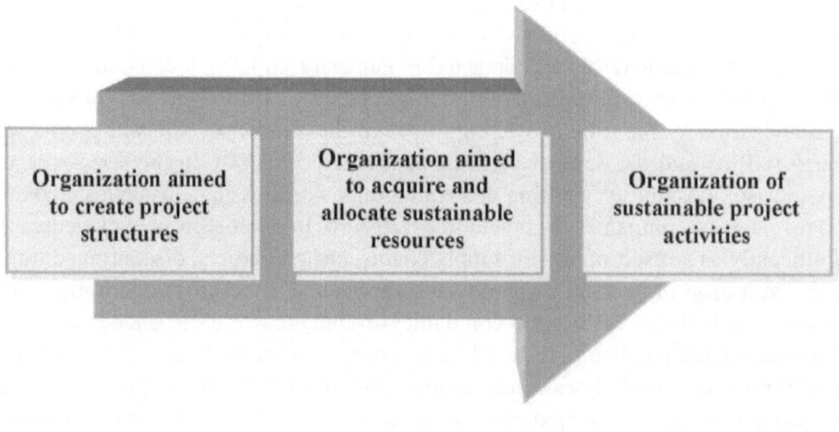

FIGURE 3.7 Areas of sustainable organization of project activities. (Own work.)

team is created. Then human and physical resources are assigned to this structure. The next step is to set this system in motion thanks to the work aimed to execute the project.

Sustainability in Organizational Structures of Project Teams

The composition of a project team and its structure must be determined in the initial phase of the project work, preferably during preparation of the project charter. The structure of the project team can be simple or complex. This depends on the type of the project and the scope and complexity of the activities it is composed of. If a project involves organization of a banquet for 100 people, the project manager either organizes it himself or herself or involves at most one or two people in the project. The organizational structure of such a project team takes the simple form of a linear structure consisting of three jobs: a manager and two employees directly reporting to him or her. The situation changes dramatically if the aim of the project is to build a solar power plant. In such a case, the organizational structure of the project team is much larger and more complex. A project of this type requires cooperation with many specialists, institutions, and companies.

The following are some of the types of organizational structures that can be useful in project execution.

Isomorphic Organizational Structure (According to the Object)

A project is divided into tasks. They are assigned to members of the project team for execution. The project manager coordinates the entirety of the project.

Expert Organizational Structure (According to the Type)

It is a variation of a matrix structure. There is a double subordination of the project team members: to the operations manager and the specialist-consultant.

Collective Organizational Structure

In this structure, there is no single leader and no clear division of tasks. Decisions are made in groups (collectively).

Surgical Organizational Structure

The team leader acts in a way that resembles a surgeon performing a surgery. He or she makes decisions and gives orders. The remaining members of the project team assist the manager by performing various types of auxiliary work.

Territorial Organizational Structure

This structure applies where different parts of a project need to be carried out in different locations away from each other.

Mixed (Hybrid) Organizational Structure

This can be a combination of an isomorphic and territorial structure: the managers responsible for executing parts of the project in a given area divide them into tasks and assign them to their subordinate team members for execution.

The organizational structure reflects the division of labor within the project team. The division of labor is based on specialization. It consists in assigning a narrow scope of tasks to an employee or a group of employees, which makes it possible to achieve greater efficiency. This is how Richard L. Daft and Dorothy Marcic see this problem: organizations perform a wide variety of tasks. A fundamental principle is that work can be performer more efficiently if employees are allowed to specialize. Work specialization is the degree to which organizational tasks are subdivided into separate jobs (Daft and Marcic 2013: 235). The tasks assigned to an employee must of course be consistent with his or her qualifications and professional experience.

Sustainability can be incorporated into the organizational structures of project teams in two ways. First, sustainable employees can be assigned to all the posts identified in these structures. In such a case, the pro-environmental and pro-social members of the team execute the project in accordance with the principles of sustainability. Consequently, there is no need to modify the structures in which they work. If, on the other hand, the members of the project team are not sustainable, then certain modifications must be made to the adopted structures. In the case of small projects and small project teams, one of the members should be formally charged with the task of taking care of the sustainability of the entire project. In the case of large projects, a sustainability specialist post or department can be created within the organizational structure. They should report directly to the project manager. Their task is not only to monitor and evaluate the sustainability of the project work being performed, but also to provide advice in this area of activity.

The members of the project team, located within its organizational structure, are assigned specific tasks to be performed. Written lists of these tasks, their descriptions, and instructions must include guidelines for their execution in accordance with the principles of sustainable development. In many cases, this is not necessary, because pro-environmental and pro-social solutions have been adopted as early as at the planning and design stage, e.g. purchase of environmentally friendly machines or organic food, replacement of light bulbs with energy-efficient ones, or installation of industrial filters on stacks.

Functioning of the organizational structure of a project team involves drawing up and circulating documents. The documents produced when applying for project funding and during project execution is often so extensive that it contradicts all the principles of sustainable development. Project documents often comprise hundreds or even thousands of printed pages. Their production consumes huge amounts of paper and energy required for their printing and the operation of office equipment. Also, a storage area is needed for the documents, which needs to be illuminated and heated during the winter months. Producing such a large number of documents requires a huge amount of work, which could be used in a more productive way. The following box presents ways to reduce paper waste during drawing up and circulation of documents in the organizational structures of project teams.

ENVIRONMENTALLY FRIENDLY DRAWING UP AND CIRCULATION OF DOCUMENTS IN THE ORGANIZATIONAL STRUCTURE OF A PROJECT TEAM

Replacing paper-based document circulation by electronic circulation
Archiving documents in electronic form
Not printing e-mails and archiving them electronically
Reducing printing of documents on paper to a minimum
Proofreading documents in the computer, rather than printed documents
Using environmentally friendly paper
Using paper of lower weight (g/m^2)
Reducing the number of document copies
Reducing the format of the paper on which documents are printed
Printing two or more pages of a document on a single sheet of paper
Making double-sided prints
Using smaller font and smaller line spacing
Using smaller page margins
Minimizing paper waste

Source: Own work.

Organization Aimed to Acquire and Allocate Sustainable Resources to Project Teams

The organizational structure of a project team needs to be filled with people and resources to function properly. The most important resource of every project team is people. Sustainable team members are found in a recruitment process. An offer to work on a project team is addressed to specific individuals – specialists in a given field or it is made public and the best applicants are selected. As mentioned earlier, it is important that the people employed on a project team are environmentally and socially sensitive and ready to act for sustainable development. The work allocated to team members should be in line with their qualifications and professional experience and should be suitable for their physical and mental abilities. The issues related to appointing a manager and recruiting project team members are discussed in Chapter 2.

One should keep in mind that productivity of project team is the greater, the better their work is adapted to their innate talents and skills. Moreover, the smaller the differences in the suitability of the members of such a group for specific tasks, the better the effects of teamwork. Attention must also be paid to proper use of the skills and experience of each team member.

Collaboration between members of a project team is very important. This is how Ward Crawford sees its essence: collaboration is not an activity performed on its own, for its own sake: rather, it is undertaken to facilitate something else of describable purpose and desired outcome. That may be the implementation of a project or change program, the development of policies or standards, the creation of an environment suitable for the accumulation of knowledge, or the support of innovation (Crawford 2017: 150).

Every project team needs specific resources to carry out its activities. These resources should not be identified only with office equipment (e.g. office furniture, computer equipment, photocopiers, and telephones) and office supplies (e.g. paper, pens, clips, envelopes, etc.). Projects are often carried out that require specialized equipment and even machines and production equipment. An example is a project aimed to make a Martian rover, which will be submitted for the international University Rover Challenge competition. To build this complex and technically advanced piece of equipment, the design team must have different materials, components, and machines at its disposal. Their more important types are shown in Table 3.19.

These resources should not be in excess, i.e., in quantities exceeding the actual needs of the project team. Also, their technical and operational parameters must be properly considered. For example, it makes no sense to purchase a large energy-intensive photocopier to make color copies if there is no need for them during project execution.

The acquisition of resources and their distribution among the members of the team is a structured activity. First, it is necessary to determine the need for specific articles, then to draw up an order, send it to the vendor, receive the delivery, pay the amount due, and distribute the delivered products among the team members. The products ordered should be sustainable, i.e., they must not harm the environment or people. The following factors may prevent the purchase of sustainable products:

- lack of sustainable equivalents for certain equipment and products in the market;
- very high prices for goods of this kind; and
- lack of sustainable products in the local or national market and the need to import them.

TABLE 3.19
Materials, Components, and Machines Needed to Make a Martian Rover

Materials	Components	Machinery and Equipment
ProfilesSheet metal	Drive motors	3D printers
Pipes	Electric actuators for the manipulator	Milling machines
Metal plates	Servomechanisms	Turning lathes
Composites	Power supply system	Welders
Bolts, nuts, washers, and pins	Directional antennas	Benders
Bearings	Cameras	Rollers
Ball joints	Electronic circuits	Precision water/laser cutting machines
	Microcontrollers	
	Sensors	
	Computers	

Source: Own work.

In many cases, team members use the resources of the organization where they are employed to carry out a project. As a result, there is no need to make numerous purchases. Whether they are conventional or sustainable resources, depends on the level of sustainability of their organization. If it is an unsustainable organization, they have unsustainable resources at its disposal. If the organization has achieved a high degree of sustainability, they will use pro-environmental and pro-social goods.

Organization of Sustainable Project Activities

The organizational activities that took place in the two previous phases have led to a situation where the members of the project team have the necessary resources and are ready to carry out the work according to the schedule. Sustainable performance of work on the project team is aimed at eliminating activities that threaten human life and health, saving materials, and ensuring ecological operation of machinery and equipment. The box below shows different possibilities to contribute to sustainable development when performing work.

PRO-ENVIRONMENTAL ASPECTS OF ORGANIZING AND PERFORMING WORK ON A PROJECT TEAM

Using environmentally friendly materials
Reduced consumption of materials
Using materials according to their intended use
Following the instructions for use of materials
Using durable, economical, and safe equipment
Shutting down or hibernating equipment if not used for a long time
Activating auto-shutdown modes
Using environmentally friendly programs
Following equipment operating instructions
Periodic inspections of equipment
Periodic maintenance of equipment based on environmentally friendly materials
Repairing equipment using environmentally friendly materials
Disconnecting chargers from the mains when devices have been charged
Work in daylight (saving electricity)
Sorting trash and waste

Source: Own work.

Work carried out on the project team should be even and rhythmic. This involves an even distribution of effort during the work, as well as adjusting its rhythm to the rhythm of the body. Wherever possible, human effort must be replaced by machinery and equipment. It is also important to eliminate unnecessary movements. Each member of the project team is bound by the principle of physical order, which is to keep the workplace tidy.

Every country has some labor regulations. For example, in Poland their collection is called the Labor Code. This Code is adapted to comply with the European Union directives and amended by the Ministry of Family, Labor, and Social Policy. It contains provisions on the following issues:

1. general provisions;
2. employment relationship;
3. remuneration for work and other benefits;
4. employer's and employee's obligations
5. material responsibility of employees;
6. work time;
7. employee leave;
8. workers' rights related to parenthood;
9. employing underage persons;
10. health and safety at work;
11. collective bargaining agreements;
12. handling disputes concerning claims pertaining to the employment relationship;
13. responsibility for violations of employees' rights;
14. statute of limitations on claims; and
15. final provisions.

Compliance with labor laws is the responsibility of every project manager. The members of a project team either are full-time employees of the companies where the projects are being carried out or perform work on the basis of contract of mandate or contract of specific work. Regardless of the form of employment, it is the responsibility of the project manager to ensure compliance with labor laws. Child labor, forced labor (e.g. use of mental and physical coercion), use of corporal punishment, verbal abuse of people, overloading with work, and many other principles contained in the legislation are unacceptable. When organizing work in a project team, there must be no discrimination against its members on the basis of nationality, age, gender, or religion. If there are people with disabilities on the team, they must be provided with appropriate working conditions. Equal opportunities for all, respect for diversity, and cooperation based on trust are important demands that should be respected when managing a project team.

> In a sustainable project organization, it is not enough to comply with labor law. Pro-social programs should be implemented that go beyond the scope of existing legislation.
>
> Source: Own work.

In the following section, we recommend pro-social solutions that go beyond standard labor legislation and should be implemented in sustainable project organizations.

PRO-SOCIAL ASPECTS OF ORGANIZING AND PERFORMING WORK ON A PROJECT TEAM

Complying with labor law
Implementing "zero-accident" systems
Creating a friendly "green" working environment
Age management (making proper use of the potential of different age groups)
Implementing "work-life balance" programs
Introducing flexible working hours
Using remote working
Implementing health promotion programs
Complying with work ethics principles
Environmental and social education

Source: Own work.

"Zero accidents" is not only a theoretical concept, but also a state that a project manager can achieve by properly organizing work on his or her team. It goes beyond the standard set of occupational health and safety regulations. Prevention, accident-free work instructions, information campaigns, and training are just some elements of a system intended to prevent accidents during execution of projects. One must keep in mind that project team members work not only at desks. They are also in places that pose a threat to human life and health (e.g. laboratories, production buildings, construction sites, and warehouses) and use various types of materials, machines, and equipment.

When organizing the work of a project team, the manager should take care of the environment in which it takes place. CBRE experts have examined the factors that are most important for employees to feel healthy and happy at work. According to the CBRE report titled "How We Want to Work," a well-arranged space that filled with plants and properly lit is the most important: three out of four people admitted that these factors make them feel more comfortable. A friendly "green" workplace makes as many as two out of three respondents feel healthier (Koprowska 2019: 136).

When defining tasks and assigning work to team members, the project manager should aim to properly use the potential of different age groups. This is called "age management." For example, older employees may have more knowledge of and experience in sustainability, which they will share during their work and training.

Work on a project team should be organized so as to ensure that its members maintain a work-life balance. Therefore, it is worthwhile to implement work-life balance programs. They involve introduction of flexible working hours and remote working. Team members with flexible working hours do not start or stop working at fixed hours, but work in intervals set by the team leader. In the case of remote working, employees work in their place of residence and contact their manager via the Internet. These systems are particularly beneficial to parents of small children.

Health-promotion programs for employees play an important role, especially in the case of large, long-term projects. Project team members should be fit, full of energy, and happy. This makes it possible to eliminate or significantly reduce inefficient presence at work. There are many reasons for inefficiency: lack of physical activity, poor nutrition, excessive emotional and mental strain, smoking, drinking alcohol, drug consumption, stress, overwork, sedentary lifestyle, and adverse climatic conditions. Taking care of the health of member of a project team can significantly contribute to its success. The manifestation of such care is providing team members with medical and psychological care, access to recreational and sports facilities, offering weight loss programs, healthy food, and relaxing massages, and organizing sports events. Physical activity is very important. Sport ensures a healthy lifestyle, strengthens, and promotes tolerance and mutual understanding. Encouraging project team members to ride bicycles rather than drive cars to commute is a good example of mobilizing them for more physical activity. Sports events can also be the subject of separate pro-social projects, such as organization of sports competitions for people with disabilities and sports activities for seniors.

Health-promotion campaigns should not be a cluster of random actions. To avoid this, "health audits" should be carried out. They help team leaders can assess whether the project activities are not in danger of a breakdown due to team members taking sick leave. Health audits provide full knowledge about the health needs of team members. Only on their basis can the right decisions be made about shaping pro-health programs.

A very important problem that has to be taken into account when organizing project activities is work ethics. Research shows that people are willing to act unethically if it benefits them. In such situations, the human mind can skillfully justify morally questionable behavior. We often look for such excuses as: everyone does it, I only follow my superior's orders, we do it for the greater good, this is not stealing, or they deserved it. The increase in unethical behavior is accompanied by high uncertainty, working late, and excessive intellectual burden. It is also facilitated by long days and series of difficult goals. Research shows that people are more likely to act unethically when they are in a hurry. In an experiment, students stopped much less often to help a stranger lying on the ground when they were in a hurry to give a lecture in class about, ironically, the biblical parable of the Good Samaritan (Kouchaki and Smith 2020: 141–142). A manager will have fewer ethical problems during a project if he or she selects his or her team members properly. The profile of a sustainable project team member is described in Chapter 2. In that chapter, we also explain how to recruit him or her. Codes of ethics are helpful in shaping ethical attitudes. Drawing up comprehensive codes of ethics is justified in the case of large, long-term projects that involve a significant number of executors. They promote establishing relationships based on honesty, trust, respect for employees' rights, and compliance with law. In the case of a smaller project, the manager may prepare only a concise list of ethical conduct rules and make them known to the team members. It is better to have one sheet of paper with such rules written on it than to ignore this problem. This is a signal that the manager attaches great importance to ethical conduct and will enforce it during the project.

It is important to continuously shape the environmental and social awareness of the project team members. This takes place not only during training sessions and workshops, but also through participation in and initiation of various types of campaigns, including charity ones. Their purpose may be to clean forests, to collect waste, to plant trees, to collect food, or to take care of animals. Volunteers, who may also be members of the project team, play a special role in conducting charity campaigns.

Educational trips, conferences, as well as exhibitions in the form of showcases or stands, located in the work places of project teams, help shape environmental and social awareness. Every team member has the right to post some interesting information on them about sustainable development (e.g. messages, press clippings, and announcements about planned charity activities). An environmental and social guide encouraging commitment to sustainable development can also be prepared and provided to project stakeholders.

Caring for project team members and providing them with pro-social working conditions can be expressed in many other undertakings. Examples of these are creation of social funds or ensuring participation in cultural and entertainment events.

Pro-social initiatives can involve project team members in two ways. They may be initiated by the project manager and concern only members of his or her team or can be implemented at the level of the organization of which the team is a part.

Organization of Meetings during Project Execution

An important aspect of the functioning of project teams is organization of meetings. They can cover a wide range of issues: reporting on progress of work, problems disrupting the execution of projects, crisis situations, personnel issues, schedules, and other topics related to the current activities of the project team. Proper organization of meetings strengthens the position and authority of the team leader and brings many tangible benefits.

Here are a few comments on organization of meetings during project execution.

Meetings should be organized only when a significant need arises. Such need may result from a problem that has to be resolved or important information that has to be shared. Meetings organized without a good reason are considered by project team members to be unnecessary and a waste of time.

Before a meeting is organized, its purpose must be identified. Only with a clearly and precisely defined goal can competent participants be selected. These should be the persons who are concerned, have the authority to decide on the matter in question, and will be responsible for implementation of the decisions reached.

Meetings should preferably be organized between 10 AM and 1 PM. In this period of time, most people demonstrate the so-called efficiency peak. It is also useful to specify the time of the end of the meeting or its duration. This allows the participants to properly organize their activities to be conducted later.

The room in which the meeting is to be held should be suitable for the number of participants and the equipment provided there (e.g. microphone, projector, and air-conditioning) should be checked before the meeting.

The best way to conduct meetings is to have a round table without a dominant position. Locating participants one next to another also contributes to reducing the tense atmosphere. We do not recommend placing participants face to face, e.g. at a long rectangular table, which may adversely affect the atmosphere of the meeting.

The following rules should apply during the meeting/conference:

- participants are required to respect the established agenda;
- participants' presentations and statements should be short, factual, and reliable;
- participants have to prepare for their presentations and discussions;
- participants should not deviate from the subject of the meeting;
- only one person should speak at any time;
- only the moderator may interrupt presentations or statements;
- personal attacks are unacceptable; and
- the atmosphere of the meeting should be free and trusting.

Meeting participants often demonstrate different behavior. It is advisable for the project manager to be able to recognize different types of behavior and react appropriately to them. A blabber should be reminded of time constraints and his or her continuing speech should be interrupted with questions to which only unambiguous answers are possible. A shy person may have good ideas, but will not reveal them without the help of the moderator. He or she needs to be helped to overcome his or her shyness. A stubborn team member criticizes the decisions and statements of the moderator. Such a person should be asked to give a concrete answer to the question, "What would you do in that case?"

Another important issue is to attract the attention of the meeting participants. Here are some useful techniques:

- using audiovisual aids (slides, films, and charts);
- changing the speaking technique (by alternating the use of loud and quiet voice, and changing the pace of speech);
- asking questions during the speech (listeners' attention increases because anyone can be required to give an answer);
- making provocative statements (they may cause aggression among the listeners, which must be neutralized later on); and
- maintaining eye contact with the participants.

Meetings should result in constructive conclusions. These can be summarized in a short report. This is not a matter of taking long and laborious minutes of the meeting that reflects its course and the subsequent statements of the participants, but about writing a conclusion implementation sheet. It should contain the most important conclusions reached at the meeting and the actions to be taken.

Ron Ashkenas and Brook Manville encourage project managers to have frank discussions with their subordinates during meetings. It is not enough to draw up a schedule of meetings during which team members will report on the measures and effects. What is needed is to use such meetings for a frank discussion about their activities. This will allow the manager to react quickly to underperformance and decide what to do in such situations (Ashkenas and Manville 2019: 183).

3.5 MOTIVATING THE PROJECT TEAM TO WORK IN THE SPHERE OF SUSTAINABILITY

Understanding motivation is the key to the successful management of people (Witzel 2017: 210). That is why a lot of different studies focus on motivation. As early as at the end of the 19th century (in the late 1800s), William James' research showed the importance of this issue. He discovered that workers use only about 20–30% of their abilities at work. High motivation results in use of 80–90% of their potential (Ghillyer 2009: 276). It is important that project team members should also be strongly motivated to undertake pro-social and pro-environmental activities.

There are many theories of motivation described in the literature. Almost every book on management contains their list and characteristics. For example, Gareth R. Jones and Jennifer M. George describe the following theories: expectancy theory, need theories, equity theory, goal-setting theory, and learning theories (Jones and George 2011: 299–315).

Linking sustainability to different theories of motivation is a difficult task. We will explain this problem using the example of Abraham Maslow's "hierarchy of needs." Maslow posited that there were five basic human needs which are presented in ascending order of importance: self-actualization, self-esteem, love or "belongingness," safety, food, and water (Witzel 2017: 208). This raises the following questions: Which category should sustainability needs be included in? Will their place in the hierarchy of needs change as -economic and environmental problems grow and how? In what order will these needs be met? What factors determine the order in which they will be met? Will and how will such needs develop? Satisfying most needs, even those of a lower order (food and water), may be compatible or incompatible with the sustainability principles. This is because hunger can be satisfied with both organic and non-organic food. In order to satisfy one thirst, one can consume drinks that harm or do not harm our health. In Table 3.20, we make a link between several theories of motivation and sustainable development activities.

TABLE 3.20
Some of the More Important Approaches to Motivation in Terms of Sustainability

Approach to Motivation			
Hierarchy of Needs	**Expectancy Approach**	**Equity Approach**	**Reinforcement Approach**
What things that I need but do not get from sustainability?	Will I improve if I try to act according to the principles of sustainability? If I improve, will I be rewarded? Do I want this reward?	Is the system for rewarding work and behavior in line with sustainability principles fair? What does it add to my motivation?	What were the consequences of my activities in compliance with/ contradictory to the principles of sustainability? Should I keep acting like this? Should I change the way I do things?

Source: Own work based on Ghillyer 2009: 289.

Motivation is very important in striving to achieve sustainability goals. Most people start a new job with energy and enthusiasm, but employees can lose their drive if managers fail in their role as motivators (Daft and Benson 2016: 470). Top managers play a special role in this area. As M. Epstein and A. Buhovac emphasize, research clearly shows that effective implementation of a sustainability strategy is possible only with commitment of top management (Epstein and Buhovac 2014: 47). The duty to motivate project team members lies primarily with the manager. The project manager has fewer problems with motivating in terms of sustainability in a team of sustainable members. Such team members are the subject of Chapter 2 of this book. These are people who want to contribute to sustainable development. More problems with motivation occur in project teams composed of wholly or partly unsustainable employees. Such people may not fully accept or even reject the social and environmental undertakings included in projects.

Creating good incentive systems requires a positive attitude to human nature, which is expressed by the Y theory and not by Douglas McGregor's X theory. The X theory assumes that most people lack ambition or interest in their work and will only work productively if coerced into doing so. Theory Y assumes that people are self-motivated and ambitious and will naturally seek responsibility and the chance to express themselves creatively (Witzel 2017: 210).

The basis for effective motivation is to recognize the motives that will encourage project team members to undertake pro-environmental and pro-social activities. The work they do is certainly such a motive. As Kyle Bruce and Chris Nyland emphasize citing N. Rose, work is an essential element in the path to self-fulfillment (Bruce and Nyland 2017: 53). However, a project manager cannot stop at this conclusion. He or she should investigate what motivates his or her team members to work efficiently, including for sustainable development.

There is a widespread belief that motivation comes from two sources. According to Gareth R. Jones and Jennifer M. George, motivation can come from intrinsic or extrinsic sources. Intrinsically motivated behavior is behavior that is performed for its own sake; the source of motivation is actually performing the behavior and motivation comes from doing the work itself. Extrinsically motivated behavior is behavior that is performed to acquire material or social rewards or to avoid punishment (Jones and George 2011: 297). The motives for sustainable development activities come from both internal and external sources. They can be divided into the following five categories:

a. high own sensitivity to ecological and social issues (a team member feels an intrinsic need to fix the world around him or her);
b. experience gained from activities in pro-environmental and pro-social organizations (a team member has worked as a volunteer and wants to show that he or she is involved in social and environmental activities and can act effectively in this area);
c. knowledge about ecological and social problems (information about the bad state of our planet presented in the media, reports, and articles encourage a team member to take remedial actions);

d. awards (a team member expects to receive an award for activities that contribute to sustainable development); and
e. penalties (a team member wants to avoid penalties for activities that contradict the principles of sustainable development).

The stimuli indicated in items a, b, and c can be classified as intrinsic motivators and those in items d and e as extrinsic ones.

The techniques used by a project manager to motivate team members have to be suitable for the unique characteristics of the listed categories. The most important motivator is high sensitivity of a team member to environmental and social issues (a). Sensitivity is largely an innate characteristic. On the other hand, environmental and social sensitivity is often shaped at different stages of life by one's own experiences, family, friends, and teachers. Ecologically and socially sensitive team members implement projects in accordance with the principles of sustainability even if the incentive systems are not functioning or are not fully operational. People in the second category (b) behave similarly. They combine social and environmental sensitivity with specific activity. They include volunteers, philanthropists, people active in foundations, and participants of community campaigns.

The third category (c) is made up of people whose social and environmental sensitivity is shaped mainly by the media, including the Internet: they find the information contained in the media credible and are willing to take various remedial actions under their influence. Their activity in the area of sustainability can be enhanced by publicizing messages that highlight the growth and effects of environmental and social risks.

The stimuli that take the form of rewards and penalties (d and e) are typical motivators that will activate even those who have no knowledge of or experience in sustainable development. Below is a wide range of areas and means of motivation, including both rewards and penalties, that can be useful for project managers in stimulating team members to work hard for sustainable development.

Formal Conditions of Participation in a Project

The source of motivation in this case is tangible and intangible conditions that result from formal project agreements and are provided by the project manager and the organization or the person who provides funding. The most important motivator in this area is remuneration for work on the project team. The amount of such remuneration is not always a strong motivator. This is due to the following reasons:

- the project budget does not provide for any pay for its executors;
- the project budget provides for only small amounts to be paid;
- the employee works on the project during his or her working hours and are not entitled to any increase in salary on this account; and
- the employee works on the project in overtime for which he or she is paid at low rates.

Remuneration for working on a project team is one of the most important motivators and should therefore meet the expectations of team members. The amount of the remuneration should be correlated with the type and amount of work, and with its results.

If the project is carried out by sustainable employees, the motivators used will encourage them to make even greater efforts for the benefit of sustainable development. They will be happy to support sustainable development because of their beliefs, sensitivity, knowledge, and experience.

Particular attention is needed when the project team is made up of people who are indifferent to or who oppose sustainable development. In order to encourage them to be pro-environmental and pro-social, various means of motivation can be used for specific achievements in this sphere, which include:

- cash prizes (additional pay and bonuses),
- in-kind prizes in the form of environmentally friendly products; and
- diplomas of recognition, medals, and statuettes.

While cash and in-kind prizes require more money, diplomas of recognition, medals, and statuettes are not expensive. After the project or one of its stages is completed, a short ceremony to summarize the results of the project may be organized to hand out such symbols of recognition for pro-environmental and pro-social activities. An example of a diploma of recognition is given below (Figure 3.8).

The importance and uniqueness of a sustainable project is also a good motivator. "I'm participating in the creation of the first electric truck depot in the country," "I'm participating in the design of the tallest autonomous building in Europe," and "I'm working on a unique technology for transforming rainwater into drinking water" – these statements confirm that the very participation in the project is a distinction and motivates the team member to make an increased effort.

DIPLOMA OF RECOGNITION

for

Marian Kowalski

for

development and implementation of pro-environmental and pro-social methods of performing work on the project

"Upgrade of road transport of company XYZ"

....

(President of XYZ) *(Project Manager)*

FIGURE 3.8 A sample diploma of recognition. (Own work.)

Relations between the Project Manager and a Project Team Member

An important source of motivation is the way the project manager exercises power. One can agree with Jonathan Gosling and Prasad Kaipa's statement that leading is never a neutral act: it requires us to make difficult choices about aims and intentions and also about the means to fulfill them (Gosling and Kaipa 2017: 88).

A sustainable manager, whose profile is presented in Chapter 2, should serve as a model for project team members. His or her authority and activities for sustainable development certainly encourage people to imitate him or her and take up new challenges in this area.

Charismatic leaders and the so-called heroes have a particularly strong motivational influence on their subordinates. A good example of a charismatic leader engaging in pro-social activities is Bill Gates, founder of the Microsoft Corporation. He is considered to be the most generous man in the world: he has already donated $28 billion to charity. An equally important category is heroes. A hero is distinguished by his or her courage and extraordinary actions, which can also take place in the area of sustainability. A manifestation of heroism can be selfless help and generosity toward other people that saves their lives, as well as participation in risky environmental campaigns. According to R. Daft and D. Marcic, such people are role models for employees – they set an example of doing something good for the organization (Daft and Marcic 2013: 70).

Every project manager, even if he or she does not have enough charisma and is not a hero, can be a role model for his or her team members. We present the possible actions in this area as follows.

The working atmosphere created by the manager plays a motivating role in the activities of the project team, including those in support of sustainable development. Ethical conduct, friendly treatment of team members, listening to their opinions and suggestions, fair evaluation, and assistance in solving problems are the most important manifestations of care for a good working atmosphere.

The manager should act in this manner in order to gain the trust of the project team members. Trusting the manager, the team members try to perform their tasks properly also in the area of sustainability. They often work with increased efficiency without supervision. They are strongly committed to achieving project goals. If they do not trust the manager, they do at most what they are told and avoid responsibility and additional workload. Worst of all, they discredit the manager, do not accept his or her instructions, and have no tolerance for wrong decisions. The following box provides some important tips on how a manager can gain the trust of project team members.

HOW TO GAIN THE TRUST OF PROJECT TEAM MEMBERS

Make important decisions after hearing the opinions of the team members
Don't take credit for achievements that are not yours
Don't avoid responsibility and do not pass it on to team members in crisis situations

Don't conceal from team members the difficulties they are going to facing on a project
Make promises only when you are absolutely sure you will keep them
Don't gossip and don't tolerate gossip
Be fair and honest, even in situations that annoy you
Don't disseminate information that is unpleasant to the team members and do not use it against them
Try to help the team members, rather than criticize them

Source: Own work.

The current activities of team members in the area of sustainability may deserve recognition or criticism. An expression of recognition by the manager motivates a team member to repeat the success. A factual criticism makes people think and helps them avoid mistakes in the future. Recognition and criticism must be expressed in a professional manner. Table 3.21 provides the examples of recognition and criticism for actions in the area of sustainability. Table 3.22, on the other hand, contains some important rules that may be helpful in contacts with project team members.

Project managers should also pay attention to their team management styles and techniques. Let us use two examples: 1. Applying an autocratic style to people who do creative work may discourage them from creating innovative solutions, including in the area of sustainability. 2. Applying a technique called "management by objectives" in relation to young and inexperienced team members can result in mistakes and underutilization of opportunities that contribute to sustainable development.

TABLE 3.21
Examples of Properly Expressed Recognition and Criticism of Activities in the Area of Sustainability

Expression of Recognition for Activities in the Area of Sustainability	Expression of Criticism for Activities in the Area of Sustainability
The new method of cutting sheet metal that you proposed has brought excellent results. As a result, waste was reduced by 12%. This is a major achievement that reduces costs and protects the environment.	Are you aware of the environmental impact of not turning off office equipment? Whenever you go to the suppliers, the computer and the photocopier are on. Please always turn off all electrical equipment remaining at your workstation before you leave.
I admire your work for sustainable development. You only order environmentally friendly materials. You use much less material than the rest of the project team. I'm very pleased.	Why are you wasting so much paper? One-sided printing, wide margins, double line spacing, a large number of badly printed pages. What do you intend to do to reduce the waste of paper?

Source: Own work.

TABLE 3.22
Important Rules for Expressing Recognition and Criticism for Actions in the Area of Sustainability

Rules for Expressing Recognition	Rules for Expressing Criticism
Only express praise if a member of the project team genuinely deserves it.	Criticize in a factual manner. Specify the exact errors in the behavior of the team member.
Don't hesitate to express your praise. Do it right after the achievement that deserves praise.	Explain to the team member what the consequences of his error are.
Don't express praise and criticism at the same time. Example: you use materials sparingly but still forget to comply with occupational health and safety regulations. Criticize a team member today and praise him tomorrow.	Allow the criticized person to respond to the criticism. Maybe he or she is not to blame at all.
When expressing recognition, focus on specific achievements and not on the characteristics of the employee.	Agree with the criticized person on a concept of a solution to prevent the mistakes from being repeated. Example: you never turn off the light before leaving office and the janitors have to it do later. When you leave the office, please come to me and tell me that you have switched off all lights.
Express your praise in the same way, regardless of whether you like or dislike the person.	Don't wait to express criticism. Don't criticize people for things that happened a long time ago.
Don't exaggerate giving praise, so that team members don't get used to it. If they do, praise loses its motivational character.	Express your criticism face to face.
	Do not use silent criticism (gestures of discouragement, ignoring a team member).

Source: Own work.

Relationships between Project Team Members and Their Associates

On the project team, as in other employee groups, there are formal and informal relationships that increase or decrease motivation for work. If a team member sees that his or her colleagues take sustainability seriously and are willing to get involved in solving environmental and social problems during the project, he or she will do the same. This is because he or she wants to be a part of the group and be accepted by it, and does not want to risk exclusion. If, on the other hand, colleagues have a negative attitude toward sustainable development and only pretend to act, a team member is likely to limit his or her activity in this area and, in time, give it up completely. Consequently, the attitudes and views of the project team members concerning sustainable development become a motivator to take or not take pro-environmental and pro-social actions when carrying out projects.

The project manager should take into account a situation where even the incentive programs that he considers best do not meet the expectations of project team members. This is proven by studies carried out in various organizations. Richard L. Daft and Alan Benson, citing a study conducted by the Society for Human Resource Management, stated: reward and punishment motivational practices dominate organizations. According to the Society for Human Resource Management, 84% of all companies in the USA offer some type of monetary or non-monetary reward system and 69% offer incentive pay, such as bonuses, based on an employee's performance. However, in other studies, more than 80% of employers with incentive programs have reported that their programs are only somewhat successful or not working at all (Daft and Benson 2016: 482). Creating good incentive programs requires consultation with employees and proper understanding of their needs.

This chapter presents many different possibilities of motivating project team members to work for sustainable development. In order to adapt to the situation, it is necessary to choose incentives that encourage team members to become strongly involved in sustainability issues for a long time.

SOME IMPORTANT SOURCES AND WAYS TO MOTIVATE PROJECT TEAM MEMBERS TO GET INVOLVED IN SUSTAINABLE DEVELOPMENT ISSUES

Additional pay (bonuses) for achievements in the area of sustainability
One-off cash prizes for achievements in the area of sustainability
In-kind prizes in the form of environmentally friendly products
Diplomas of recognition, medals, and statuettes
Additional benefits for achievements in the area of sustainability, e.g. financing of vocational training
Trustworthy project management
Adaptation of management styles and techniques to the type of work performed by and the professional qualifications of project team members
Making decisions concerning sustainability taking into account the opinions and suggestions of the project team members
Thorough evaluation of achievements in the area of sustainability
Oral recognition of achievements in the area of sustainability
Oral and written criticism for lack of achievements in the area of sustainability
Assisting the project manager in solving issues related to sustainability
Good working atmosphere on the project team
Attitudes and views of colleagues concerning sustainability
Good working conditions
Project manager's exemplary personality and setting an example of commitment to sustainability

Source: Own work.

3.6 CONTROLLING THE WORK OF THE PROJECT TEAM AND ITS RESULTS

Generally speaking, controlling involves evaluating results in relations to plans or objectives and deciding what action to take next (Doh and Luthans 2018: 398). More specifically, controlling is comparing the actual performance of the project tasks with their normative states. A typical control process related to sustainability activities consists of the steps listed in Table 3.23.

TABLE 3.23
Sustainability Project Activity Control Process

Phases	Specification of Activities
1	Determination of normative states in terms of sustainability
2	Measurement of the actual level of performance of project tasks in the area of sustainability
3	Comparison of the actual execution of the project tasks with the normative states
4	In case of discrepancies, taking corrective actions

Source: Own work.

It would be very expensive and unreasonable to control everyone and everything in the course of project execution. Therefore, controlling covers key areas that have a fundamental impact on the success of the overall project. The key areas related to sustainability include:

a. controlling the timeline of project tasks in the area of sustainability;
b. controlling the use of resources in terms of sustainability; and
c. controlling the spending of cash on tasks related to sustainability.

Tables 3.24–3.26 show the application of the control process to these key areas.

TABLE 3.24
Controlling the Timeline of Project Tasks in the Area of Sustainability

Phases	Specification of Control Activities
1	The normative states are defined in the project work schedules. The schedules indicate the planned start and end dates for individual tasks and the activities they comprise, including those that contribute to sustainable development. Example: completion of work on the sustainable building project is scheduled for 30 April 2020.
2	The measurement of the actual level of task performance consists in obtaining information on the actual dates of completion of the project work related to sustainability. In our example, on 30 April 2020, the project was 90% completed.
3	The comparison of the actual performance of the project tasks with the normative states involves comparing the deadlines set in the schedule with the actual completion dates of the tasks. The comparison shows that the project completion is six days late.
4	No corrective action is needed if the deadlines are met. If there are discrepancies, corrective actions are required. There is a delay in our example. The project manager assigns one more person to help the designer, which reduces the delay time from six days to one day.

Source: Own work.

TABLE 3.25
Controlling the Use of Resources in Terms of Sustainability

Phases	Specification of Control Activities
1	The normative states in relation to sustainability should be included in the project plan. Example: the plan includes arrangements for the designer to use environmentally friendly devices: a computer, a printer, and a photocopier.
2	The measurement of the actual level of completion of project tasks related to sustainability is be based on determination of whether the project team members have been equipped with sustainable resources and whether and to what extent they are being used. In our example, it was found that: – the designer has environmentally friendly equipment at his workstation; – the printer and the computer are operational while the photocopier is not working; and – the designer uses this equipment when working on the design.
3	In this phase, it is determined whether the sustainable resources set out in the project plan are at the workstations, whether they are operational, and whether the team members use them. In our example, it turned out that the photocopier is broken.
4	No corrective action is taken if there are no differences between the status of the sustainable resources set out in the project plan and the status of the sustainable resources provided to the project team. Otherwise, corrective actions are required. In our example, the project manager ordered the replacement of a broken photocopier with one that works.

Source: Own work.

Control Timeline – Monitoring of Activities Related to Sustainability

Control should be an ongoing process. It cannot be applied only in relation to the final results of the work. We will explain this using the example of the sustainable building project we presented in Table 3.24. The execution of the entire project is set in the plan for 30 April 2020. On that day, the project manager, when performing the control, expected the project to be completed. However, it turned out that the work on the project is still in progress – it is 90% advanced and will be completed in six days. Why did this happen? Could the project manager have prevented the delay? This situation was possible because the manager did not monitor the progress of the project work or did it improperly. By monitoring the project, the project manager could have avoided the delay.

Monitoring is nothing more than a staggered control. It consists in observing the progress of the project, comparing this progress with the standards and taking corrective action. Monitoring is based on information contained in reports. Reports are drawn up and submitted to the project manager by the persons executing the project tasks.

Reporting as a Basis for Monitoring Activities Related to Sustainability

The purpose of reporting is to check the progress of the project. A useful approach to this problem is provided by the Scrum methodology. Using this methodology, the

TABLE 3.26
Controlling the Spending of Cash on Tasks Related to Sustainability

Phases	Specification of Activities
1	The normative states related to spending on tasks related to sustainability are specified in the project budget. Example: the project budget assumes the cost of construction of a sustainable building to be $20 million. These costs include the earthworks and the foundations (1 million), the shell and roof construction (8 million), and the installation and finishing works (11 million).
2	The measurement of the actual level of performance consists in tracking the actual costs of execution of individual tasks and the entire project. In our example, the project manager determines in an ongoing basis the expenditures related to the construction of the sustainable building. It cost $10 million to complete the earthworks, the foundations, the shell, and the roof.
3	Comparison of the actual performance with the normative states involves comparing the amounts specified in the budget with the actual costs incurred for a task. In our example, the project budget was exceeded by $1 million after completion of the work specified in the previous item.
4	No corrective action is taken if there is no difference between the costs specified in the budget and those actually incurred. If there are discrepancies, corrective actions are required. In our example, the project manager can apply for additional funds for the project or look for savings on the installation and finishing works (using cheaper materials or reducing labor, transport, and other costs).

Source: Own work.

project manager asks his or her subordinates the following questions about tasks related to sustainability:

- What has been done in terms of sustainability so far?
- What will be done in that area in the near future?
- What problems have occurred in achieving the sustainability goals?

Reporting is intended to demonstrate whether activities related to sustainability are being carried out according to the schedule and whether the costs of their execution are within the budget. Attention should also be paid to the working atmosphere and collaboration of the team members. Growing conflicts can constitute a serious barrier to timely achievement of planned goals.

The frequency of reporting depends on the type of work and the duration of the project. If the duration of the project is several days, it is clear that reporting will take place daily or even more often. If the project is to be carried out for several years, reporting at weekly, bi-weekly, or monthly intervals can be considered sufficient.

In determining the frequency of reporting, managers should take into account the professional qualifications, the experience, and the reliability of their subordinates. Professional and reliable employees can be fully trusted. They are very likely to make every effort to complete the work on time and maintain high quality standards. In this case, the reporting frequency can be reduced.

Sometimes a manager does not know his or her subordinates well enough. There may be specialists recruited for the project team with whom the project manager may have never worked before. In such cases, we suggest that more frequent reporting should be required in the first phase of the project and if the work turns out to be timely and of high quality, the frequency of reporting can be reduced.

Reporting takes different forms, which raises two important issues. First, the frequency and level of detail of reports should not be excessive. Let us remember that preparation of reports, regardless of their form, is an additional workload for team members, which distracts them from performing their tasks. The more often we require reporting and the more detailed the reports are, the less time is left for work on the project. Exaggeration and lack of moderation in the approach to reporting are harmful to project activities and arouse negative emotions. Excessive formalism and bureaucracy cause the emphasis to shift from creative project performance to "creative" drawing up of reports. Such reports show progress and proper execution of tasks, although in reality this is not the case. Some managers require frequent and detailed reporting, due to their lack of trust in the team members.

Reports can be prepared in written or oral form. The ways in which information is communicated depend on whether team members are concentrated in one place or dispersed around the country or the world.

If team members are concentrated in one place, e.g. at the headquarters of the organization that commissioned the project, the project manager can convene meetings and require oral or written reports during the meetings. Meetings should last up to one hour and be convened regularly at equal intervals, e.g. on Mondays between 9 AM and 10 AM. Following these rules is important because it allows team members to manage their time rationally.

If project team members are scattered across the country or the world, the following reporting communication methods may be used:

- e-mails;
- text messages;
- phone calls;
- instant messengers, e.g. Skype;
- videos of the meeting;
- report templates included in the project management software; and
- courier mail.

Scattering of project team members does not exempt them from the obligation to report on the progress of the project work in which they are involved on time and in a proper manner.

EXAMPLE OF A SHORT REPORT ON PROJECT WORKS

Report of 16 March 2020

Goal of the project works: preparation and printing of the jubilee folder on environmentally friendly paper in the quantity of 300 copies. The deadline for completion of the work as indicated in the schedule is 30 April 2020.

Work completed by 16 March 2020: the structure of the folder content (table of contents) has been prepared, texts for all chapters have been prepared.

Work planned for the next week: collecting photographs for the folder, submitting the texts and photographs to the graphic designer in order to make a graphic design of the folder and its cover.

Expected problems: there are many photos available concerning the history of the company and its products; there are no professional photos showing the current, modern infrastructure of the company (e.g. main building, production building, production machines, and means of transport). Recommended alternative solutions to the problem: 1. buy a good camera for PLN 3,000–4,000, e.g. NIKON D5600 SLR, and take photos on our own; 2. hire a professional photographer, e.g. Mr. R.G. – the cost of taking and processing the photos that we need will be about PLN 5,000.

Source: Own work.

4 Material Resources in Sustainable Project Management

4.1 TYPES OF MATERIAL RESOURCES AND THEIR IMPORTANCE IN PROJECT IMPLEMENTATION

In our model 4 × SUSTAINABILITY IN PROJECT ACTIVITIES approach, sustainable project team members use sustainable resources to execute a project in a sustainable manner and achieve sustainable goals. The concept of sustainable project organization that meets these requirements is presented in Chapter 1 (Table 1.4). As this concept implies, integration of sustainability into projects and project activities requires knowledge concerning:

a. sustainable project staff;
b. sustainable construction infrastructure;
c. sustainable equipment for production and office spaces;
d. sustainable modes of transport; and
e. sustainable project activities.

The profiles of sustainable project team members are presented in Chapter 2 (sustainable project staff). Chapter 3 (sustainable project activities) focus on managing and execution of work in a sustainable manner. In this chapter, we focus on sustainable material goods (sustainable construction infrastructure, sustainable equipment for production and office spaces, and sustainable modes of transport) that should be used by the project organization and be the result of its activities (Figure 4.1). We will characterize these types of goods, which should facilitate understanding their essence and selecting specific products for projects and project activities.

In this chapter, in our discussion of sustainable material goods, we do not divide them into:

1. goods located at the inputs of a sustainable project organization (goods needed to execute a project);
2. goods that a sustainable project organization is equipped with; or
3. goods that are the goal and content of projects.

It is not necessary to consider each type of these goods separately, since the same types of products can be found in groups 1, 2, and 3 alike. Let us use a mobile phone

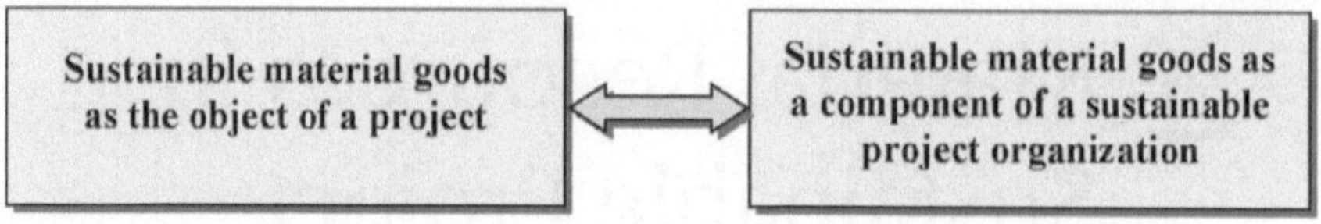

FIGURE 4.1 Sustainable material goods in projects and project activities. (Own work.)

as an example. A mobile phone can be purchased for a project organization (1), can be a part of the company's resources made available to its employees for the duration of the project (2), or can be the object of the project (3).

Sustainable Material Goods as the Object of a Project

Very often the goal of a project is to create various kinds of material goods. These goods are divided into consumer and industrial products. They include durable and non-durable products. Building infrastructure in the form of buildings, production shops, warehouses, and other structures is also a material resource. With a view to sustainable development, it is recommended that standard material goods be replaced on projects with their sustainable equivalents. For example, instead of a traditional building, it is possible to design and make an autonomous building and to finish and equip its interiors in such a way that they contribute to sustainable development. Of course, this is not always possible. Many products still do not have sustainable equivalents. Projects can contribute to their creation.

The result of project activities is innovative products. Nomita Sharma right in her opinion that innovation has been described as the industrial religion of the 21st century (Sharma 2019: 212). Some innovations deserve to be called breakthrough innovations. As C. Christensen and M. Raynor say, breakthrough innovations, as opposed to conservative ones, try to destroy the existing trajectory and redefine it. They offer new values in the form of simpler, more convenient, and cheaper products (Christensen and Raynor 2008: 53). Examples of breakthrough innovations are cameras, light bulbs, telephones, motors, TV sets, radios, computers, and plastics. In the last decade of the 21st century, many innovative products were also developed. These include tablet computers, 3D TV sets, e-book readers, game consoles responding to movement, and many other material goods that affect our lives and contribute to the development of modern civilization.

From the point of view of sustainability, particularly important are innovations that contribute to sustainable development. They are often called eco-innovations. According to F. Halila and J. Rundquist, eco-innovations are those innovations that contribute to a sustainable environment through ecological improvements (Halila and Rundquist 2011: 278–302). Many innovative products have been developed which are considered as eco-innovations. Examples of these are facilities for the production of energy from renewable sources, wastewater treatment facilities, and facilities for eliminating or reducing harmful emissions of gases and particulate matter into the atmosphere. However, it is wrong to equate sustainable development only with eco-innovation. Sustainability is not only

TABLE 4.1
Stages of Creation and Marketing of New Products

Author	Stages
W. Pride, O. Ferrell, *Marketing*, Cengage Learning, United States 2016: 358	Idea generation, screening, concept testing, business analysis, product development, test marketing, and commercialization.
Greg Elliott, Sharyn Rundle-Thiele, David Waller, *Marketing*, John Wiley and Sons, Australia, Ltd. 2012: 224–225	Idea generation, screening, concept evaluation, marketing strategy, business analysis, product development, test marketing, and commercialization.
R. Kerin, S. Hartley, W. Redelius, *Marketing*, McGraw-Hill, New York, 2009: 266	New-product strategy development, idea generation, screening and evaluation, business analysis, development, market testing, and commercialization.
O. Omar, *International Marketing*, Polgrave Macmillan, New York 2009: 263–265	New product idea generation, screening of new product ideas, valuating new product ideas, developing a prototype of new product, market testing of new product, and full-scale marketing of new product.
P. Baines, Ch. Fill, K. Page, *Marketing*, Oxford University Press 2008: 369	Idea generation, screening, business plan and market analysis, product development and selection, test marketing, and commercialization.

Source: Own work.

about pro-environmental but also about pro-social activities. Many different types of innovative products are used to combat social problems. Such goals are achieved thanks to diagnostic devices and medicines that help cure disease and addiction, modern wheelchairs, and personal protective equipment that prevents accidents.

Creation and marketing of innovative products consists of several stages (phases). Table 4.1 shows the stages of creation and marketing of new products defined by different authors. This process starts with the creation of ideas for a new product and ends with its commercialization.

Every project can contribute to sustainable development to some extent. The greatest contribution to this development is made by eco-innovations and products useful in pro-social activities. If the aim of projects is to create a different kind of products, it is always possible to introduce some pro-environmental and pro-social solutions to their design. Such opportunities should be fully exploited.

Sustainable Material Goods as a Component of a Sustainable Project Organization

Every project team or its head office is located in a place that enables the project to be completed. Project executors have their locations in the buildings and, while working on a project, use various types of equipment (e.g. computers, photocopiers, telephones, cars, etc.) and materials (e.g. paper, document folders, toners, and many others). With a view to sustainability, standard products used in project activities should be replaced, where possible, with their sustainable equivalents. Let us look into this in more detail.

Building infrastructure is mainly the buildings in which the project teams do their work. Most buildings that currently exist do not meet sustainability criteria or meet them only to a small extent. This is due to the fact that sustainable construction is in its infancy. The number of fully sustainable buildings is still small compared to the entire building infrastructure used by people. Members of project teams have little influence over the sustainability of their locations. Either they work in spaces where they have worked so far for their employer or they are assigned to other premises intended solely for carrying out the project activities. Changing the structure of existing buildings and the equipment installed in them to a sustainable version is not possible until an upgrade or major renovation has been carried out. It is upgrades and major renovations that create an opportunity to introduce pro-environmental and pro-social solutions. There are also rare cases where buildings are built for project teams. If the aim of a project is to build a large industrial plant, a large power plant, or a stadium, the construction of permanent or temporary premises for the project team at the future construction site can greatly facilitate the management of the entire project.

In practice, there are few possibilities to introduce sustainability into the building infrastructure that a project team has at its disposal. The greatest potential lies in construction projects carried out by project teams. Section 4.2 of this chapter presents the essence and characteristics of sustainable building infrastructure. The solutions presented there are intended to inspire designers to take sustainability into account in all types of building infrastructure they deal with in their work. One should keep in mind that taking sustainability into account when designing and erecting new structures, as well as when upgrading and renovating existing infrastructure is very important for sustainable development. A building constructed today will be used for decades. During this operation, either it will be friendly to the environment and its inhabitants, or it will cause them harm.

For a building to be suitable for use and for the project team to work in it, it is necessary to:

a. perform finishing works, which consist in installation of windows and window sills, installation of doors, installation of radiators, installation of flooring, painting of walls and ceilings, installation of electrical sockets and other equipment, the type of which depends on the purpose of a specific space; and
b. after completion of the finishing works, put furniture in the offices, install computers, photocopiers, telephones, and other equipment; install lighting fixtures, hang chandeliers, and decorate the interiors; set up machines, assemble process lines, prepare handling equipment, equip workstations with tables, chairs, containers, and tool sets; and provide adequate lighting and ventilation of the workspace in production spaces.

In Sections 4.2 and 4.3, we present a wide range of sustainable products that can be used in the finishing and furnishing of production and office spaces. This list is useful in following two cases:

- when the goal of a project is not only to erect the structure of a building, but also to carry out finishing works and furnishing the interior; and
- when the team has the opportunity to shape their workspace before and during the project.

Various types of equipment are often purchased for a project and the spaces are adapted to the needs of the project teams. This is an excellent opportunity to replace standard finishing and furnishing elements with their sustainable equivalents. The situation is similar for means of transport.

In the following chapters of this book, we present many different types of solutions that contribute to sustainable development and can be applied in projects and project activities.

4.2 SUSTAINABLE BUILDING INFRASTRUCTURE

Sustainable building is still in development. According to Adolpho Guido Araujo, Arnoldo Manoel Pereira Carneiro, and Richael Perez Palha, the first articles related to the topic of sustainability in construction were published in 1993 (Araujo, Carneiro and Palha 2020). A. Pabian defines sustainable construction as a sphere of economic activity which deals with the erection, modification, reconstruction, upgrade, and maintenance of buildings in accordance with the principles of sustainable development (Pabian 2011: 5–25). Sustainable construction has been recognized by the European Commission as a leading sector with high innovative potential and key importance for the development of a modern European economy. Traditional construction is criticized for its massive amount of resource consumption and pollutant emissions. It is material- and energy-intensive. European buildings consume as much as 42% of energy and produce 35% of the EU's greenhouse gases. More than 50% of materials extracted from the ground (after processing) are used in the construction sector (Bunikowska 2015). The situation is similar in other countries of the world. China is a good example. According to recent studies, in China, the existing building stock is responsible for approximately 29.6% of the total energy consumption and 27.9–34.3% of the total greenhouse gas emissions. In addition, construction activities account for 40% of the total wastes generated in mainland China (Yu, Shi, Zuo and Chen 2018: 93–103).

Today, sustainable construction takes the forms shown in Figure 4.2.

The triangle shown in Figure 4.2 symbolizes the hierarchy and market shares in the construction market of each type of construction. Majority of the buildings are energy-efficient ones and this is why they are located at the base of the triangle. Compared to other types of construction, energy-efficient construction is the most widespread, easier to implement, and also requires financial outlays. In traditional buildings, heat loss occurs through the walls, the roof, the windows, and the stack ventilation system. To guarantee the proper functioning of a traditional building,

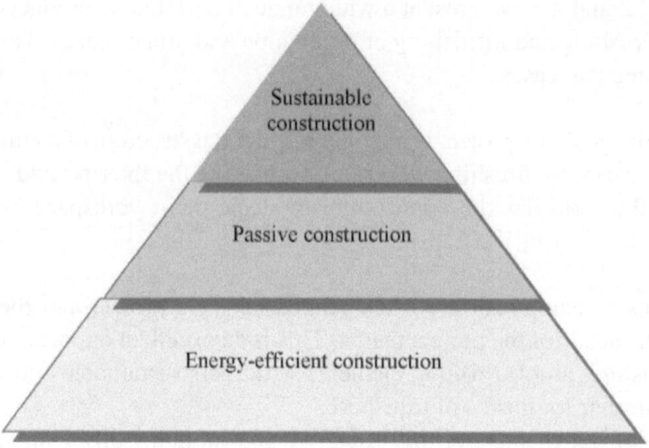

FIGURE 4.2 Types of construction that contributes to sustainable development. (Own work.)

approximately 180 kWh of energy per square meter per year is needed. Energy-efficient buildings are characterized by lower energy loss compared to traditional buildings. In energy-efficient houses, the consumption usually does not exceed 70 kWh. Heat loss is prevented by airtight thermal insulation of the walls and the roof, as well as by appropriate design of the windows and the doors. Energy-efficient buildings are equipped with traditional solid-fuel stoves or with more modern heating systems, e.g. high-performance gas stoves. There are many building insulation systems and energy-efficient heating devices available in the market, which people have been using for many years.

Higher in the hierarchy there are passive buildings. Passive buildings have an extremely low energy demand. The annual energy demand for heating purposes does not exceed 15 kWh/m^2 and the energy demand for hot water production and operation of household appliances does not exceed 120 kWh/m^2. Although passive buildings consume little energy, they usually receive it from external sources. The low energy consumption of this type of structures is mainly due to its very high air-tightness. It is assumed that the amount of air flowing through all leaks in the building should not exceed 60% of its volume. Energy is obtained from energy-saving systems, including renewable sources.

At the apex of the triangle (Figure 4.2) are located autonomous buildings. Buildings of this type have no connections to external infrastructure. They operate on the basis of their own sources of electricity, heat, and water, and do not require stormwater drainage and drainage of waste water to external systems. Consequently, they are self-sufficient, which requires installation of many technically advanced devices. Autonomous construction is therefore much more expensive compared to energy-efficient and passive buildings, more difficult to implement, and least widespread.

In Section 4.2, we present model solutions for sustainable construction in the 21st century, which are a synthesis of solutions used in energy-efficient, passive, and autonomous construction.

Sustainable Construction in the 21st Century

A sustainable building is an environmentally friendly structure that has a positive impact on the people who stay inside. Before its location is specified, a wildlife inventory of the site in which the building is to be erected must be conducted. There must be no endangered species of fauna and flora in the site.

A sustainable building was constructed using clean production processes based on natural, renewable, and healthy materials of local origin (e.g. wood, bricks, and clay). A building like this does not disturb the landscape, is durable, has a simple and lightweight construction, and is recyclable at the end of its life. Its simple and compact structure, as well as its modern wall, window, and roof insulation systems prevent heat loss. Thermal bridges, i.e., places in external partitions with an increased thermal conductivity coefficient, are eliminated from the structure. The seals, as well as the walls and roof, should not impede drainage of excess water vapor from inside the building. This prevents its condensation in spaces and formation of mold and fungi. The location and size of windows in a sustainable building allow maximum use of the heat from sunlight and also protect indoor spaces from overheating. Large windows should be located on the southern side and small windows – on the northern side of buildings. Shade in the summer can be achieved naturally with deciduous trees planted near the building. In the winter, they will not inhibit the heat supply because they are leafless then.

In the case of windows, it is not only the low thermal conductivity coefficient that is important, but also the high solar energy transmittance coefficient. Using triple glazing is a very good solution. Glass panes are separated by chambers (the wider the chambers, the more insulating the window is) filled with an inert gas. A gas called krypton isolates better than argon, but is more expensive. The gas should not leak from the windows, as this will impair their insulation. External blinds/shutters protecting windows and doors are another component of a sustainable building. They reduce energy losses on cold days and prevent the building from overheating in the summer. Of note are the smart windows, which optimize access of natural light and prevent reflection of light from computer screens.

Energy for sustainable buildings is obtained from natural sources (renewable energy). Solar thermal collectors and solar cells (solarthermy) enable conversion of sunlight into heat (domestic water heating, support of central heating). Photovoltaic cells convert solar energy into electricity. Electricity can also be generated by wind turbines. In addition, geothermal energy sources and biogas plants are used. If the location is suitable, energy can also be obtained from a home hydropower plant. Domestic appliances such as cookers, ovens, toasters, and even people in the building are also sources of heat. The correct human body temperature varies between 36 and 37 degrees Celsius, so our body is a natural source of heat. Proper management of electricity requires installation of storage batteries. If possible, surpluses energy should be fed into the power grid. Elevators, which convert kinetic energy into thermal energy, can also be a source of energy.

Operation of the heating system is controlled automatically. As a result, heating in spaces where there are no people is switched off or reduced to a minimum. This helps avoid unproductive operation of heating equipment and overheating of rooms.

An important element of energy-efficient buildings is energy-efficient indoor (LED type) and outdoor (solar-powered lanterns) lighting. Use of artificial lighting can be significantly reduced by maximizing the use of daylight inside the building.

In sustainable buildings, standard stack ventilation is replaced by recuperation, i.e., ventilation with heat recovery. The recuperator recovers heat from the air exhausted from the building and heats the fresh air supplied to the inside. Also, the supplied air is filtered to remove bacteria, viruses, and allergens. Grilles and filters also stop dust, mites, flies, mosquitoes, and other insects. Due to the high air quality provided by ventilation systems with heat recovery, windows that do not open can be installed.

In a sustainable building, it is important to manage water rationally. Therefore, it is equipped with rainwater tanks, which enables use of rainwater, as well as with water purification and treatment stations that enable recirculation of water. Water from these springs is usually used to water plants and flush toilets. To save water, taps with motion detectors and special aerators are installed. The same purpose is served by dual flush toilets. Tightness of the water system is very important. Water dripping from taps and leaking toilet cisterns are the cause of considerable waste.

If the building is to be self-sufficient, it may have its own deep water intake. Such water goes through a treatment system. Self-sufficiency is also ensured by home wastewater treatment plants. It is advisable to recover thermal energy from wastewater.

A sustainable building has biologically active surfaces, which include natural vegetation-covered roofs, facades, patios, inner walls and even gardens where vegetables or herbs are grown. The flora present in buildings should not require intensive watering (to save water) or use of chemicals that are harmful to the environment and humans. Contact of employees with nature can also be ensured by placing aquariums, bird feeders, and apiaries in or in the vicinity of buildings. According to scientists, eye contact with nature for 5–20 minutes a day promotes concentration and reduces stress. Research shows that mental regeneration is also facilitated by appropriate sounds. Sounds present in nature are 40% more conducive to mental regeneration than those of a big city (Hb Reavis 2020: R11). It is worth mentioning that as early as in the 1970s, there was a trend in building design called biophilia, which draws inspiration from nature. The term "biophilia" means "the love of nature and all living things." According to this trend, design uses patterns, colors, and principles found in nature. Examples are construction of building facades in the shape of tree bark, staircases resembling snail shells, and use of natural materials (e.g. wood, stone, cork, or bamboo) in construction, as well as for interior decoration (Hb Reavis 2020: R12).

The social aspects of use of buildings by people are as important as environmental protection. The priorities for users are the comfort of staying in buildings, aesthetic impressions, and protection of life and health. In order to ensure appropriate conditions, construction and finishing materials that are not harmful to health are used, the internal microclimate in the rooms (e.g. temperature, humidity, air filtration, and ventilation) is regulated, the interiors are protected from noise, and proper lighting is provided. Users should be able to adjust the air temperature and humidity to suit their needs. Optimization of the indoor microclimate is also possible by computer control.

Research shows that people working in buildings want access to natural light and a view outside the windows. Lack of such light and view makes employees feel worse. However, according to research, more than a third of them do not have sufficient access to natural light. For this reason, 47% of employees feel tired or very tired, and 43% feel gloomy. It was also found that the more time employees spend with electronic devices, the longer their eyes need to rest. Although a walk is most advisable, a view outside the window can also help the eyes recover. Research has shown that people working in an office with access to daylight are less likely to have tired eyesight, have fewer headaches, and feel sleepy less often (Meister 2019: 12–13). Research shows that people working in green office buildings take sick leave 35–55% less often (Janicka 2014: 62).

Creating pro-social working conditions in buildings also involves including special rooms in their structure to meet various additional needs of employees. Bars and restaurants, especially those serving healthy food, are best suited to solve food problems. In properly equipped relaxation rooms, employees rest and regain strength for further work. If they feel sleepy, they can use a special box during a break to take a nap. A good alternative to relaxation rooms in the workplace is a gym. It is particularly suitable for employees who spend a lot of time sitting at a desk. Instead of a gym, it is possible to provide for a place near the workplaces for a treadmill. Employees may also be allowed to bring their favorite animal, such as a dog or a cat, to work from time to time.

Sustainable construction is mainly buildings that are used not only for residential, commercial, service, and office purposes, but also for production and storage. Production and storage buildings can be fitted with many different types of equipment that contribute to sustainable development. They include:

- systems based on renewable energy sources, e.g. installation of photovoltaic systems on the roofs of production buildings;
- energy-efficient heating and cooling systems, e.g. cooling systems based on CO_2 technology (using CO_2 as the refrigerant);
- energy-efficient air conditioning and ventilation systems;
- energy-efficient lighting systems, e.g. smart LED zone lighting controlled by motion detectors; and
- systems that control and optimize the use of production inputs, including water and electricity.

Higher costs of construction of sustainable buildings are compensated by both current and long-term benefits. Researchers emphasize that the costs associated with the construction of green buildings are about 5% higher than those of standard buildings, but the investment payback period is 5 to 15 years. Green buildings save 30–50% of energy, use about 30% less water, and reduce CO_2 emissions to the atmosphere by about 40%. Last but not least, green buildings produce as much as 70% less waste compared to standard buildings (Bunikowska 2015).

It is also worth mentioning the methods and systems for evaluating sustainable buildings. The first of them were developed in the early 1990s. In the UK, the Building Research Establishment Environmental Assessment Method was published in 1990, which makes it possible to assess buildings in terms of their environmental friendliness and future user comfort. The method set the standards for sustainable design. In the USA, the Leadership in Energy and Environmental Design building assessment system was developed in 1998, which covers assessment of the entire life cycle of a building from design (including location, quality of materials, and technical solutions), through construction and applied building practices and standards, to operation and management of the property. In Germany, on the other hand, the Deutsche Gesellshaft für Nahchaltiges Bauen – German Association for Sustainable Construction has developed a building assessment system that covers six areas: ecology, economics, the socio-cultural factor, and functional topics, such as technology, processes, and location. The National Australian Built Environment Rating System was developed in Australia, which measures and compares the environmental performance of Australian buildings and leases (Siew, Balatbat and Carmichael 2013: 106–139).

SUSTAINABLE CONSTRUCTION

The building occupies a site where there are no endangered species of fauna and flora
The building does not disturb the landscape
The building was built using pure production
The earthworks do not permanently deform the terrain
Building structure: durable, lightweight, compact, and without thermal bridges
The structure is made of natural, renewable, and healthy materials of local origin
The building structure is recyclable at the end of lifetime
Modern wall, window, and roof insulation systems
Environmentally friendly heating systems
Windows with a low thermal transmittance coefficient and a high solar energy transmittance coefficient
The size and location of windows enable maximum use of solar heat and protect rooms against overheating
Large windows on the southern side and small windows on the northern side
External blinds/shutters
Energy is obtained from natural sources: solarthermy, photovoltaic systems, geothermal, wind turbines, and home hydropower plants
Energy-efficient outdoor and indoor lighting
A ventilation system with recuperation (heat recovery and air purification)
Rainwater storage tanks
Water purification and treatment stations
Own deep water intake
Home wastewater treatment system
Biologically active external and internal surfaces
Appropriate microclimate and noise protection
Additional rooms to meet the various needs of employees (bars, restaurants, relaxation rooms, gyms, nap boxes, etc.)

Source: Own work.

4.3 SUSTAINABLE EQUIPMENT OF PRODUCTION HALLS AND OFFICES

Any activity in buildings is possible only after the finishing works have been carried out and the buildings have been properly furnished. In this section, we address important issues concerning environmentally friendly interior finishing and furnishing of offices, production buildings, and warehouses.

Environmentally Friendly Interior Finishing

Every room requires finishing work before it can be used. Flooring needs to be installed and walls and ceilings need to be painted, covered with wallpaper, or fitted with other types of lining. Environmentally friendly interior finishing involves the use of materials that do not harm either people or the environment. It is best to use natural materials from local, easily renewable sources, including wood and stone. Recycled wood is particularly recommended for the sake of forest protection. Wood can be used for floors in offices, as well as in production rooms (industrial parquet). Floors should not be painted. Oiling is a better solution from the environmental point of view. When performing finishing work, all kinds of plastics must be avoided. For painting walls and ceilings, environmentally friendly paints or linings made of natural materials are the best. Their color is not indifferent either. Bright colors enable better use of the sunlight, which they reflect.

A significant potential lies in the lighting of rooms. It is obvious that it should be energy-efficient, e.g. of the LED type. The ability to adjust the light intensity is very important. Reduction of electricity consumption is made possible by zone lighting, based on motion detectors and dusk to dawn sensors. They automatically adjust the light intensity to the time of day and the weather conditions and switch off the light in places where there are no people. Employees should also be able to change the light intensity. Although the requirements for light intensity in workplaces are regulated by standards, the needs of employees must be taken into account. These needs change with age. Research has shown that people aged 40 need almost twice as much light to see as people aged 20 (Buczkowski 2019: R16).

Employees should influence not only the intensity of the light, but also its color. Some colors, e.g. yellow and red, stimulate increased effort, while others, e.g. green and blue, calm down. Changing the color of light, e.g. yellow to green during rest periods, certainly has a positive effect on the employee's mood. It is also important, as we have already mentioned, for employees to be able to adjust the air temperature and the humidity according to their needs.

When finishing interiors, it is worthwhile to provide space for environmentally friendly decorations. They can be placed on walls, ceilings, floors, and furniture. An austere design of workplaces does not promote employee well-being. The most desirable are decorations made of ceramics, glass, wickerwork, other natural materials, but also ones made of plants as they purify and moisturize the air. Vertical gardens and walls made of natural plants are more and more often placed in the working rooms of various companies.

Inside rooms, space should be provided for eco-bins. Eco-bins enable convenient sorting of waste. They are usually made in sets of at least four bins for putting, plastic, paper, and organic waste. An even more environmentally advanced are baskets made of renewable raw materials such as braided jute. Studies from 2019 show that Europeans' waste sorting habits have improved significantly in recent years. On average, six out of ten (59%) respondents from Germany, the UK, Poland, and Belgium say they now sort and process more waste than five years ago (Szmith 2019: R10).

Environmentally Friendly Furniture

Furniture is used both in offices and in production facilities. The raw materials used in the production of environmentally friendly furniture originate from organic farms and contain no harmful substances. Wood is harvested from certified forests (Forest Stewardship Council [FSC] and Programme for the Endorsement of Forest Certification [PEFC] certificates). Such forests are managed in ways that are beneficial for nature. Endangered tree species are protected there. Environmentally friendly furniture can be made from materials other than wood. It can also be wicker, rattan, bamboo, compressed hemp fibers, and other natural materials. They should be plants that are fast-growing and easy to transport and transform into finished products. Recycled materials are also suitable for production of environmentally friendly furniture.

An unconventional material that is used to make furniture is specially processed cardboard. Its strength is similar to that of plywood, but it is lighter and easier to form. It consists of overlapping glued layers of cardboard. Furniture made of this material (e.g. chairs, cabinets, and tables) are light, durable, deformation-resistant, and flame retardant.

Environmentally friendly furniture is lighter than its standard counterparts. This means that less material is used in its production and less fuel is used for its transport. It also causes fewer problems in the end-of-life phase. When no longer in use, environmentally friendly furniture can be recycled.

Environmentally friendly furniture is made using varnishes, adhesives, and stains that contain natural ingredients. These include water-based paints and adhesives with environmental certificates. Environmentally friendly furniture is upholstered with natural leather, silk, linen, cotton, and filled with sheep wool, straw, and other natural materials. If the filler is synthetic foam, it does not contain environmentally harmful freons.

Long life of furniture contributes to environmental protection. Frequent replacement of furniture causes an increase in demand for it, which results in increased production, with all the negative consequences for the environment. Consequently, it is better to renovate furniture and to make new purchases only when it is really necessary.

Environmentally Friendly Office Equipment

Working in the office requires use of various types of devices. The most typical include computers, photocopiers, and telephones. Although these devices are very useful to humans, their production does not contribute to sustainable development. A good example is computers. A computer consists of 1,800–2,000 components. These components are sourced or manufactured in many countries around the world. Manufacturers, in their search for savings, use the resources and labor of poor countries in Africa, South America, and Asia, and this in turn becomes a source of social problems. These include inhumane working conditions, excessive working hours, low wages, failure to meet safety standards, forced relocation, and child labor. Production of the numerous components that make up a computer requires huge amounts of materials. Production of a single desktop computer requires more than 240 kg of fossil fuels, 22 kg of chemicals, and 1,500 kg of water. More than 1,000 different materials are used in the production of computers and computer hardware. The negative feature of many of these is high toxicity. Computer chips containing lead and cadmium, monitors contain mercury and barium, and lithium, nickel, and cadmium are found in batteries (Pabian 2012b: 798).

Also, the frequent replacement of computers, their low quality, and their energy consumption are contrary to the principles of sustainable development. A serious threat to the natural and human environment is posed by waste computer hardware that does not undergo special disposal. Fortunately, there are more and more computers in the market that are manufactured and used in ways that are less harmful to humans and the nature. Here are some examples (https://www.ekologia.pl/styl-zycia/oszczedzaj/5-najbardziej-ekologicznych-laptopow,8209.html).

Lenovo ThinkPad X301

The laptop housing is free of cadmium, lead, and arsenic compounds. It is 90% recyclable. It uses mercury-free LEDs. The computer has software to extend battery life and low power consumption components.

ASUS Eee PC 1000HE

It is one of the "greenest" and best-looking laptops in the market. The 1000HE model has a 10-inch screen and weighs only 900 grams. The super-efficient atom processor consumes no more than 3 watts of power and the intelligent power supply module can adjust the power consumption and the brightness of the LCD display, which makes the computer extremely energy-efficient.

Apple MacBook Air

It has an arsenic- and mercury-free display, and its housing is made of 100% recyclable aluminum.

Devices that work with computers and their components are also harmful to humans and the natural environment. An example of this is toner cartridges used in computer printers. Every year more than 375 million empty laser printer toners and inkjet printer cartridges are disposed of worldwide. In order to prevent this problem to some extent, refabricated toner cartridges, i.e., toner cartridges made from parts of original cartridges, are increasingly used (Daniluk 2019: R15).

When deciding to purchase devices that work with computers, it is a good idea to choose ones whose use contributes more to sustainable development. Let us use the example of inkjet and laser printers. It turns out that inkjet printers are more environmentally friendly than laser printers. Inkjet printers produce 90% less waste compared to lasers (thanks to the Replaceable Ink Pack System [RIPS] technology). They do not require replacement of toner cartridges, drums, developers, transfer belts, or fuser units because they do not have them. They consume 80% less power due to the technology used, which does not generate heat. They are user-friendly because they do not need toner (it is a source of released micro dust that irritates the eyes, the skin, and the respiratory tract, and causes headaches), emit no ozone at work and make less noise when printing (https://www.hicopy.gdansk.pl/porfolio-item/redukcja-kosztow-utrzymania/).

Environmentally Friendly Office Supplies

The most important material used in every office is paper. The global paper consumption is still too high. The situation is aggravated by the use of standard paper made using the harmful chlorine bleaching process. Companies and their employees can contribute to sustainable development by using environmentally friendly paper. Environmentally friendly paper has different characteristics. It is mainly associated with a product made from recycled paper. However, its origin may be completely different. Here is an example. In Thailand, a paper producer sources the raw material for paper production from farmed trees without exploiting natural forests. As a result of research and development work, they developed a hybrid, fast-growing eucalyptus tree called "Paper Tree." It is cultivated on previously unused strips of land, as well as by 1.5 million farmers who plant it around their rice fields (thus increases the green areas). Tree bark, wood shavings, lignin, and black lye are used to produce energy from biomass, which is in turn used to power the factory (https://www.hicopy.gdansk.pl/porfolio-item/redukcja-kosztow-utrzymania/). In addition to paper itself, the way it is used is important. Minimizing the amount of paper documents in circulation, minimizing the number of copies, using double-sided prints, and using smaller paper formats are examples of responsible activities that contribute to sustainable development.

ENVIRONMENTALLY FRIENDLY CURTAINS

Environmentally friendly curtains fit into the trend of creating innovative pro-environmental and pro-social solutions. An example is the GUNRID air-purifying curtains. Air purification is possible thanks to an innovative technology based on a photocatalytic mineral-based coating. The sunlight-activated coating decomposes particles of typical pollutants (nitrogen oxides found in the exhaust gases of gas stoves and formaldehyde released into the air from plastic objects, paints, and furniture). These unique curtains do not require electricity and can also be washed less frequently than ordinary curtains. Moreover, they are made of recycled PET bottles.

Source: Own work based on http://www.propertydesign.pl/architektura/104/nowosci_ikea_na_luty_marka_zacheca_do_zrownowazonego_stylu_zycia,27507.html

When discussing sustainable indoor furnishings, we cannot overlook the principles of environmentally friendly consumption of beverages in the workplace. This is because such furnishings comprise coffee makers, kettles, cups, and glasses. Beverage consumption in the workplace is a very big environmental problem. Beverages are consumed in millions of companies around the world. The products used during beverage consumption pollute the environment. To reduce the scale of this pollution, the principle of "as little plastic as possible at the place of consumption of beverages" must be applied. Instead of buying water in small plastic bottles, the company can use environmentally friendly water dispensers with bottles used more than 50 times. Another solution is to use filter jugs. Plastic cups can be replaced by paper cups or, preferably, reusable glass or ceramic cups. Thermal mugs are also a good idea. The beverage poured into them stays warm for a long time, which reduces the frequency of coffee and tea brewing. Energy-efficient coffee machines and kettles are also advisable. Environmentalists criticize capsule coffee machines. It is estimated that up to 20 billion coffee capsules are disposed of every year in British landfills alone (https://www.rp.pl/Handel/191109729-Lavazza-wprowadza-ekologiczne-kapsulki-z-kawa.html). Standard capsules harm the environment because the aluminum used for their production is not recycled. Aluminum is made from bauxite. Bauxite is mined in open pit mines where workers' rights are often violated. What is more, in order to mine bauxite, forests, including the Amazon rainforest, are often cleared. Aluminum production requires very high-energy consumption, which also harms the environment (https://finanse.wp.pl/kawa-w-kapsulkach-niebezpieczna-dla-srodowiska-organizacje-ekologiczne-apeluja-do-nestle-koncern-odpowiada-6111805322053761a). Manufacturers are looking for new solutions – they are trying to replace traditional aluminum and plastic capsules with capsules that are biodegradable.

SUSTAINABLE EQUIPMENT OF ROOMS

Equipment made of natural materials of local origin
Equipment made of recycled materials
Equipment coated with environmentally friendly paints and varnishes
Energy-efficient lighting
Zone lighting based on motion and dusk to dawn sensors
Adjustable light intensity and color
Biologically active indoor surfaces, including vertical gardens with natural plants
Environmentally friendly furniture made of natural or recycled materials
Environmentally friendly machinery and equipment
Environmentally friendly interior decoration

Source: Own work.

4.4 SUSTAINABLE TRANSPORT

Transport is currently the third sector, after the power industry and the manufacturing sector, that emits the largest amount of carbon dioxide (CO_2) (Wajer 2019: 36). The two main branches of transport are passenger and cargo transport. Taking into account the type of means of transport and their mode of movement, transport is divided into air, land, and water transport. In this chapter, we focus land transport using cars. This type of transport does most damage to the environment and has a negative impact on human health. In the European Union, almost 30% of the total CO_2 emissions come from the transport sector, 72% of which is from road transport. Passenger cars are a major source of pollution, accounting for 60.7% of all CO_2 emissions (https://www.europarl.europa.eu/news/pl/headlines/society/20190313STO31218/emisje-co2-z-samochodow-fakty-i-liczby-infografika).

The number of cars in the world is growing rapidly. It is estimated that there will be 1.5 billion of them in 2025 and 2 billion in 2040. In the future, the greatest increase in the number of cars is expected in developing countries, including China and India. There were four vehicles per 1,000 people in China in 2000 and 40 in 2010, and it is estimated that this number will reach 310 in 2035. According to the European Automobile Manufacturers' Association, 54.1% of European vehicles run on petrol and 40.97% on diesel. Cars that use alternative fuels represent only 4.94%. The average age of cars in use in many regions of the world is ten years and more (https://www.motofakty.pl/artykul/liczba-samochodow-na-swiecie.html). This is not beneficial to the environment because older cars are less environmentally friendly compared to those manufactured today. The vehicles manufactured in recent years have a number of modern solutions that reduce fuel consumption and exhaust emissions. Examples include the auto start–stop technology that allows the engine to be automatically switched off at a standstill, or the ECO PRO program that reduces fuel consumption.

Car transport has a negative impact on the environment, which also harms people. It is a source of the following pollutants in the form of greenhouse and tropospheric gases (http://www.eere.energy.gov/vehiclesandfuels, 19 February 2012):

a. carbon dioxide (CO_2) – at high concentrations, it causes headaches and dizziness, difficulty in falling asleep, and field of vision loss;
b. carbon monoxide (CO) – at higher concentrations, it is lethal and causes vision and coordination disorders, headaches and dizziness, disorientation, and nausea;
c. nitrogen oxides (NOx) – they affect the respiratory system; and
d. sulfur dioxide (SO_2) – it causes aggravation respiratory diseases (bronchial diseases and asthma).

Furthermore, transport is a source of noise and vibration. Noise worsens the mental and physical condition of people (damages hearing, causes headaches, and disturbs concentration) and causes animals to migrate from areas adjacent to traffic routes. Vibrations contribute to destruction of infrastructure and have a negative impact on the human body.

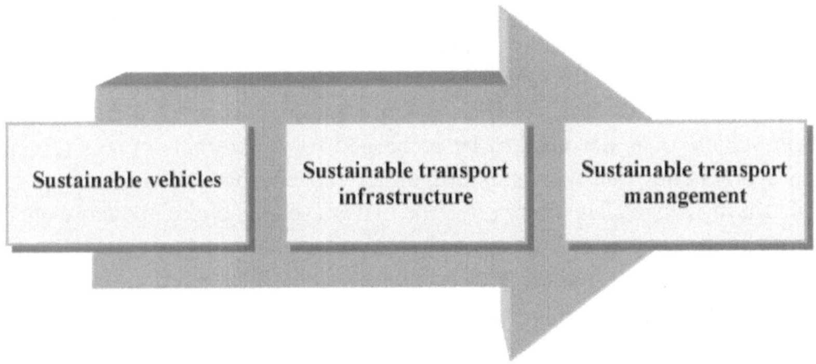

FIGURE 4.3 Basic components of sustainable transport. (Own work.)

Means of transport vary in terms of energy consumption and emissions of harmful gases and substances. With the same energy input, goods can be transported by ship over a distance of 370 km, by train over a distance of 300 km, and by truck over a distance of only up to 100 km. A ship emits 33.4 grams of CO_2 per kilometer, a train – 48.1 grams, and a truck – as much as 164 grams (http://klasterip.pl/wp-content/uploads/2016/11/aar-2.jpg).

Sustainable transport enables people and cargo to be moved with respect for the environment. It consists of the three components shown in Figure 4.3. In the further part of this section, we analyze these components in terms of sustainability.

Sustainable Vehicles

In the model approach, the characteristics of sustainable vehicles and their utilization are:

a. design and fitout made of sustainable materials;
b. transport without emissions or waste polluting the natural environment;
c. operational parameters enabling efficient, comfortable, and safe transport of people and cargo; and
d. carrying out repairs and maintenance in a pro-environmental and pro-social manner.

There are currently no vehicles in the market that meet all the conditions listed in items (a)–(d). These conditions reflect the state that automotive companies and vehicle users should strive for. Progress in this area is manifested in designing increasingly modern cars powered by alternative energy sources. The key designs of this type are presented below.

Hybrid Vehicles

Hybrid vehicles provide a bridge between vehicles with internal combustion engines and electric vehicles (they have internal combustion-electric engines). The most important part of the hybrid system is the planetary gearbox, which connects the internal combustion engine, the generator, and the electric motor. The hybrid drive makes it possible to start the vehicle with the electric motor and to use this motor to cover certain distances at urban speeds. Since energy is recovered during braking, a hybrid vehicle does not need to be recharged from external sources (except for plug-in hybrids equipped with standard, larger-capacity batteries to ensure a longer electric driving range). The more often the driver uses the brake, the more energy is recovered by the generator. This causes hybrid vehicles to consume much less fuel in urban traffic where the frequency of braking is higher compared to driving outside such areas. Due to their design, they are also more durable.

Vehicles Fueled by CNG, LNG, and LPG

Many vehicles run on natural gas (NG) or a mixture of petroleum gases (LPG). Natural gas is used in compressed (CNG – compressed natural gas) or liquefied (LNG – liquid natural gas) form. The mixture of petroleum gases is liquefied (LPG – liquefied petroleum gas).

The main component of natural gas (CNG and LNG) is methane. The significant advantage of this gas over other fuels results from lower emissions of particulate matter (PM) – by 95% and nitrogen oxide (NO_2) – by 90%, and a significant reduction of CO_2 emissions. (https://www.trucks.com.pl/2020/03/02/iveco-nowoczesna-stacja-tankowania-gazu-ziemnego-w-turynie/). Natural gas is therefore a source of low emissions – the exhaust gases are almost completely free of particles, smoke, and odor. Experience with the use of natural gas in different transport sectors is positive. Vehicles powered with liquefied gas (LNG) reduce emissions of pollutants by 90–95% compared to those with diesel engines and emissions of CO_2 particles by 95%. This means that LNG is less harmful not only to the environment, but also to human health. An LNG truck consumes up to 10–15% less fuel than a diesel truck and after refueling, it can cover a distance of up to 1,600 km (http://laj.pl/transport/5012/grupa-hegelmann-kupuje-pojazdy-ciezarowe-napedzane-skroplonym-gazem-lng/). The cost of CNG-fueled buses is up to 50% lower than that of electric buses. The same is true of the range, which is up to 350–400 km (https://pim.pl/rewolucja-gazowa-w-transporcie-towarowym/).

A mixture of petroleum gases (LPG) consists of propane and butane. It is produced in the process of refining of crude oil and during extraction of natural gas. The advantage of using this mixture as a fuel is that it does not require use of toxic antiknock agents.

Electric Vehicles

The number of models of electric cars available worldwide is constantly increasing. According to the International Energy Agency, there are already more than 1 million electric cars on the road and the number expected by 2030 is over 100 million (https://www.motofakty.pl/artykul/liczba-samochodow-na-swiecie.html). Car companies are working on better and better versions of such vehicles. Table 4.2 shows a part of the wide range of electric passenger cars available in the market at the end of 2019.

TABLE 4.2
Examples of Electric Passenger Cars Available in the Market at the End of 2019

Model	Energy Consumption kWh/100 km	Range in km
Smart	12.9	150
Renault Zoe	13.3	300
Volkswagen e-Golf	12.7	300
Renault ZOE	14.6	300
Nissan LEAF	20.6	270
Hyundai Kona (136 hp power)	15	289
BMW i3	13.3	235
Hyundai Kona (204 hp power)	15.4	449
Nissan e+LEAF	18	385
Jaguar I Pace	21.2	480
Tesla X 75D	20.8	417
Tesla S 75D	18.9	490
Tesla X P100D	22.6	542

Source: Own work based on Motosalon 2019: 31.

The environmental advantages of the BMW i3 electric car are presented below as an example. It is manufactured using energy from renewable sources (hydro and wind energy). 95% of the car is recyclable. It drives without exhaust emissions. It also emits hardly any sounds or odors. The integrated ECO PRO mode increases the car's range and reduces power consumption. Innovative aerodynamic solutions that reduce drag also contribute to reduced energy consumption. Inside the car, renewable or recycled materials are used, including kenaf, pure wool, eucalyptus wood, and leather tanned with olive leaves (BMW i3 Catalogue 2016: 20–23).

Not only are the production volumes and the range of electric cars increasing, but also the demand for such vehicles. People are increasingly willing to buy electric cars. This is not just because of their concern for the environment. Low operating costs are a serious incentive. The cost of electricity needed to drive such vehicles is much lower compared to the purchase of gasoline or diesel. The demand for electric cars would be even greater if it was not for the barriers, which include high prices, still too few charging stations, long recharging times, and short range on a single charge.

According to an analysis conducted by the Center of Automotive Management, China is currently the world's largest market for electric and plug-in hybrid cars. From January to June 2019, approximately 628,000 such cars were registered there. In the first half of 2019, 48,000 electric cars were registered in Germany, 29,000 in France, 27,000 in Great Britain, and 20,000 in Holland (https://moto.rp.pl/tu-i-teraz/29120-sprzedaz-aut-elektrycznych-na-swiecie-polska-daleko-w-tyle).

Hydrogen-Powered Vehicles

Hydrogen powered vehicles are modern, environmentally friendly means of transport that are used in some transport sectors. We briefly describe this type of vehicles using the example of the Solaris Urbino 12 hydrogen bus manufactured by Solaris Bus & Coach S.A. This innovative vehicle was presented in 2019 at the Global Public Transport Summit in Stockholm where it found further buyers. Solaris Urbino 12 hydrogen buses use a 70 kW fuel cell set. A single fueling makes it possible to cover a distance of up to 350 km. Electricity in a hydrogen fuel cell is generated by reverse water electrolysis and is transferred directly to the drive system. These vehicles do not emit any harmful substances. The only by-products of the chemical reaction taking place in the cell are heat and steam. Hydrogen-powered buses are equipped with a Solaris High Power traction battery with the capacity of about 30 kWh, which is designed to support the fuel cell at times of peak demand for electricity. The battery is charged with energy from hydrogen and by recuperation during braking. The electricity produced by electrolysis drives the axle with integrated electric motors. Hydrogen is collected under the pressure of 350 atmospheres in five tanks located on the bus roof. A set of composite cylinders placed longitudinally above the first axle of the vehicle has the capacity of 1,560 liters and allows the storage of 37.5 kg of hydrogen. The bus also uses many modern technologies to improve passenger safety and comfort, which goes along the pro-social aspects of sustainable development (https://www.trucks.com.pl/2020/03/16/solaris-kolejne-miasta-zamawiaja-wodorowe-autobusy/).

Biomethane-Powered Vehicles

Biomethane and biogas are clean motor fuels. Biogas is produced from biomass and then converted into biomethane. Biogas is produced by anaerobic digestion as a result of decomposition of organic substances (e.g. plants, animal feces, wastewater sludge, and agricultural and food waste) by microorganisms. The use of agricultural and municipal organic waste for biogas production is particularly important for environmental protection. Compressed biomethane gas is normally used to power motor vehicles. Using biomethane as a fuel significantly reduces NOx, particulate matter, and greenhouse gas emissions. It also enables reduction of noise, compared to traditional fuels.

Compressed Air-Powered Vehicles

A car powered by compressed air has been developed in Europe. It does not emit any pollutants. During its compression, air passes through filters, which makes it cleaner than atmospheric air when it leaves the exhaust pipe. The engine of this car can also work in the reverse direction as a compressor. Thanks to the installation of the motor-alternator, the car can be filled with compressed air in two ways:

at a compressed air station (filling up takes about 3 minutes) or by plugging the car into a power socket. In the latter case, the motor-alternator works as an electric motor and powers the car's pneumatic motor. The pneumatic motor acts as a compressor and fills the tanks with air from the atmosphere (the "fueling" takes about 4 hours). The energy needed to drive the compressor can be drawn from solar batteries, windmills, and other unconventional sources. Compared to electric cars, such vehicles are lighter and have a greater range. At the end of their service life there is no problem with disposal of batteries containing lead compounds, electrolytes, and other harmful substances. The high air pressure in the cylinders creates risk of explosion in the event case of a collision with an obstacle. However, it should be emphasized that vehicles powered with petrol and hydrogen, which are flammable substances, have the same disadvantage (https://wolnemedia.net/samochody-na-sprezone-powietrze/).

The list of possible more environmentally friendly means of transport contains many more solutions than those presented above. Even standard vehicles can be modified to make at least some degree of sustainability. A good example is the solutions adopted by the global logistics company DHL for its British customer in the retail sector. The customer decided to reduce CO_2 emissions during road transport from suppliers to distribution centers. In order to reduce fuel consumption and the number of trips, a decision was made to use aerodynamic trailers. Their streamlined shape saved 10% of fuel while increasing the volume of transported cargo by one tenth. The introduction of 399 such trailers has made it possible to reduce CO_2 emissions by 2,000 tons per year (https://www.rp.pl/Analizy-Rzeczpospolitej/310099988-Ekologia-to-nie-tylko-redukcja-emisji–z-wielkich-tirow.html).

THE PERSONAL RAPID TRANSIT (PRT) SYSTEM AT THE UK HEATHROW AIRPORT

The PRT system is an example of implementation of the concept of fast individual urban transport worldwide. The system enables travelers to travel between a business car park and the new Terminal 5 of the Heathrow Airport located about 2 km away. There are 21 automatically controlled electric vehicles on this route. Each has four seats for passengers with luggage. The vehicles carry people along a separate route at speeds of up to 40 km/h. The ride takes about 5 minutes. The vehicles arrive "on request" or are available immediately. The waiting time is zero for 70% of users and very short for others. According to estimates, the investment costs are roughly half as high as those for a comparable tram system with similar capacity in terms of passengers carried.

Source: Own work based on http://www.rupprecht-consult.eu/uploads/tx_rupprecht/NICHES_overview_concepts_PL.pdf

Sustainable Transport Infrastructure

Sustainable transport requires sustainable infrastructure. Sustainable infrastructure not only enables the operation of sustainable vehicles in an area, e.g. charging of electric vehicles, but can also contribute in various ways to sustainable development through modern technology. Some examples are given below.

Environmentally Friendly Filling Stations

These include passive or autonomous buildings, as well as electric vehicle charging stations, and natural gas, biomethane, and other clean fuel dispensers. Electricity for charging vehicles as well as for the station's own use comes from renewable sources. Rainwater collected in tanks can be used for washing cars.

Environmentally Friendly Lighting

This includes both road and pavement lighting, and traffic lights. Energy for lighting along transport routes comes from renewable sources, including solar panels and wind turbines.

Roads that Generate Electricity

Photovoltaic solar panels integrated into the roadway produce electricity that can be used for lighting, powering road systems, or charging electric cars, as well as in homes. It has been calculated that 100 meters of road surface made of solar panels generates 30,000 kWh of electricity per year. Such solutions are already used in the Netherlands (https://polonia.nl/2019/03/07/holandia-sloneczna-droga/). Electricity can also be generated by the roadway as a result of the stress caused by the passing vehicles, as well as vibrations.

Roads with Addition of Rubber

Rubber pellets added to the asphalt are made from used tires. It therefore contributes to environmental protection not only by reducing harmful waste, but also by reducing noise. The noise emitted by cars driving on such roads is 3–6 decibels less than on traditional surfaces. The construction of 1 kilometer of rubber-modified asphalt road makes it possible to use 400–1,200 used tires. Rubber surfaces are more resistant to cracking, aging, and low temperatures, and are cheaper to maintain (https://www.rp.pl/Analizy-Rzeczpospolitej/310099988-Ekologia-to-nie-tylko-redukcja-emisji–z-wielkich-tirow.html).

Environmentally Friendly Traffic Lanes

On motorways and other multi-lane roads, lanes are provided for both alternative fuel vehicles and petrol vehicles, provided that they at least two people (driver plus at least one passenger) travel in them. The aim is to promote practices whereby several passengers use a car at the same time, as opposed to just the driver, thus significantly reducing the number of vehicles on the road. Environmentally friendly lanes are a very effective way to force pro-environmental behavior. Drivers are keen to use them because traffic on environmentally friendly lanes is usually much lower than on adjacent standard lanes, so traffic jams are avoided and the journey to the destination is faster.

COMPONENTS OF SUSTAINABLE TRANSPORT

Hybrid vehicles
Vehicles fueled by CNG, LNG, and LPG
Electric vehicles
Hydrogen-powered vehicles
Biomethane-powered vehicles
Compressed air-powered vehicles
Environmentally friendly filling stations
Transport route layout in compliance with the principle of sustainability
Roads made of environmentally friendly materials
Environmentally friendly road lighting
Road structure as a renewable energy source
Environmentally friendly traffic lanes

Source: Own work.

Sustainable Transport Management

The third important component of sustainable transport is management. Its aim is to make the operation of vehicles pro-environmental and pro-social. The objectives of sustainable transport management should be to minimize fuel consumption, optimize use of means of transport, and ensure the safety of operators, passengers, and cargo. An important role in transport management is played by telematics. The box below shows important environmental and social activities that are a part of sustainable transport management.

PRO-ENVIRONMENTAL AND PRO-SOCIAL ASPECTS OF TRANSPORT MANAGEMENT

Reduction of the number of vehicles
Reduction of the number of kilometers traveled
Optimization of the travel routes
Optimal use of vehicle capacity
Avoidance of overloading of vehicles
Elimination of empty runs (runs without passengers and cargo)
Reduction of fuel consumption and tire way through proper driving techniques
Sustainable maintenance and repair management
Pro-social management of human resources in transport
Driver training in eco-driving
Installation of breathalyzers in vehicles

Source: Own work.

4.5 SUSTAINABLE PRODUCTS AS MANUFACTURING OUTPUT

The executors of every project aim to achieve a goal. As a result of their work, new products, services, and technologies are created and various types of actions are carried out. Increasing environmental and social risks lead to the search for solutions that contribute to sustainable development. Every project should, as far as possible, contribute to this development and thus create pro-environmental and pro-social goods. In this section, we present the potential inherent in this area and the innovative solutions that have already been created or are in the development phase.

Projects result in sustainable, partially sustainable, or unsustainable goods as shown in Table 4.3.

Sustainable goods are fully pro-environmental and pro-social. Organic, plant-based food products, which are an example of such goods, come from organic, renewable farms, and do not harm either people or the environment. Partially sustainable goods are not fully pro-environmental or pro-social, but have certain attributes that contribute to sustainable development. An example of this is a hybrid car that needs less gasoline than a standard car, an energy-efficient washing machine, or an environmentally friendly computer from which a significant part of harmful substances has been eliminated. Unsustainable goods have a negative impact on human health and the environment (e.g. plastic objects, coal-fired ovens, sweet beverages containing sugar and chemical substances, and many other products). Unsustainable goods are the most common in the market and sustainable goods – the least common. The range of partly sustainable goods continues to grow as more and more people and organizations want to contribute to sustainable development. The search for new solutions in project activities should be directed toward designing and making fully sustainable products. If this is not possible in some cases, they must be at least partly sustainable. However, it is becoming necessary to minimize the number of projects whose goal is to create products that are harmful to people and the environment. The following box shows important features of sustainable products, which are briefly discussed later in the section.

TABLE 4.3
Types of Goods Resulting from Projects – from the Perspective of Sustainability

Goods Resulting from Projects		
Sustainable	Partly sustainable	Unsustainable
Durable physical goods		
Non-durable physical goods		
Services		

Source: Own work.

SUSTAINABLE PRODUCTS

Safe products
Durable and reusable products
Economical products
Products powered by energy from renewable sources
Emission-free products
Products made of renewable materials
Products made of recycled materials
Reusable products
Products that are easy to disassemble, repair, or modify
Products that decompose rapidly and harmlessly

Source: Own work.

Safe products do not endanger human life or health. They are made from materials that are not harmful to people or the environment. They are also safe to operate. Physical products with a long service life are ergonomic; contain the necessary housings and covers for moving parts, as well as safety systems to protect the health and life of their users.

Durable products are characterized by a long service life. Currently, manufacturers use various ways to cause rapid wear and tear of goods in order to force consumers to buy again. Many products start to deteriorate after their warranty period has expired. It is also common to launch seemingly new products in the market. The goal is to attract customer attention and increase sales. The practices described here have a disastrous impact on the environment. The greater the production volume, the more materials, energy, water, and other goods are needed for manufacturing processes. Harmful emissions are increasing, as is the amount of waste. Prematurely discarded products are landfilled, posing further risks to people and nature. Long service lives of products reduce the scale of these negative phenomena as it reduces the scale and frequency of purchases. As a result of lower demand, the supply and, consequently, the production volume decrease.

Economical products, depending on their purpose, consume small amounts of electricity, water, gas, and other substances needed for their operation. Particularly noteworthy are autonomous products, i.e., ones that are not powered by traditional energy sources at all. For example, calculators and watches equipped with solar batteries that convert light into electricity. They do not require standard batteries or rechargeable batteries with chargers. Solar batteries do not reduce the amount of electricity from traditional sources.

Products supplied with energy from renewable resources use energy generated from sunlight, wind, water, and thermal energy from rocks, water, and the ground below the Earth's surface. This energy comes from the nature and does not require exploitation of non-renewable resources.

Emission-free products do not emit substances that are harmful to people and the environment in the form of solid, liquid, or gaseous pollutants, as well as harmful heat, noise, vibrations, and electromagnetic fields. It is enough to replace the cars currently on the road with emission-free vehicles to end emission of huge amounts of nitrogen oxide, CO_2, CO, hydrocarbons, sulfur oxide, particulates, and other pollutants resulting from the combustion of fossil fuels into the atmosphere.

Products made from renewable materials are those made from wood, stone, bamboo, cane, straw, leather, clay, flax, and other useful materials that nature has to offer. Many of these materials are pre-processed so that they can be easily used in practice. For example, when building an environmentally friendly house, one does not have to buy straw or clay. These types of materials have been prepared for use in an appropriate form. Straw has been pressed into cubes and is available for sale as blocks. Bricks are formed from clay to build walls.

Products made from recycled materials are manufactured from recycled waste. Waste is therefore not landfilled, but is processed and returned to the market as finished products. Many materials, e.g. glass, can be processed almost infinitely. Some waste is used directly to make various types of products. For example, recycled plastic is used to make pens, bottles, toys, furniture, and many other products. Some waste is not processed, but valuable materials used in production are recovered from it. An example of such waste is used mobile phones, from which aluminum, silver, and gold are recovered.

Reusable products are a broad category of different types of products. We have been used to practices in this area for a long time. For example, cars often have several or even over ten owners during their life cycle. They are reused by each subsequent owner until they are scrapped. The market for second-hand products comprises tens of thousands of different types of goods. Instead of buying new products, many people buy used products. The environment benefits from this because production of new goods can be reduced. Another environmentally friendly solution is refurbishing used products to restore their original appearance and functionalities. For example, instead of being thrown away, furniture can be renovated.

Products that decompose quickly and harmlessly are only a part of the waste that is deposited in landfills. Organic waste, such as food waste and plant waste (e.g. grass, leaves, flowers, branches, etc.), decomposes most rapidly. The decomposition process takes from two weeks to several months. Decomposition of paper takes the same amount of time. Plastics need 100–1,000 years or even longer to decompose. Metals (except precious metals), on the other hand, decompose in a period of 50–200 years. Manufacturers try to replace hard-to-degrade materials with their environmentally friendly equivalents. An example of this is the ecoplastic.

When designing and manufacturing any products as a part of projects, one must strive to create goods that are fully or at least partly sustainable. Table 4.4 can help to achieve this goal.

Green, environmentally friendly products, created as a result of projects, can undergo a certification process. A certificate is a guarantee that the product meets certain requirements concerning its composition and manufacturing process. As products from different sectors of the economy differ in composition, characteristics, production methods, and intended use, certification requirements and procedures are

TABLE 4.4
Is the Product Designed or Manufactured as a Part of the Project Sustainable?

Questions	Condition Met
Is the product safe?	
Is the product durable?	
Is the product economical?	
Is the product powered by energy from renewable sources?	
Is the product emission-free?	
Is the product made of renewable materials?	
Is the product made of recycled materials?	
Is the product reusable?	
Does the product decompose rapidly and harmlessly?	

Source: Own work.

not uniform. A certificate entitles the manufacturer to place proprietary eco-labels on the products. Examples of these are given in Table 4.5. In most countries, there are entities that award certificates and conduct audits to confirm compliance with natural environment protection criteria.

Ecolabels placed on products provide a special distinction in the market: they communicate that the product is environmentally friendly and contributes to

TABLE 4.5
Examples of Environmental Certificates

Name	Label	Description
Blue Angel		The oldest European certificate for environmentally friendly products. The label is placed on products that are safer than other products of the same type and recognized as environmental leaders in a given group.
The EU Flower		A multi-sector European Union label. It has the widest geographical coverage of all labels. It can be obtained in any EU country. This label may be applied for by: the manufacturer, the importer, the service provider, or the distributor of a product in any European market.
BIO-organic product		Products from controlled organic production. Certified in accordance with European Union standards by certification bodies.

(Continued)

TABLE 4.5 (*Continued*)
Examples of Environmental Certificates

Name	Label	Description
Carbon Neutral		This certificate is given to carbon-neutral products. It means that the greenhouse gas emissions associated with the production of such a product are offset by credits that finance renewable and emission-free energy projects.
Eco Garantie		A registered trademark for laundry and cleaning products that meet the criteria of the Belgian certification institute Probila Unitrab and are checked annually by the Belgian Ecocert organization.
Fair Trade		Fair Trade stands for a partnership in trade based on dialogue, transparency, and respect. Fair Trade organizations are actively engaged in awareness raising and campaigns aimed to improve the rules and practices in international trade.
Green Seal		A private eco-labeling program in the USA. It establishes environmental standards for certain products that take into account their characteristics and operation.
Nordic Swan		The best known label in Norway, Sweden, Denmark, Finland, and Iceland. It can be obtained by the manufacturers, the importers, and the vendors of a product who comply with specific environmental criteria for both the product itself and its production process.
Oeko-Tex Standard		The world's leading safety label for textile products. Products bearing this label are free from harmful substances in concentrations that adversely affect health (e.g. pesticides, chlorophenols, formaldehyde, allergenic dyes, etc.).
Recycled		This label means that secondary materials have been used to make the product.
100% energia verde		This label means that the product has been produced using electricity from renewable sources only.

Source: Own work based on https://greencom.pl/s22-certyfikaty.html.

sustainable development. They also confirm the good attributes of the manufacturer. As a result, they have a positive impact on the image of products and the companies that make them. Products with eco-labels attract the attention of environmentally and socially sensitive consumers, which can result in increased sales.

Find out which eco-certification organizations are active in your country in the sector of the product involved in the project and which eco-labels can be used based on their certificates. Familiarize yourself with the requirements and procedures applied by these organizations. If you are sure that the product and/or its manufacturing process meets these requirements, apply for an eco-certificate.

Source: Own work.

Pro-Environmental and Pro-Social Production

In bookstores, one can find specialized publications on sustainable production. The following publications can be mentioned as examples: 1. Editors: Rainer Stark, Gunther Seliger, Jeremy Bonvoisin, *Sustainable Manufacturing. Challenges, Solutions and Implementation Perspectives,* Springer, Berlin 2017. 2. Editors: Giampaolo Campana, Robert J. Howlett, Rossi Setchi, Barbara Climatti, Sustainable Design and Manufacturing 2017, Springer International Publishing AG 2017. These books present a variety of pro-environmental and pro-social solutions used in many manufacturing sectors of the economy. We encourage studying this type of literature and learning about solutions for the industries in which the Readers of this book are employed.

Manufacturing technology presents ever more ambitious challenges to manufacturers of various types of goods. According to Jeremy Bonvoisin, Rainer Stark, and Gunther Seliger, they are as follows: how things are produced; what is being produced; in which organizational context; and how to make a systematic change (Bonvoisin, Stark and Seliger 2017: 3).

There is no doubt that the goal of sustainability engineering is to develop production processes that create as little waste as possible while depending on as few resources as possible (Cohen 2011: 21). Production carried out in an environmentally and socially responsible manner is called sustainable production or clean production. Clean production results in sustainable products, which are discussed in Section 4.5. Sustainable production is based on renewable, recycled, and rapidly and harmlessly degradable raw materials and consumables. For example, instead of using standard plastic to make disposable cups, a manufacturer uses biodegradable plastic (Ecovio). The raw materials and consumables used in sustainable production must meet high environmental and social standards. This requires the appropriate selection of suppliers. The products they supply in the form of raw materials, consumables, components, and parts should not contain harmful substances and should be manufactured in conditions that respect workers' rights and ethics. Organic farming of animal husbandry is a good example of sources of raw materials for sustainable food production.

ORGANIC FARMING AND ANIMAL HUSBANDRY AS A SOURCE OF RAW MATERIALS FOR FOOD PRODUCTION

Organic farming uses crop rotation, i.e., a rotational change in the type of plants grown in a given area. This way, the soil is protected against depletion of nutrients. Because organic farming uses natural fertilizers, including compost and manure, it is good to combine plant cultivation with animal husbandry. No industrial fodder is allowed to be fed to the animals: the bio-fodder should come from the same farm. The animals are traditionally kept in a barn on litter to enable the manure is easily taken. Administration of antibiotics and hormones to animals is prohibited. The Swiss Research Institute of Organic Agriculture provides as many as 90 arguments in favor of expansion of organic farming. Organic vegetables and fruit contain much more antioxidants that prevent cancer, including resveratrol, which delays the ageing process. They contain more fiber, minerals, and vitamins. Plants in conventional farms are fertilized with nitrogen, which supports their growth. Its excess accumulates in the leaves, forming nitrites. In the human body, they turn into harmful substances. This phenomenon does not occur in organic products. Vegetables and fruit from organic farms have a longer shelf life thanks to the higher content of vitamin C, which is a natural preservative. Organic animal products are also recommended. They have not only taste better, but also have more nutritional value. Animals on organic farms eat more varied feed and their meat is less fat and watery. Only up to 5% of additives are allowed in organic food. They are used to prevent rapid spoilage of meat and cured meat products. The European Union allows organic producers to choose from 48 artificial dyes and flavor and odor enhancers. Standard producers may use up to 316 such food additives.

Source: Own work based on https://wyborcza.pl/TylkoZdrowie/1,137474,17025203,Co_jest_bio_a_co_jest_eko_Jak_rozpoznac_zdrowa_zywnosc.html

Sustainable producers carry out audits of their suppliers, which focus on their social responsibility (labor standards, environmental assessment, and business ethics). They require their suppliers to obtain eco-certificates for their products. They also educate them on sustainable development.

Fully sustainable production is based on a closed-circuit economy. Products, consumables, and raw materials stay in circulation as long as possible and waste is treated as recyclable and reusable materials. Production processes minimize water and energy consumption, as well as the use of harmful chemicals. Plastic is eliminated from supply chains. High quality production is preferred. Product are expected to serve customers for a long time and do not require repair. Longer warranty periods are granted for products of higher quality. Material handling systems are also being rationalized. An example of such rationalization is replacement of forklifts with internal combustion motors with electric forklifts, reduction of their number, and extension of the life of their batteries.

Zero-defects programs contribute to elimination of waste in sustainable production. A zero-defects program involves increasing quality by increasing everyone's impact on quality (Rue and Byars 2009: 443). A zero-defects program attempts to create a positive attitude toward the prevention of low quality. The objective of a zero-defects program is to heighten awareness of quality by making everyone aware of his or her potential impact on quality (Rue and Byars 2009: 443–444).

Sustainable production takes into account customers' individual needs. Only those products that have already been ordered leave the production line. This prevents waste and disposal of unsold products. As a result, less storage space is needed and savings are achieved on everything associated with the operation of warehouses. Systems that take this into account have long been in place in many companies worldwide. An example is the Just-in-Time production system introduced by Toyota. Traditional production systems work according to the push principle. Raw materials and consumables are "pushed" into the production system and the resulting finished products are "pushed" into the market for sale. The Just-in-Time system works according to the pull principle. Production only starts when the customer has ordered the product. Production is initiated by sales, not by supply. The sales department, upon receipt of a purchase order, files a production request for the product to the production department and the production department "pulls" the materials needed for its production from the procurement department and the procurement department "pulls" them from suppliers. As a result, application of the just-in-time principle benefits the entire production cycle from procurement to sales. It enables savings on storage of raw materials and consumables (supplies), semi-finished products in technological processes (production), and finished products (sale).

Product packaging is still a serious environmental problem. The problem is the huge amounts of packaging that are disposed of, as well as the materials they are made of. Plastic packaging and the large amounts of plastic they contain are a threat to the environment. Less harmful is packaging made of recycled paper that is supplied from certified sources and recyclable. What benefits the environment is use of reusable packaging, but also complete abandonment of packaging. It is also important that packaging should be properly adjusted to the size of the product, so that no fillers are needed. Many irregularities in this area occur in packaging and delivering products purchased online to customers. Products sent to customers are often packed by online retailers in too large boxes, which they fill with paper, plastic film, and other environmentally harmful fillers. The purpose of the filler is to immobilize the purchased product in the box in order to protect it from damage during transport.

Systems for collection of used products developed by manufacturers are beneficial from an environmental and social point of view. The manufacturer collects or buys back used products, then repairs them and sells them at a reduced price, recycles them, or, in the worst case, recovers some parts from them.

4.6 IMPACT OF SUSTAINABILITY SOLUTIONS ON PROJECT COSTS AND BUDGET

A project budget is a list of costs related to the use of resources that are necessary to carry out a project. The budget is approved by the person/organization that finances the project and by the project manager. Preparation of the final detailed project budget, which is submitted for approval, is usually preceded by a preliminary cost estimate. A detailed draft budget is based on a detailed division of labor and estimated costs for all tasks and work packages.

When drawing up a project budget, the bottom-up or top-down method is used. The bottom-up method consists in determining the cost of each work package and task and then adding them together. The top-down method first sets a target budget for the entire project and then allocates it to tasks and work packages. The budget includes costs of labor, materials, and energy, as well as financial, subcontracting, overhead, and other costs. The cost structure depends on the type and size of the project.

The planned staggered financing of the project reflects the so-called base line. The executors should be motivated to carry out the project in such a way that the actual expenses conform to the base line. It is important not to exceed the expenditures planned in the budget. The budget provides for a financial reserve for unforeseen circumstances.

INCLUDING SOCIAL AND ENVIRONMENTAL COSTS IN PROJECT BUDGETS

The purpose of this chapter is to discuss the impact of sustainability on project costs. Let us start with a concrete example. In Chapter 3, we divided a project aimed at preparing the 50th anniversary of the XYZ Company into tasks and work packages, including pro-environmental and pro-social activities. The impact of these activities on the costs will be illustrated using the example of task 3, which consists in making a commemorative folder. The folder, made in the A4 format, is to be printed in 300 copies. It consists of 40 pages, which are planned to be filled with texts and photographs. The cover will bind the entire content of the folder. The work on the folder consists of the following three stages:

1. preparation of the folder design;
2. editorial work; and
3. printing the folder.

The folder is to be printed on environmentally friendly paper. In this way, task 3 is to contribute to sustainable development. Regardless of the type of paper used, the costs of the folder design and editorial work (steps 1 and 2) will be the same. Consequently, all we have to do is make a calculation for step 3 (folder printing) and compare the printing costs for two cases: printing on environmentally friendly paper (Table 4.6) and printing on standard paper (Table 4.7).

In our case, the folder printing cost for environmentally friendly paper is USD 105 higher for standard paper. This is not a big difference and it can certainly be accepted in the project budget. However, one should keep in mind that the folder is

TABLE 4.6
Folder Printing Costs for Environmentally Friendly Paper (Wood-Free Paper COLOR COPY 100 g/m²)

	Designation	Costs
Medium	A3 100 g/m² paper	USD 360.00
	0.12 cents × 3,000 sheets	
	Print	USD 1,320.00
Cover	A3 160 g/m² paper	USD 60.00
	0.20 cents × 300 sheets	
	Print	USD 240.00
Sewing		USD 60.00
Total		**USD 2040.00**

A sheet is one A3 sheet (four folder pages).
Source: Own work.

printed in a small print run of 300 copies. If the circulation increases to 3,000 copies, the costs will increase by USD 1,050. This case gives rise to the following proposition: projects that involve environmentally friendly physical goods require higher budgets compared to their traditional equivalents. This proposition is also confirmed by examples from other industries. Let us take a look at construction, e.g. Siddharth Jain, Prateek Gupta, and Deepa make a cost comparison of conventional building and green building, as reflected in Table 4.8.

The authors make the following comment to the results of the calculations contained in the table: total development costs for the green buildings ranged from 9 to 18% above the costs for comparable conventional affordable housing (Jain, Gupta and Deepa 2019: 200). They supplement this statement with this opinion: green

TABLE 4.7
Folder Printing Costs for Standard Paper (Standard Paper MONDI 100 g/m²)

	Designation	Costs
Medium	A3 100 g/m² paper	USD 270.00
	0.09 cents × 3,000 sheets	
	Print	USD 1,320.00
Cover	A3 160 g/m² paper	USD 45.00
	PLN 0.15 × 300 sheets	
	Print	USD 240.00
Sewing		USD 60.00
Total		**USD 1,935.00**

A sheet is one A3 sheet (four folder pages).
Source: Own work.

TABLE 4.8
Cost Comparison of Conventional Building and Green Building

Sr. No.	Item Name	Cost in Conventional Home	Cost in Green Home
1	Windows and openings	140,800	217,350
2	Lighting fixtures	15,800	46,150
3	Plumbing fixtures	45,885	108,300
4	Flooring	230,540	295,295
5	Doors	79,830	165,510
6	Paints	166,380	168,880
7	Bricks	60,175	40,105
8	Cement	976,000	995,250
9	Rainwater harvesting system	0	90,700
Total		**1,715,410**	**2,127,540**

Source: Own work based on Jain, Gupta and Deepa 2019: 200.

houses are costlier than conventional houses but only in short run. As per the need of society and livelihood, green houses are very much required and will surely be much cheaper than conventional houses in long run (Jain, Gupta and Deepa 2019: 206).

Environmentally friendly goods require higher financial outlays mainly because they consist of environmentally friendly raw materials, consumables, and components, which are more expensive than their traditional counterparts. However, this perception of the impact of sustainability on project costs is superficial and inappropriate. It is an excellent excuse for the anti-environmental and anti-social attitudes of business people who do not want to carry out projects that contribute to sustainable development. If a business person claims that projects contributing to sustainable development are much more expensive and it does not pay to carry them out, he or she only takes into account his own short-term benefits. In fact, the problem of the impact of sustainability on project costs is much broader and more complex. The higher cost of pro-environmental and pro-social projects is only apparent because the prices of standard goods are understated. When setting these prices, the costs of the negative impact of the products and services on the environment and people are ignored. Let us look at this in more detail.

Projects involving sustainable physical goods now require higher budgets compared to standard goods. This is because standard goods consist of standard components that are underpriced. The prices are underestimated because the costs of the negative environmental and human impact of these components are not taken into account in their calculation.

Source: Own work.

Sustainable Prices and Their Impact on Project Budgets

People would not be able to produce any goods without nature. The Earth is the largest producer of natural goods and provides services to people. It reproduces and makes available natural resources from which people produce energy and thousands of physical products. It provides the growing plants and the multiplying animals, fish, and birds that are the basis for the food industry. It purifies the air and naturally treats waste. These examples are only the beginning of a long list of services provided free of charge by the Earth to humans. A global study on the assessment of the economic value of the services provided by the Earth's ecosystem has led to the conclusion that the value of the entire biosphere (most of which is assessed in non-market terms) is estimated to be between $16 and 54 trillion per year, or an average of $33 trillion per year. This value should be considered as a minimum estimate, because the nature of the services assessed is uncertain and difficult to determine clearly (Constanza et al. 1997: 243–253). For example, let us consider one of the components of the above value, i.e., the value of the work of bees in pollination of flowers of fruit, vegetables, and oil plants. This value is estimated at 150 billion dollars (Bendyk 2013: 6). Moturu Venkata Rajasekhar, Krishnaveer Abhishek Challa, Dharmavaram Vijaylakshmi, and Nittala Rajyalakshmi state: the biosphere supports life on Earth. It ranges from the atmosphere's top layer to the soil's bottom layers, both on the continents and in the ocean. Society and all earthlings depend on the biosphere for food, fresh water, a habitable climate, and to maintain nature's integrity and diversity (Rajasekhar, Challa, Vijaylakshmi and Rajyalakshmi 2019: 230).

The Earth is unable to enforce payment for the goods and services it provides to people. Consequently, this aspect of product pricing is neglected in practice. The essence of the problem is appropriately reflected in the following questions, asked by F. Belz and K. Peattie: Have you ever asked why you can buy a radio receiver for less than 10 euros? Is such a price really commensurate with the cost? Does it fully cover the extraction of natural resources at the beginning of the production cycle, e.g. crude oil for the manufacture of plastic components or copper or silicon for the integrated circuits and transistors? What about the packaging and transport costs? Does the price include the impact of the product on the global warming and climate change? What about the manufacturing costs? Where and in what operating conditions are the radios that cost less than 10 euros assembled? Last but not least, what about the cost of disposal of the product at the end of its service life? Who pays for it? (Belz and Peattie 2010: 218). According to these authors, the price of such a radio receiver does not cover all the costs related to the environment and the social aspects. In most cases, the price paid for various goods is only a fraction of the actual total cost borne by others (now and in the future), i.e., future generations who will be affected by global warming and climate change. The pricing system in place does not cover external costs related to environmental and social issues. As a result, the prices of many products available in the market are completely unreasonably low. This leads to a biased competition mechanism that favors unsustainable products. Conventional products will be priced more favorably than sustainable products as long as their prices do not reflect the actual social and environmental costs (Belz and Peattie 2010: 218).

Thus, when prices are considered, producers of sustainable goods are at a competitive disadvantage in the market. To increase their competitiveness, project funding bodies often put pressure on project teams to find solutions to reduce the costs of production of sustainable goods and services. As a result, decisions are made to replace sustainable components of products with their cheaper, unsustainable equivalents in projects, which is harmful to sustainable development.

The main reason for the higher costs of projects involving sustainable goods and the resulting competitive disadvantage of their producers and vendors are incorrectly calculated prices of standard goods. The prices of standard goods are unsustainable. A sustainable price takes full account of the cost of production and marketing, not only in economic terms, but also in environmental and social terms, thus ensuring a benefit to the consumer a fair profit for the business (Martin and Schouten 2012: 171). In the case of sustainable prices, the cost category is significantly extended, as explained later in this chapter.

A properly determined price should cover the costs of production and sales and ensure a fair profit. In reality, most prices set in the standard manner do not include all costs. For example, the price of a product does not take into account the cost of the consequences of water pollution. Omitting this cost means assuming that water pollution has no negative consequences and is economically neutral. Meanwhile, such pollution as a side effect of production processes depletes drinking water resources, reduces fish populations, and destroys recreational areas. All this has the following negative economic effects:

- an increase in the price of the water supplied to houses, because it needs to be purified and treated;
- an increase in fish prices as the supply of fish in the market decreases; and
- the loss of businesses in the tourism sector, because tourists are not interested in recreation at polluted bodies of water.

These costs are in fact already incurred, but are not taken into account when setting the product prices. They are not taken into account because they are difficult to estimate and to assign to specific organizations or people, and even more difficult to enforce. The lack of sufficient knowledge, procedures, and legal provisions for the enforcement of total production and sales costs, taking into account the environmental and social effects, leads to an accumulation of negative phenomena and to hiding of real costs.

The unpaid environmental and social costs for most goods and services are referred to as externalized costs. The difference between the retail price and the real cost of the product, including the externalized costs, can be very large. D. Martin and J. Schouten refer to the study conducted by the International Center for Technological Research. It showed that the real cost of a gallon of gasoline at that time was about 15 US dollars. The actual price at the pump in the United States was set at about $1.30 per gallon. In calculating the real cost, the researchers took into account the direct government subsidies, the fuel supplier protection costs, as well as the healthcare, the environmental protection, and the social costs. When added up, the externalized costs were more than a trillion dollars a year, or more than $24,000 per family of four (Martin and Schouten 2012: 172–173).

If the social and environmental costs were included in the price calculations, the prices of sustainable products and services would be lower than those of standard goods. This would result in lower budgets for sustainable projects compared to those for unsustainable ones.

Source: Own work.

So far, we have considered the problem of replacing traditional physical goods with their sustainable equivalents in projects. We have come to the conclusion that the costs of a project that uses sustainable goods are higher than those of a project where standard goods are used. This difference is due to incorrect calculation of prices. This is because the prices of standard goods available in the market do not take into account the high social and environmental costs. If these costs were included in the calculations, the prices of sustainable products and services would be lower than those of their unsustainable equivalents. As a result, the costs of implementation of projects that are based on sustainable goods, and thus their budgets, would be lower than those of projects that use unsustainable products and services.

According to Anjala Karol and C. Mashood, green pricing or environmental pricing is a pricing strategy that encompasses environmental responsibility in pricing products and services (Karol and Mashood 2019: 21). Now let us move on to the costs of creating and operating a sustainable project organization.

Costs of Creating and Operating a Sustainable Project Organization

As can be seen from the 4 × SUSTAINABILITY IN PROJECT ACTIVITIES rule, a sustainable project organization is based on sustainable human and material resources. Its work on the project is also carried out in a sustainable manner. The types of costs related to the establishment and functioning of a sustainable organization are shown in Table 4.9. We discuss them below.

TABLE 4.9
Costs of Creating and Operating a Sustainable Project Organization

Costs of recruitment and employment of sustainable project team members
Costs of sustainable construction infrastructure
Costs of sustainable equipment for production and office spaces
Costs of sustainable modes of transport
Costs of other sustainable goods
Costs of work on a project carried out in a sustainable manner

Source: Own work.

The first cost source listed in Table 4.9 is recruitment and employment of sustainable project team members. Replacement of standard recruitment with recruitment that aims at attracting and employing sustainable project team members practically does not change the associated costs. Recruitment for a sustainable organization, as described in Chapter 2, follows general principles. The change consists in introduction of sustainability requirements in the recruitment notices and in examination of whether candidates meet these requirements. Sustainability does not change the recruitment procedure, but only the scope of the recruitment process. A company may want to hire a specialist to evaluate candidates in terms of sustainability. Even in this case, it will not require high financial outlays.

Project work in a sustainable organization is done in a sustainable way. The members of the project team use the materials needed to execute the project economically, save light, use equipment and means of transport in a rational way, and observe the rules of occupational health and safety. All this leads to savings in different phases of the project.

Another item listed in Table 4.9 is the cost of sustainable building infrastructure in which members of the project team carry out their work. In a model sustainable project organization, the project team works in a sustainable building. In practice, this condition is met only if the company or institution whose employees carry out the project is located in a sustainable building. In any other case, the location of the project team is either partly sustainable or unsustainable. This does not apply to the unusual situation where a separate building has to be erected for the team. As one can easily guess, renting any premises for a project involves costs (lighting, heating, etc.) that are charged to the project budget. Such costs are certainly lower if the building in which the project team works has been built with sustainability in mind and the energy comes from own renewable sources.

The other sources of costs listed in Table 4.9 are related to the purchase of sustainable room furnishings, means of transport, and materials for the project team. In practice, such purchases are not always possible. In many cases, project team members have, as employees of companies and institutions, already assigned means of transport, as well as fully furnished rooms, which they use for the project. They may be sustainable, partly sustainable, or unsustainable. The situation in this regard is similar to that of a project team using building infrastructure. On the other hand, if any resources are to be purchased for the project team, they should be sustainable, which reduces costs during their utilization.

As has been established so far, the establishment and operation of a sustainable project organization are simple in some areas and do not require large financial outlays, while in other areas the situation is more complicated. Recruitment and employment of sustainable project team members, as well as their work, are not a problem. Sustainability, taken into account in recruitment and work on a project, does not increase costs, but contributes to their reduction. The situation is different with regard to building infrastructure and resources. They may be sustainable, partly sustainable, or unsustainable. A project team in most cases has no influence on the degree of sustainability as it uses an already existing infrastructure with fully equipped rooms, as well as the means of transport and equipment allocated to it. This is the case when the members of the project team are full-time employees of business entities and use their infrastructure and equipment to carry out the project. The costs charged for this should decrease as the degree of sustainability of the premises and of the equipment put into service for the project team increases.

The above-mentioned conditions do not undermine the principle that, wherever possible, traditional elements of project organizations should be replaced by their sustainable counterparts.

Functioning of a project organization based on sustainable goods leads to cost reductions and contributes to sustainable development.

Source: Own work.

More and more organizations are interested in sustainable development and are investing in projects in this area. This is due not only to the increasingly pro-environmental and pro-social attitudes of companies themselves and their customers, but also to the behavior of shareholders. Shareholders are entering more and more boldly into the area of sustainable investment. As of 10 August 2018, 476 shareholder resolutions on environmental and social issues had been registered in the United States. The percentage of all resolutions related to these issues had increased from about 33% in 2006–2010 to about 45% in 2011–2016. In 2017, this ratio slightly exceeded 50%. Research shows that investing in sustainable development pays off. Companies that measured, controlled, and communicated environmental, social, and governance (ESG) performance in the early 1990s were in better financial shape for the next 18 years than a carefully selected control group. Another study showed a positive correlation between good ESG performance and above-average financial performance. Evidence gathered by investors confirms this relationship: a survey conducted in 2017 by the Nordea Equity Research group (the largest financial services group in Scandinavia) showed that between 2012 and 2015, the companies with the highest sustainability rating achieved 40% better financial results than the lowest rated organizations. In 2018, the Bank of America Merrill Lynch found that companies with better ESG results than comparable organizations generated higher three-year profits, were more valued by investors (their shares were considered high quality securities), had less frequent significant drops in share prices, and were less likely to become bankrupt (Eccles and Klimenko 2020: 129, 132).

As practice shows, it is possible to achieve high financial results from business activities and at the same time do good and care for the environment.

Source: Own work.

Revenues from Sale of Sustainable Goods Depend on the Customer

If a project concerns sustainable goods to be marketed and offered to consumers, then in addition to their cost of production, the project budget must also estimate the revenue from their sale. The difference between sales revenue and costs is the seller's profit. The level of sales revenue depends on the demand for sustainable goods. In order to estimate the demand and the potential revenue, it is best to use marketing research. Information on marketing research can be found in marketing books. Marketing research is a starting point for any well-conducted marketing activity, alongside marketing intelligence. Marketing research is also the subject matter of various books. Their authors include Anne E. Beall (Beall 2019), Harrison M., Cupman J., Truman O., Hague P. (Harrison, Cupman, Truman and Hague 2016), Chapman C., and McDonnel Feit E. (Chapman, McDonnel and Feit 2019). Marketing research starts with identification of the research purpose. Its next steps are: to establish the research objectives, t estimate the value of information, to design the research, to collect the data, to prepare and analyze the data, and to report the research results (Aaker, Kumar, Day and Leone 2011: 48).

If the project team is not able to carry out marketing research, it should commission one of the many marketing research agencies offering their services in the market. We are of the opinion that properly conducted marketing research is the most reliable source of information on the demand and the sales revenue for goods involved in a project. Use of secondary sources, i.e., all kinds of published and unpublished market and sales data, is risky. Such data sources can only be considered if the product is the same as or very similar to products already sold in the market. As we have already mentioned in this book, projects are aimed at creating new and innovative products and services. Such products or services have not been offered in the market so far, so there is no experience related to their sales. In such cases, information from secondary sources may not be useful. Therefore, it is necessary to obtain information from the original source of marketing research.

Consumers are a very complex and unpredictable part of the market. Their purchasing behavior is influenced by many different factors. These include social and group forces, psychological forces, situational forces, and information from commercial and social sources. Also, their purchasing decision-making process, especially in the case of durable goods with long service lives, is complicated and consists of the following phases: problem recognition, information search, information evaluation, purchasing process, and post purchasing behavior. In the following part of this chapter, we will present a few remarks about consumers' attitudes toward sustainable goods and ways to increase their sales. This will enable more realistic project budgeting.

Buying decisions are made by customers based on an analysis of expected benefits and costs. Customers try to maximize benefits and minimize costs, so they ultimately choose those products that are better than competing goods in the categories considered. Sustainable products are subject to the same principle: in order to be sellable, they should be seen by consumers as superior to conventional products. This perception is negatively affected by prices. Sustainable products are usually more expensive than their unsustainable equivalents. Including externalized costs would result in a significant increase in the prices of the latter. It is unlikely that the market will accept such prices. Nevertheless, producers and retailers of sustainable goods can count on increased demand and decent profits. This is enabled by the life-cycle costing and the promotion of the results of this valuation among consumers. Such valuation is more advantageous compared to the valuation of conventional goods. Let us explain its essence.

When considering the purchase of a product, the customer takes into account not only its price, but also other aspects related to the purchase, use, and disposal of the product. A good example is the purchase of a new car. For the customer, in addition to the price, the following issues may be important: Can car X be bought in the customer's own town or must he or she go to a showroom located in another town? How much gasoline does the car use per 100 km? Is it reliable? How much does it cost to service it? How much does the vehicle lose in value each year? How much will the customer be able to sell it for in a few years? Consequently, the concept of total customer cost has been introduced, which includes, in addition to the retail price:

- the product purchase costs;
- the product use costs; and
- the postuse costs.

The product purchase cost includes all costs associated with searching for a product, collecting and comparing information to facilitate selection, and transport of a product to the customer's home or business. The cost of use is mainly related to the purchase of the materials needed for its use, maintenance, and servicing. The post-use costs include, but are not limited to, charges for the removal and disposal of the product.

The concept of total customer cost provides producers and sellers of sustainable goods with an important tool to influence the market, which is particularly useful in situations where the prices of such goods are higher than those of their conventional equivalents. It can encourage customers to buy by demonstrating lower costs of use and environmentally friendly disposal of sustainable products. The electricity that powers an electric car costs a fraction of the cost of gasoline; solar thermal collectors help save money on hot water and house heating; and environmentally friendly washing machines use less water and electricity, thus reducing bills. Consequently, despite the higher retail prices of these products, the total customer cost is lower compared to their cheaper conventional equivalents. The source of savings is lower costs of use. This aspect should therefore be used to promote sustainable goods. This does not require any additional costs, but only modifications to the content and appearance of marketing messages. In marketing communication with customers, it is a good idea to use the so-called savings calculators. They contain comparisons of sustainable products with their conventional equivalents. Use of savings calculators is justified in cases where a sustainable product is cheaper to use and its disposal is environmentally friendly. Transparent, concrete arguments supported with numbers concerning the costs of use and disposal of sustainable products in marketing communications are an effective incentive for consumers to buy them despite their higher prices.

The amount of revenue from sales of sustainable goods depends on their attractiveness, their ability to meet needs, their prices, and the attitudes of consumers towards sustainability. B. Emery divides these attitudes into favorable and unfavorable. He gives the following names to consumers with a favorable attitude to sustainability:

a. guilty – a consumer who is aware of sustainability issues and occasionally becomes involved in sustainable consumption, although he or she does not do so consistently; the consumer feels guilty but not enough to become more sustainable;
b. practitioner – this consumer has more knowledge and understanding of sustainability than a consumer from the previous group and, whenever possible, his or her consumption becomes sustainable; he or she seeks to deepen his or her knowledge of sustainability and maintain a sustainable lifestyle; and
c. sustainable – this consumer is completely and enthusiastically committed to sustainability; he or she tries to do as much as possible to make his activities fully sustainable.

On the other hand, B. Emery classifies consumers with an unfavorable attitude to sustainability as follows:

a. ignorant – this consumer has no knowledge of sustainable development and often belongs to a lower socio-economic group;
b. fatalist – this consumer does nothing because he or she feels it is too late to influence anything, also with regard to his or her life and imminent death;
c. in denial – this consumer is not convinced by evidence, especially when opposing views on sustainability are presented;
d. cynical – this consumer fights to act despite sustainability concerns, but is skeptical and recognizes the fact that his or her contribution is irrelevant;
e. disinterested – this consumer is not interested in sustainability issues; and
f. fed-up – this consumer treats sustainability issues as a whim, considering it appropriate for the media and companies to no longer focus on this issue (Emery 2012: 80–81).

Consumers with a favorable attitude toward sustainability are the most attractive market segment for sustainable products. They are most often bought by people classified as sustainable, followed by people classified as practitioners and guilty. Consumers with unfavorable attitudes do not show interest in sustainable goods. Moreover, many consumers associate high prices of such goods with unfair practices. Empirical research conducted in the UK has shown that a majority of customers believe that higher prices of sustainable products are just a trick to get as much money from them as possible, not to raise money to save the environment or to achieve social goals (Belz and Peattie 2010: 209). As we have mentioned in Chapter 2, many consumers are willing to pay more for a product that supports environmental and social goals.

When working on the project budget, the problems of market research and consumer behavior cannot be overlooked. This is because customers are the most important source of revenue and decide on the success or failure of a product or service to be put on the market.

5 Sustainable Project Management from the IT Perspective

5.1 INFORMATION TECHNOLOGY IN PROJECT MANAGEMENT

The concept of sustainable development requires using appropriate information technologies. Effectiveness of sustainable project management from the information technology (IT) perspective depends on the effectiveness of the actions taken, such as cooperation and readiness to implement new technologies, networking, and supporting key processes that enable faster access to information and data updates. Sustainable project management should be accompanied by formulation of the role and importance of innovative IT solutions for businesses and their environment and treatment of IT aspects as an element that supports all processes that constitute its part.

A strategic and prospective approach to sustainable development should focus on investments in IT (Figure 5.1).

At present, the high level of complexity and the scope of projects is associated with numerous failed decisions. Project failures are often defined as the LOOP syndrome (Late, Over Schedule, Overtime, and Poor Quality). Consequently, in the concept of sustainable development, management should mainly focus on:

- sustainable team management;
- sustainable production processes; and
- use of sustainable information technologies in production and management.

The IT methods and tools implemented by managers should be appropriate for the sustainable management of the personnel, the manufacturing processes, and the technologies used (Flasiński 2006). Incorrect adaptation of management methods or IT tools that support management and production processes to an IT project results in untimely realization of project tasks, as well as certain reluctance and lack of energy of the team that executes the project (Lock, 2009; Boehm and Papaccio 1988).

Modern IT solutions undoubtedly contribute to the development of businesses and societies. Technological inspirations with the use of IT tools lead to formation of an organization that can be called sustainable, i.e., one that uses sustainable production, sustainable marketing, sustainable finances, and sustainable logistics (Figure 5.2) (Pabian 2017).

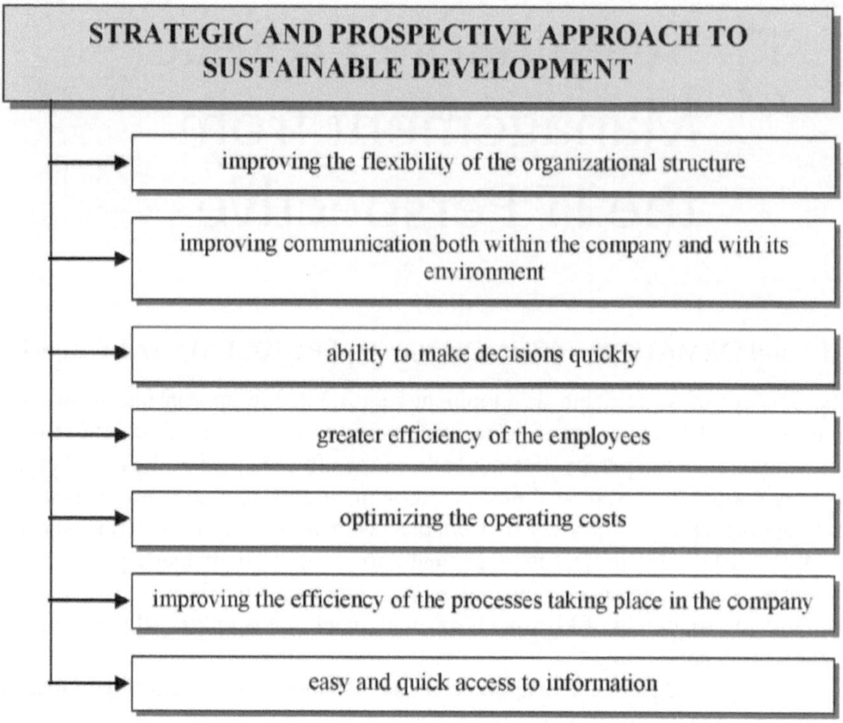

FIGURE 5.1 Strategic and prospective approach to sustainable development. (Own work based on Adamczyk 2009.)

The IT industry has been developing and improving very dynamically in recent years, offering more and more sustainable and creative IT solutions. However, there appears to be a shortage of specialized workers in this sector, which appears to be a kind of dysfunction. An acceleration of the IT industry and the permanent professionalization of workers are extremely important for economic growth, according to the concept of sustainable development, on a global scale (Werewka 2013).

The technological evolution in recent years has caused an extraordinary global escalation of public goods. In the sustainable development concept, the greatest impact on people's lives and activities of organizations has been exercised mainly by the development of information and communication technology (Kotler, Armstrong, Saunders and Wong 2002: 59), which, also in terms of other branches of the economy, has contributed to increased labor productivity and higher quality and innovation of products and services.

In the 19th century, the meaning of the term "technology" started to be limited to activities mainly related to industry. Technological development proceeds together with the increase in the knowledge and the level of education of the society. The consequences of the work of the human mind and the introduction of technological

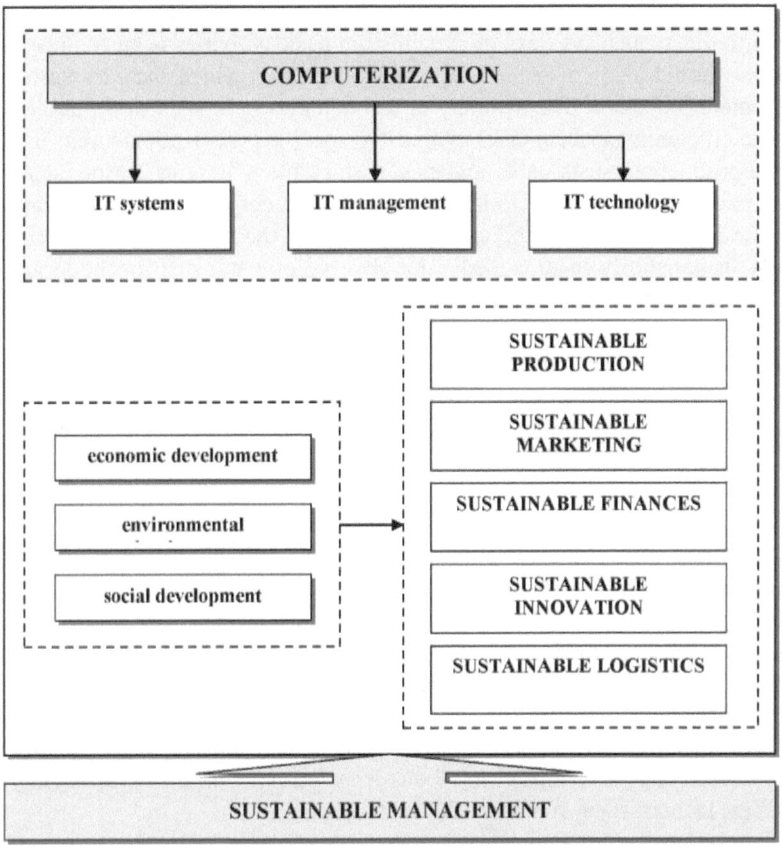

FIGURE 5.2 Sustainability in terms of IT. (Own work.)

innovations are progress and economic development (Gregor 2002: 24). M. J. Hatch interprets this term very broadly as the means to achieve set objectives, which include (Hatch 2002: 136):

- physical objects and by-products that arise as the software develops;
- procedures, treatments, and production processes; and
- knowledge necessary to implement the planned objectives.

According to the authors of this book, technology and its goals can be considered from two standpoints (Kozłowski 2010: 72):

1. from the standpoint of the sustainable environment of the organization that uses it (providing the goods needed);
2. from the standpoint of a sustainable external environment (analysis of the methods and qualifications needed for production and performance of services).

However, interpretation of technology should be much broader. Limitation of this concept to the means and ways of carrying out basic activities is far too restrictive. The term should also cover the scope of its handling, which includes sustainable management processes. The diversity of technologies in today's world provides the ability to efficiently perform tasks assigned to specific organizational units (e.g. sustainable production, sustainable logistics, sustainable marketing, sustainable sales, etc.). It is therefore advisable to identify one main technology with which a majority of the project tasks is to be carried out, so that the company can generate the greatest sustainability in its added value. Every company, also in the sustainable development concept, should ensure exchange of information between its individual departments and the external environment; therefore, the information system of a given organization should be properly selected according to its organizational structure and to the conditions in which it operates (Nogalski and Ronkowski 2007: 86). This is extremely important in times of continuous and dynamic changes in the environment.

Information technologies (telecommunications and Internet) are changing the environment and the modern world. In the modern world, operation of the economy and the society without the use of IT would be very difficult, if not impossible. The overarching objective of IT should be to sustainably support management processes, especially those related to environmental and social aspects.

For information technologies to function properly, they must have a set of IT tools that make it possible to create new databases and to update them. J. F. Lyotard argues that databases change the way knowledge is acquired, qualified, disseminated, and used, which results in an evolution of the society. He also stresses that the development of technology has shifted the focus from goals to means of achieving them (McAuley, Duberley and Johnson 2007: 259–260).

The past decades have seen a very rapid development of information technologies, leading to a convergence that has blurred the distinction between telecommunications, IT, and media. At the same time, technological convergence has had an impact on cooperation activities between entities that deal with its different areas. Currently, we are also witnessing a very fast development of digital techniques. According to A. Grove, "the world is heading into digital space. With digital infrastructure, distance will no longer matter" (Grove 2003: 61). A. Grove also claims that the borders between the United States and the rest of the world will be minimized, since national borders are not a barrier to digital technologies and talented individuals living in different corners of the world contribute to their development (Grove 2003: 61). Therefore, the question is: should we not aim to use sustainable information technologies in managing projects on a global scale to achieve concrete benefits (Figure 5.3)?

Although a lot of attention is paid nowadays to advanced technologies, why are these not sustainable technologies? The problem lies in defining sustainability criteria for classifying technologies as advanced or not advanced. The difficulties arise from constant changes in and modifications to existing technologies. A sustainable technology is a technology that changes organizational systems without requiring the use of management that is the condition for productivity, efficiency, quality, or motivation of the employed staff. According to the criteria for qualification of technologies proposed

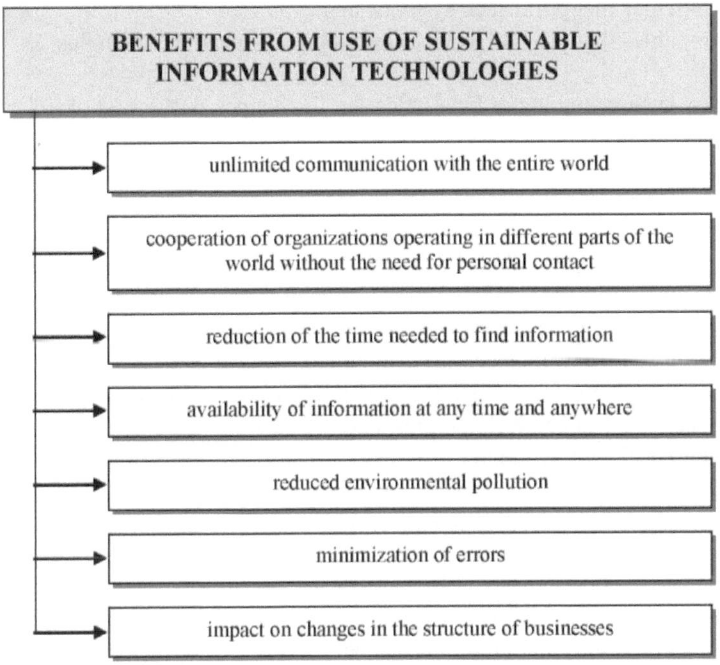

FIGURE 5.3 Benefits from use of sustainable information technologies. (Own work.)

by K. Weick, the contemporary qualification of technologies differs from those proposed earlier and the aforementioned author describes it as (Weick 1990: 1–44):

- stochastic – the interactions between the vast number of components leads to unpredictability of the processes taking place with the involvement of these technologies;
- continuous – technologies are subject to constant change and, consequently, users are obliged to constantly improve expand their knowledge related to their application and to implement constantly modernized procedures;
- abstract – advanced technology processes take place in the real world and in the minds of users, and the effects of its operation are not fully visible to users.

In view of the increasing scope of application of modern advanced technologies, steps have been taken to identify criteria that would make it possible to specify groups in this segment. C. A. Brook has divided companies that use advanced technologies into the following groups (Brook 1983):

- companies that carry out their tasks and grow in the area of advanced technologies;
- companies that make products that involve advanced technologies;

- companies that build such systems; and
- companies that provide services based on advanced technologies.

In the past, new technologies have often led to changes in the way of life of people and the operating principles of organizations. A prospective assumption can be made that the existing technologies and those that will be used in the future will contribute to similar important changes, also with regard to sustainable project management (Kozłowski 2010).

This is where the directions of development of advanced technologies and their impact on economic and social life in the concept of sustainable development should be outlined. As these directions depend on many factors, it is necessary to identify the determinants that influence the development of advanced technologies and those that prevent it. These factors are the organization's environment, which forces the development of advanced technologies, and the barriers (Figure 5.4).

Technological and economic progress in relation to the natural environment is minimal (Grądzki and Matejun 2009: 4). Work on the next versions of technological solutions will certainly be focused on minimizing their burdensome impact on the natural environment, as well as on their faultless operation and user safety. Recently, more and more attention has been paid to the use of so-called clean production technologies. They enable production processes to run in harmony with the environment, without any pollution, and enable the use of non-hazardous components during production processes, thus reducing the risk of degradation and contamination of the environment. R. Grądzki has qualified these technologies as tools for implementing sustainable development (Grądzki 2008: 6). This position results in major changes in, among other things, sustainable project management processes, sustainable production processes, sustainable selection of raw materials, and development and implementation of sustainable recycling of used products. Advanced technologies contribute to increased demand, reduced product prices, faster growth of companies, and increased profits. Productivity and competitiveness depend on the pace of technological progress, but is this progress sustainable? This applies not only to organizations, but also to the entire country, which places great emphasis on the development of advanced technologies that stimulate economic growth, thus enabling improvement of the financial situation of its citizens. Advanced technologies are rapidly spreading in the era of globalization and thus provide an opportunity for economic growth on a global scale (Jay 2000: 302). Those who use advanced technologies are often very enthusiastic about them because they are rightly convinced that they improve their professional project work and make their private lives easier and more interesting. However, it is worth noting that only sustainable implementation of advanced technologies enables organizations to achieve positive economic results.

New decisions are made not only when selecting a technology, but also when extending or updating it; therefore, it is very important to ensure proper management that takes into account the concept of sustainable development. When choosing to implement a new advanced technology in a company, its further development should be taken into account. This task is difficult and requires the decision makers to have appropriate knowledge.

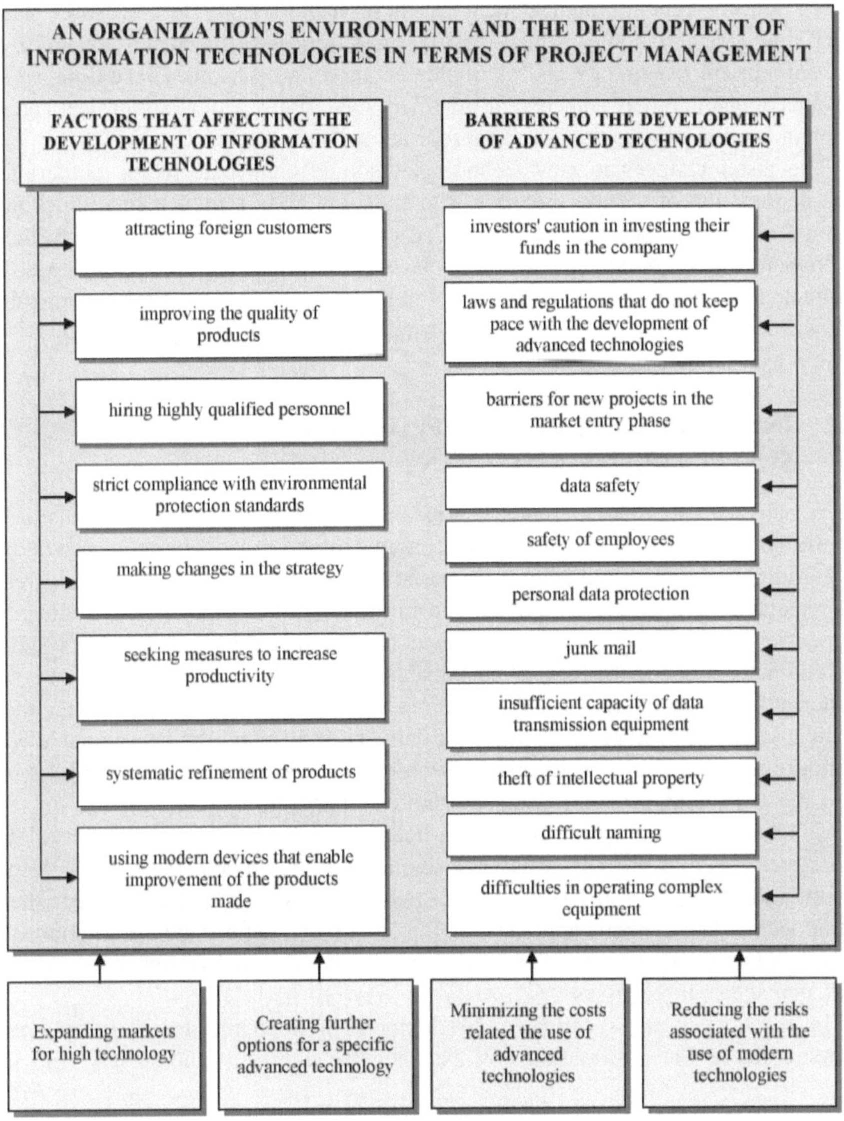

FIGURE 5.4 The impact of an organization's environment on the development of information technologies in project management. (Own work based on Kozłowski 2010.)

It is worth noting that, in the concept of sustainable development, through the use of newer technologies, technological progress contributes to:

- an increase in the functionalities of manufactured products;
- an improvement of their quality;
- a reduction of the production costs; and
- a reduction of adverse environmental impact;

which require rational management of these technologies (Rokita 2005: 217). Such management should include the two most important stages, i.e., selection of the appropriate technology and its implementation and start-up. Every time a new advanced technology is launched or modified, it is usually a standard project and its implementation enables the use of appropriate tools to manage it.

The faster changes in new technologies should contribute to the obliteration and degradation of certain sectors of the economy and its implementation should force a change in the expectations placed on the management. The effectiveness of implementation of changes that take place as a result of upgrades of the existing technologies depends on the knowledge and experience in the field of sustainable management from the perspective of information technologies.

5.2 INFORMATION SYSTEMS APPLIED TO SUSTAINABILITY ASSESSMENT

Sustainable development is a dynamic balance between three types of goals: economic, social, and environmental. The economic dimension is economic growth that is not inhibited, but stimulated by increased efficiency and technological progress. The social dimension is an improvement in the quality of life. The environmental dimension is elimination of harmful effects of human activity. Information systems for computer-based assessment of sustainable development are a collection of components that work together to collect data in a sustainable way (input), change their content and shape (processing), transmit data and information in a sustainable way (output), as well as provide feedback, in order to achieve the intended goal, taking into account social, economic, and environmental aspects (Figure 5.5).

The static approach presented herein defines a multi-level structure that allows the system user to process sustainable input information into the desired output information using appropriate procedures and models with a balance between these components. The dynamic approach, on the other hand, defines the information system based on the structure of the sphere of real processes and the sphere of sustainable management processes.

In the concept of sustainable development, it becomes necessary to know the sources of the information flow between the economy, the society, and the

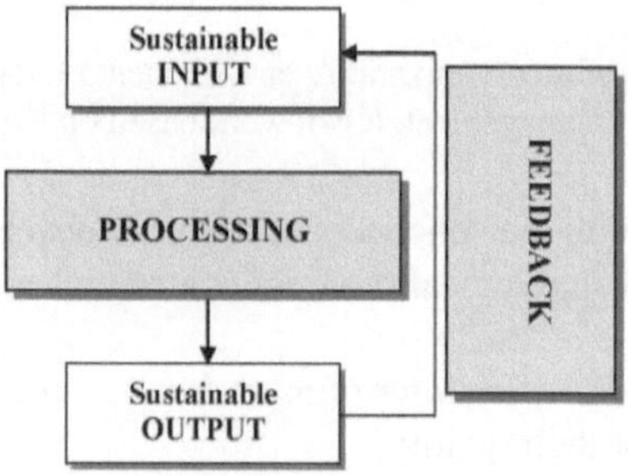

FIGURE 5.5 Components of a sustainable information system. (Own work.)

environment, and, above all, to make the information channels more unobstructed. Omissions and gaps in the flow of information lead to conflicts and errors, the consequence of which is usually the deterioration of the quality of a product or a service.

Sustainable economic growth depends on the profitability of organizations and on maximum use of human resources, raw materials, and financial resources, as well as on proper adaptation of projects to needs, sustainable effective management, and sustainable planning and control. Sustainable social development depends on the perception of the needs of the entire society. Sustainable environmental development, on the other hand, requires safe use of natural resources and avoidance of environmental degradation (Abidin and Pasquire 2007: 277).

An environmental information system must contain data that reflects the phenomena taking place throughout the system and should follow the common scheme used to investigate the problem, referred to as a DPSIR. DPSIR is a model based on the relationship between the drivers (D), the pressure exerted on the environment (P), the state (S), the impact on health and environment (I), and the responses (R). This model contains (Figure 5.6):

- information about the drivers;
- information about the pressure exerted on the environment;
- information about the state of the environment;
- information about the impact of the environment on health and development; and
- information about the social responses to the phenomena taking place.

Environmental information systems can be classified into two groups (Sej-Kolaska 2002):

- traditional systems, which are large databases that contain information on specific topics, without relationship to space;
- systems based on the GIS technology (geographical information system) – the data collected in the systems is spatial in nature (it refers to space).

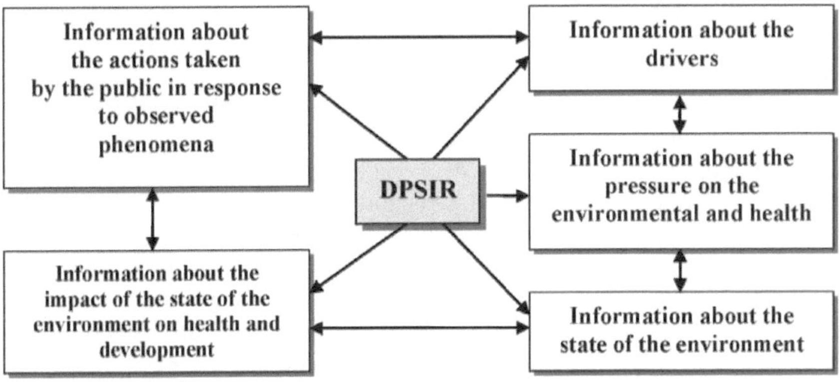

FIGURE 5.6 Information in the DPSIR model. (Own work based on Krupanek 2004.)

Standard systems are data banks that contain a variety of data, not only data related to environmental protection. They operate in various government agencies, banks, and institutions.

The best developed information system is currently the business information system, which is the most advanced tool for collecting, processing, and sharing information. This is undoubtedly due to the globalization of the economy, which creates the need for quick and effective decision-making. This system allows users to ask interactive questions, analyze spatial information, and edit data on maps.

Another group of information systems for assessment of sustainable development in the social dimension should be applications that will contribute to the creation of an information society, taking into account the growing importance of information resources among all social goods, greater access to information, changing social preferences, and changes involving unlimited communication. The complexity of the socio-economic system that results from sustainability depends on the individual subsystems that constitute its parts, the inter-relationships between its components, and the pace of change. Since the social system and the economic system are closely interlinked, they are usually analyzed together. Changes in the social system affect the economic system and vice versa, so they can be direct or indirect.

An extremely important feature of information systems is the possibility of their integration, which can take place on two levels: inside the organization and outside, by connecting the internal systems of a given organization with systems located in their surroundings (Kolbusz 2005). The intensive development of information systems makes them applicable in every area of economic activity. However, in order for management to be comprehensive and seamless, they should not only apply to one system. This would create the need for systems that integrate data processing throughout the organization. Functional and physical integration are two types of information system integration. Integration on the functional level allows all functions to be used, thanks to a single, properly selected interface. On the other hand, integration on the physical level takes place during a complex combination of components of integrated IT systems in the software and hardware area (Kolbusz 2005). Full integration is only possible with modular systems that guarantee preservation of elements of sustainable development (Figure 5.7).

Today, as a result of the globalization of business activity and the increasing capacities of advanced information technologies, integration between organizations is becoming increasingly important for sustainable development. Integration of IT systems of many organizations (external integration) is possible through the development of the Internet. In order to introduce selected concepts and instruments of environmental protection for sustainable development in a company in an effective and targeted manner, technical information support systems are used. The best support is provided by systems that provide information on the state of the environment used in a company (BUIS). The BUIS system enables targeted formulation, control, and determination of values, as well as presentation of data relevant for environmental protection in a company (Arndt 2013). Some authors treat BUIS systems and eco-controlling as synonyms. The authors of the book interpret the BUIS system more broadly as any IT solution that is used in a company to compare data on the environmental impact of its activities, thus supporting various and complex tasks related to

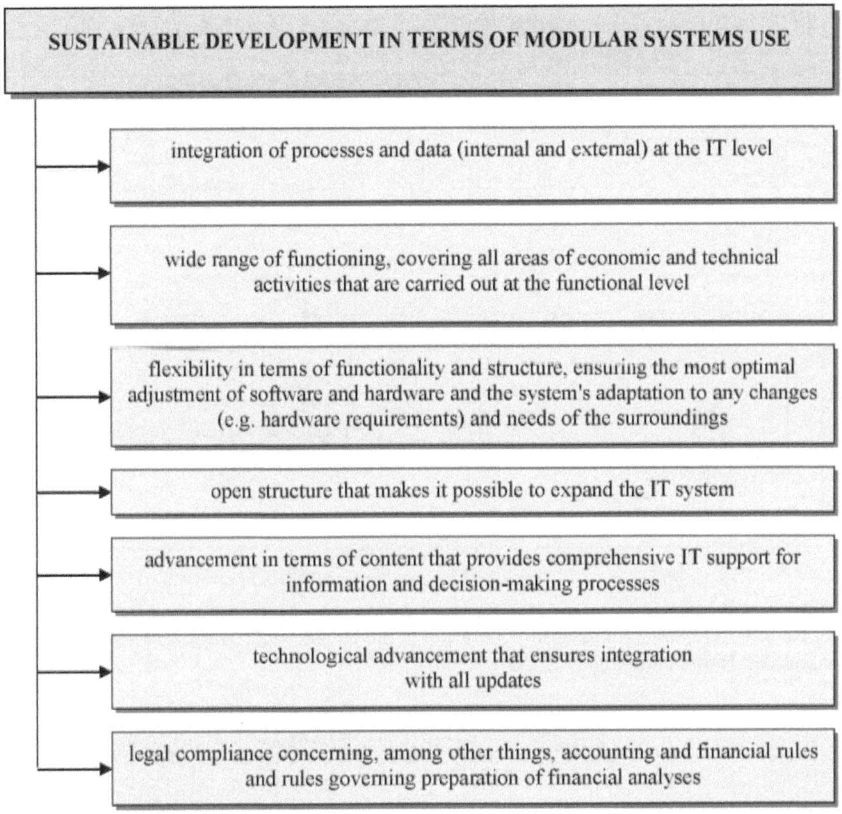

FIGURE 5.7 Sustainable development in terms of modular systems use. (Own work based on Kolbusz 2005.)

environmental protection and eco-controlling (Isenmann and Rautenstrauch 2007). BUIS systems are therefore responsible for the exchange of data and information in three areas: company, electronic data processing, and environmental protection. Furthermore, they can contribute to integration of environmental protection in certain areas of a company's activity, such as sustainable sourcing, sustainable production, etc. (Möller and Schaltegger 2012). However, the choice of a BUIS system is also determined by the selected supporting instrument. In addition to a quantitative depiction of materials and energy flows, individual BUIS systems (e.g. Audit® and Umberto®) offer a graphical presentation in the form of so-called program operation images, as shown in Figure 5.8 and enable identification of complex structures and relationships between processes. Based on the amount of materials and energy, calculations or simulations can be performed. The result often takes the form of environmental balance sheets. In addition to the amount of materials and energy, the associated costs can also be presented graphically. Figure 5.9 shows, using the example of the Umberto® software, the distribution of the costs of materials and energy, as well as other cost components, in the form of a Sankey diagram. The width of the

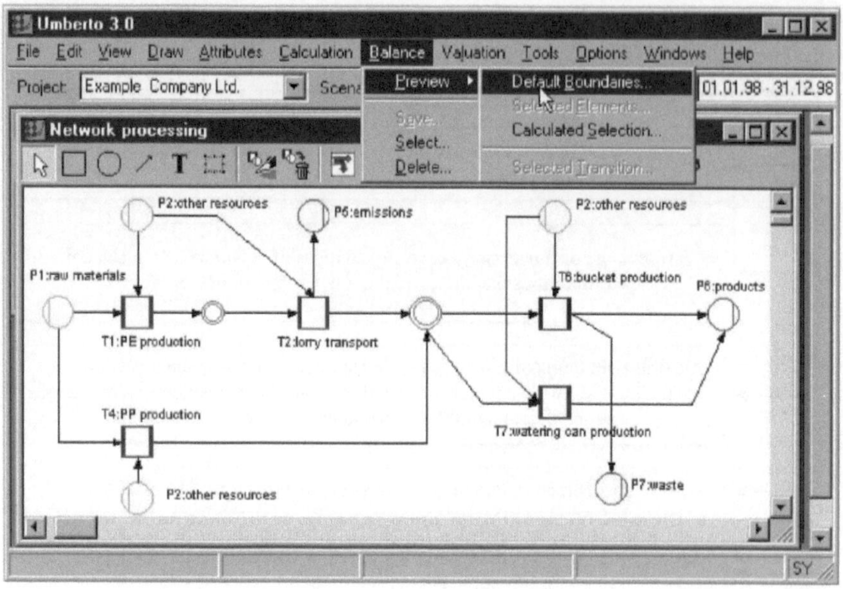

FIGURE 5.8 Depiction of program operation in the Umberto software. (Own work based on Brzozowska, Bubel and Pabian 2015.)

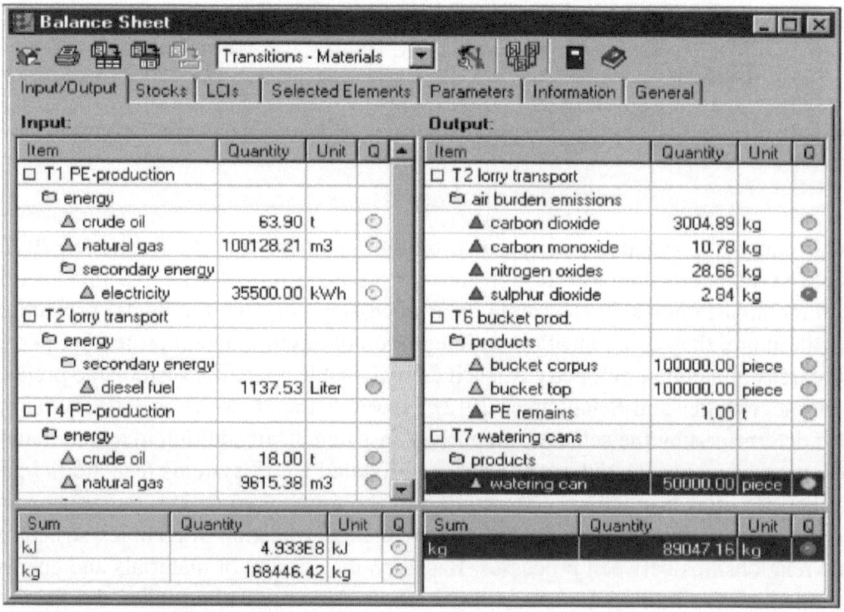

FIGURE 5.9 An environmental balance sheet in the Umberto® software. (Own work based on Brzozowska, Bubel and Pabian 2015.)

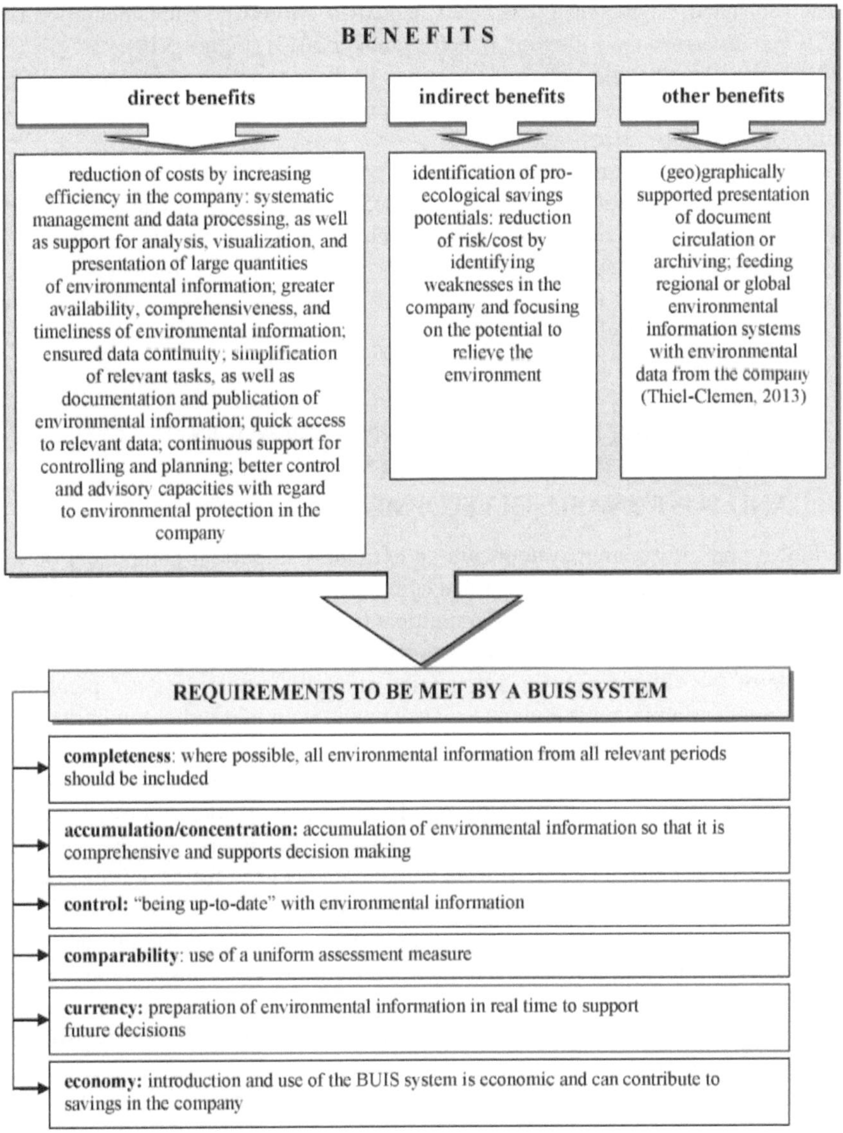

FIGURE 5.10 Benefits of implementation of a BUIS system. (Own work based on Brzozowska, Bubel and Pabian 2015.)

arrow indicates the size of the cost, while the colors of the arrows indicate the type of material or energy. In addition, individual BUIS systems (e.g. Umsys® software) contain geo-information modules that present environmental data in map-based geo-information systems to provide insight into the most common data volumes. This allows the user to quickly find out where, with what results, and what sampling has been carried out in the company or where the various waste treatment plants store waste (Solsbach, Lipnitskaya and van Vliet 2013). Moreover, implementation of a BUIS system brings the following benefits (Junker 2013) (Figure 5.10).

However, these requirements are contrary to the estimation of the costs of their use, e.g. with regard to completeness of data presentation, which relativizes the firm nature of the requirements.

Companies that care about the environment get better business results (Brzozowska, Kalinichenko and Minkova 2015: 7–29). IT is nowadays an excellent instrument for implementing sustainable development strategies. Sustainable development enables cost reduction, generates new revenue streams, improves the competitive position, and at the same time reduces the ecological footprint, i.e., the use of natural environmental resources.

5.3 THE RELATIONSHIP BETWEEN INFORMATION SYSTEMS, PROJECT MANAGEMENT SYSTEMS, AND SUSTAINABLE DEVELOPMENT FEATURES

Technical and information systems are an extremely important component of support for environmental management in a company. There are many different options for their implementation that perform multiple functions, which, when considered in relation to the effects of implementation of systems that provide information about the state of the environment in a company, strongly emphasize the typical areas of their application in environmental management, with particular emphasis on the assessment of their practical significance.

Implementation of IT systems used for project management in terms of sustainability is a very important stage in the whole process of creation of effective operation of companies. Knowledge of software packages, the directions of their progress, and the areas in which they can be used is the main decision factor in implementing such systems.

IT systems were initially developed mainly for specific organizations or specific computer hardware makers. They were intended to improve the level of management of the core business. The dynamic development in the field of IT applications for management purposes has contributed to the creation of highly specialized software packages that support more and more management areas. In terms of the management areas they support, the systems are divided into: partial systems (so-called segmented systems), systems that covering one area, and systems that cover many areas, as shown in Figure 5.11.

Project management requires appropriate skills and tools, and consequently: sustainable management of the project plan, sustainable management of project execution, sustainable project risk management, sustainable project quality management, and reporting on project progress. IT is an industry that bases its activity primarily on execution of projects, and the products created in this industry are the result of specific projects (Parsons 2002) (Figure 5.12).

The ever-growing importance of sustainable development contributes to the growing importance of project management issues, especially in the IT sector. The classification of IT projects is shown in Figure 5.13.

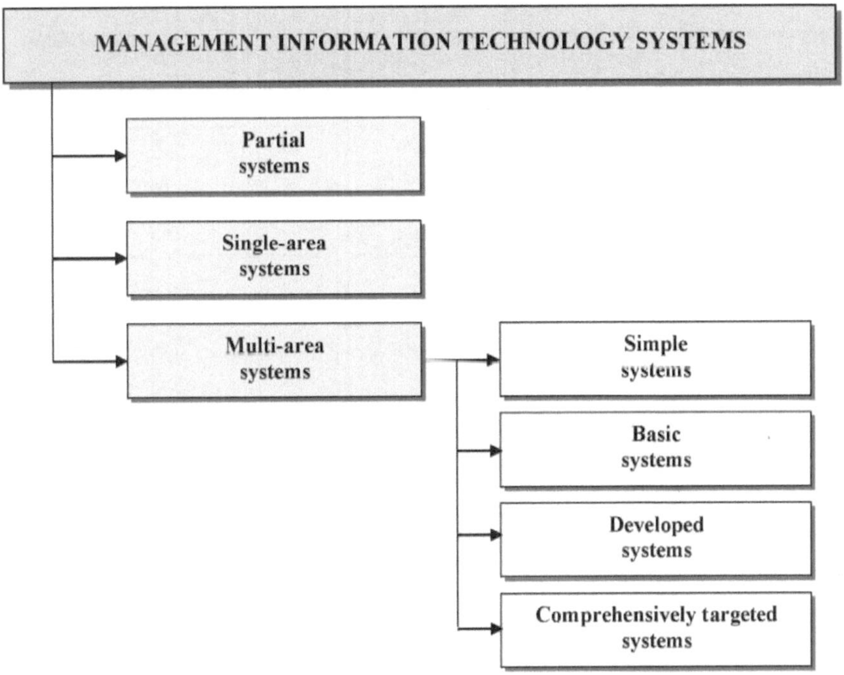

FIGURE 5.11 Division of management IT systems. (Own work based on Krupanek 2004.)

The civilizational changes taking place in the society require a continuous increase in the level of computerization in all branches of the economy (Ziemba 2013: 401). Organizations, which operate in an ever-changing environment, are forced to seek new solutions that will increase their competitiveness in the marketplace and create the conditions for greater financial benefits. Priority should be given to use of modern information technologies, which contribute to the generation of specific gains.

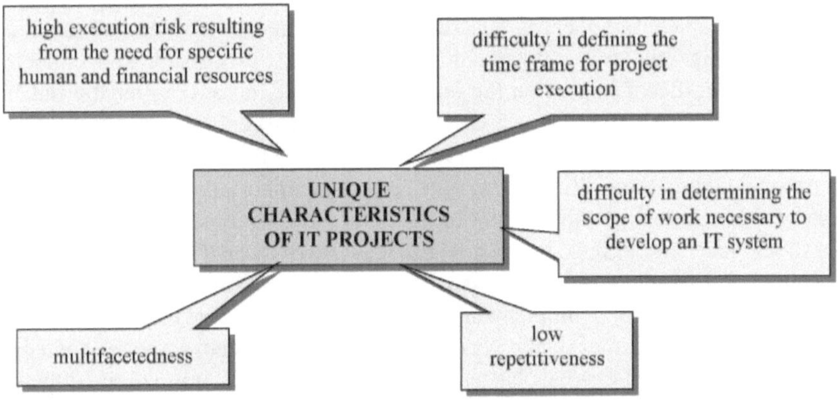

FIGURE 5.12 Unique characteristics of IT projects. (Own work based on Parsons 2002.)

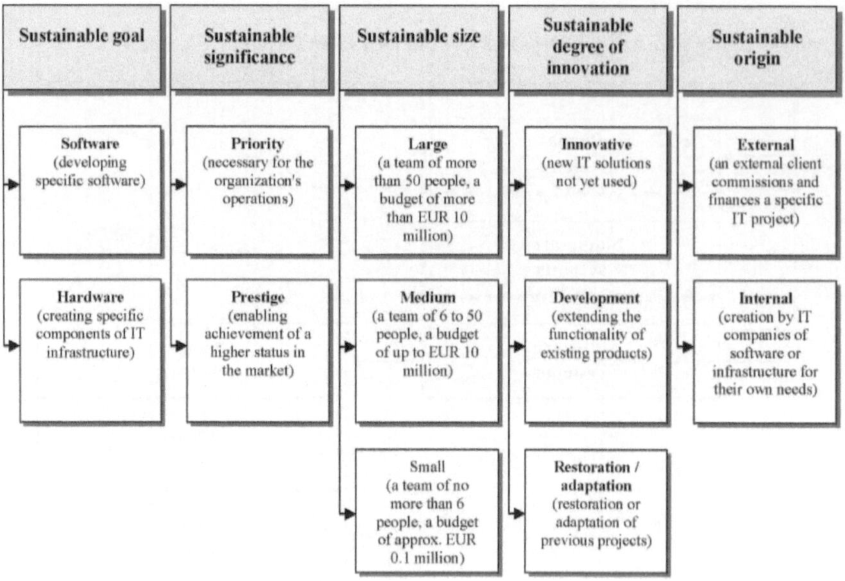

FIGURE 5.13 Classification of IT projects. (Own work based on Frączkowski 2003.)

These technologies should be environmentally friendly and their actions should be aimed at reducing the negative impact of the civilizational evolution on the environment and at rational and sustainable use of resources (Płaczek 2012: 83).

Development in practically every area of life depends on implementation of new information technologies. Computerization provides access to almost all areas of social life and eliminates digital exclusion. The modern civilization is increasingly trying to implement the vision of a sustainable information society and sustainable development aims to create a vision of civilization that is oriented towards achieving specific economic, social, and environmental goals (Hilty and Hercheui 2010: 227–235).

An inseparable component of sustainable development is information technologies that change the way information is transmitted, processed, and collected, and have a significant impact on the economic, social, and environmental balance (Szkudlarek and Milczarek 2014: 232). As mentioned earlier, the concept of sustainable development is based on minimal interference with the resources of the natural environmental and their rational use. Since it is very important for the environment to survive in the best possible condition for future generations, the current population should take care of it, so as not to cause loss and damage (Gechev 2005: 1). The concept of sustainable development in the period of globalization and rapid growth is more and more willingly implemented and becomes a vision of the development of a wealthy society (Adamczak and Nitkiewicz 2007: 14). Human activities contribute to pollution. This applies to air, water, and soil. In order to minimize the effects of such activities, modern IT solutions are used to support sustainable development. Computerization can only have a positive impact on sustainable development if it determines the negative impact and only those projects that are sustainable will bring benefits to the society. Therefore, the most important tasks are those that ensure (Szkudlarek and Milczarek 2014: 235):

- sustainable but constant monitoring of energy consumption;
- minimized energy consumption in buildings; and
- integrated sustainable management of project processes.

Computerization and implementation of IT technologies are the basic assumptions for the development of the economy and the society in the area of innovative forms of management (Abramowicz 2013). The relationship between them is shown in Figure 5.14.

In modern times, distance is not an obstacle to transmitting any information, which is one of the most valuable resources. The society in the era of computerization and development of information technologies is more and more often referred to as information society, where information is the most important element of activity in the economic and social spheres and the changes taking place in them. Nowadays, it is increasingly common for all information (such as image, sound, etc.) to be saved and quickly shared through a computing cloud and this aspect should be used in and implemented for project management, especially in the context of sustainable development. Thanks to computerization, economic and social capital should also be built efficiently.

The idea of sustainable development also involves use of the available resources to achieve efficiency, savings, and effectiveness, while avoiding a harmful impact on the environment. Sustainability plays a major role in almost all areas of life. The contemporary development of technologies involves constantly new and improved forms of information circulation and IT systems. Computerization also plays an important role in sustainable development, including its three main aspects. In social terms, it facilitates communication, in economic terms, it helps minimize costs and save time, and in environmental terms, it saves natural resources.

Flow of information is one of the most important factors that determine the level of socio-economic development. Competent and effective information management

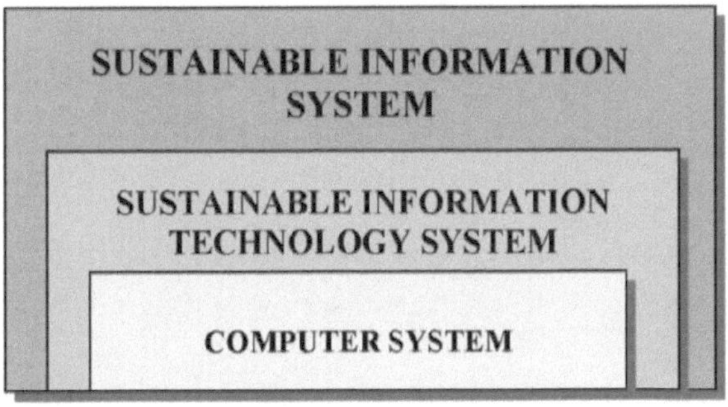

FIGURE 5.14 The relationship between information systems, IT systems, and computer systems. (Own work based on Florek and Klimasara 2003.)

in the area of the economy, the society, and the environment is the starting point for efficient, sustainable, and long-term development in a knowledge-based economy.

To sum up the discussion concerning project management in the concept of sustainable development in terms of IT, it should be stated that (Brzozowska, El. Emary and Bubel 2020: 40):

- advanced technologies are an indispensable tool in the modern world;
- conscious use of new technologies requires having the relevant skills;
- when selecting new technologies, their capabilities should be adapted to current needs and the possibility of integration with those already existing in the organization should be checked;
- the existence of technological areas must be taken into account in order to properly select the technology to be used for projects at a later stage;
- the existing widely available solutions, which are based on advanced information and communication technologies, enable effective management of the knowledge gained during execution of projects; and
- the technologies should be properly selected and managed to ensure reaping the benefits of their use.

Organizations that operate based on the concept of sustainable development should take pro-environmental and pro-social aspects into account in their activities. In such organizations, a comprehensive, long-term approach to issues related to the acquisition, collection, and management of resources becomes necessary. The goals and tasks of the organizations should be correlated with the concept of sustainable development. The development of modern organizations depends to a large extent on their ability to use advanced information technologies whose functionality complies with environmental protection laws.

References

Aaker D. A., Kumar V., Day G. S. and Leone R. P. 2011. *Marketing Research*. New York, John Wiley & Sons (Asia) Pvt Ltd., p. 48.

Abidin N. Z. and Pasquire C. L. 2007. Revolutionize value management: A mode towards sustainability. *International Journal of Project Management*, vol. 25, p. 277.

Abramowicz M. 2013. *Społeczeństwo informatyczne a informatyzacja, konferencja zamykająca projekt: E-zdrowie w województwie świętokrzyskim, rozbudowa i wdrożenie systemów informatycznych w jednostkach służby zdrowia – etap I*. 8 October 2013, Kielce, ŚCO.

Acharya A. and Gupta M. 2019. Green marketing: The next marketing revolution. In: *Green Consumerism. Perspectives, Sustainability and Behavior*, edited by Malyan R. S. and Duhan P., USA, Canada, Apple Academic Press, CRC Press Taylor and Francis Group, p. 13.

Achua C. F. and Lussier R. N. 2010. *Effective Leadership*. United States, South-Western, Cengage Learning, pp. 6–8, 297.

Adamczak J. and Nitkiewicz T. 2007. *Programowanie Zrównoważonego Rozwoju Przedsiębiorstw*. Warsaw, PWE, p. 14.

Adamczyk J. 2009. *Społeczna Odpowiedzialność Przedsiębiorstwa. Teoria I Praktyka*, Warsaw, PWE.

Al Ali H. M., Ajmal M. M., Gunasekaran A. and Helo P. T. 2019. Managing change in constant evolving sustainable energy market. An exploratory study of motivators, enablers and barriers, *Sustainable Production and Consumption*, vol. 20, pp. 84–97.

Aldy J. E. 2019. Przyszłościowa strategia klimatyczna dla organizacji. *Harvard Business Review Polska*, October 2019, vol. 200, pp. 153–156.

Amrutha V. N. and Geetha S. N. 2020. A systematic review on green human resource management: Implications for social sustainability. *Journal of Cleaner Production*, vol. 247, pp. 1–65.

Andrews J. C. and Shimp T. A. 2018. *Advertising, Promotion, and Other Aspects of Integrated Marketing Communications*. United States, Cengage Learning, p. 10.

Araujo A. G., Carneiro A. M. P. and Palha R. P. 2020. Sustainable construction management: A systematic review of the literature with meta-analysis. *Journal of Cleaner Production*, vol. 256, pp. 1–11.

Arens W. F., Weigold M. F. and Arens C. 2009. *Contemporary Advertising*, Irwin, Boston, McGraw-Hill.

Ariansen P. 1999. Sustainability, morality and future generations. In: *Towards Sustainable Development: On the Goals of Development the Conditions of Sustainability*, edited by Lafferty W. M. and Langhelle O., London, McMillian, p. 84.

Arndt, H. K. 1997. *Betriebliche Umweltinformationssysteme: Gestaltung und Implementierung eines BUIS-Kernsystems*. Wiesbaden, Gabler.

Ashkenas R. and Manville B. 2019. *Harvard Business Review. Podręcznik Lidera*. Poznań, Rebis, p. 183.

Avlonas N. and Nassos G. P. 2014. *Practical Sustainability Strategies. How to Gain a Competitive Advantage*. New Jersey, John Wiley and Sons, Inc., pp. 3, 249.

Ayesha N., Yousuf Z. S. A., Muhammad W. and Ali K. S. 2020. Education for sustainable development (ESD): Effects of sustainability education on pre-service teachers' attitude towards sustainable development (SD). *Journal of Cleaner Production*, vol. 250, pp. 1–12.

Baines P., Fill C. and Page K. 2008. *Marketing*. New York, United States, Oxford University Press Inc., p. 369.

Beall A. E. 2019. *Strategic Market Research: A Guide to Conducting Research That Drives Businesses*, Third Edition, Kindle Edition.

Belch G. E. and Belch M. A. 2018. *Advertising and Promotion*, New York, Mc-Graw-Hill.

Belz F. and Peattie K. 2010. *Sustainability Marketing. A Global Perspective*, United Kingdom, A John Wiley and Sons Ltd Publication, pp. 13, 84, 209, 218.

Bendyk E. 2013. Co wiemy o zmianach klimatycznych. *Polityka*, special issue no. 9/2013 titled: *Zagrożenia dla globu. Jak ich uniknąć? Czas apokalipsy*, pp. 6–7, 11–12.

Bhandari D., Kr Singh R. and Garg S. K. 2019. Prioritisation and evaluation of barriers intensity for implementation of cleaner technologies: Framework for sustainable production resources. *Conservation and Recycling*, vol. 146, July 2019, pp. 156–167.

Bickler G., Morton S. and Menne B. 2020. Health and sustainable development: An analysis of 20 European voluntary national reviews. *Public Health*, vol. 180, March 2020, pp. 180–184.

Blakeman R. 2018. *Integrated Marketing Communication. Creative Strategy*, New York, Rowman and Littlefield.

BMW i3 catalogue, 2016, p. 20–23.

Boehm B. W. and Papaccio P. N. 1988. Understanding and controlling software costs. *IEEE Transactions on Software Engineering*, vol. 14, no. 10, pp. 1462–1477.

Bonvoisin J., Stark R. and Seliger G. 2017. Field of research in sustainable manufacturing. In: *Sustainable Manufacturing. Challenges, Solutions and Implementation Perspectives*, edited by Stark R., Seliger G. and Bonvoisin J., Berlin, Springer, p. 3.

Bossink B. 2012. *Eco-Innovation and Sustainability Management*. New York, London, Routledge Taylor & Francis Group, p. 1, 65

Hb Reavis. 2020. Natura wie, jak pracować lepiej. *Harvard Business Review Polska*, February–March 2020, vol. 2/3, pp. R11, R12.

Brinkmann R. 2016. *Introduction to Sustainability*. United Kingdom, John Wiley & Sons Ltd, pp. 1–2.

Brones F., Monteiro de Carvalho M. and de Senzi Zancul E. 2014. Ecodesign in project management: A missing link for the integration of sustainability in project development. *Journal of Cleaner Production*, vol. 80, 1 October 2014, pp. 106–118.

Brook C. A. 1983. *The Rapidly Changing Field of High-Technology Development and Science Park*. Paper presented to the School for Advanced Urban Studies at Oxford Polytechnic, Oxford.

Bruce K. and Nyland C. 2017. Human relations. In: *The Oxford Handbook of Management*, edited by Stark R., Seliger G. and Bonvoisin J., United Kingdom, Oxford University Press, p. 53.

Brzozowska A., Bubel D. and Pabian A. 2015. *Implementation of technical and information systems in environmental management*. 20th International Scientific Conference Economics and Management-2015 (ICEM-2015), Elsevier.

Brzozowska A., El. Emary I. M. M. and Bubel D. 2020. *Management of Organizational Culture as a Stabilizer of Changes. Organizational Culture Management Dilemmas*. Boca Raton, London and New York, CRC Press Taylor & Francis Group, p. 40.

Brzozowska A., Kalinichenko A. and Minkova O. 2015. *Ecological Perspective of IT in Environmental Management*. Poltava, Poltava State Agrarian Academy, pp. 7–29.

Buczkowski R. 2019. Pięć głównych błędów w oświetleniu miejsca pracy. *Harvard Business Review Polska*, February 2019, vol. 2, p. R16.

Bunikowska J. 2015. Przyszłość europejskiego sektora budowlanego. Zrównoważone budownictwo. www.parp.gov.pl, accessed on 18 March 2015.

Carbo J. A., Dao V. T., Haase S. J., Hargrove M. B. and Langella I. M. 2018. *Social Sustainability for Business*. New York and London, Routledge Taylor and Francis Group, pp. 9, 68, 138, 155–158.

Carson, R. 1962. *Silent Spring*, Boston, Houghton Mifflin Company.

Certo S. and Certo T. 2009. *Modern Management. Concepts and Skills*. London, Pearson Education International, pp. 121–123, 179–570.

Chapman C. and McDonnel Feit E. 2019. *R for Marketing Research and Analytics*, Springer.

Christensen C. and Raynor M. 2008. *Innowacje. Napęd Wzrostu*. Warsaw, Wydawnictwo Studio Emka, p. 53.

Cohen S. 2011. *Sustainability Management*. New York, Columbia University Press, pp. 1–21, 132–158.

Constanza R., D'Arge R., De Groot R., Farber S., Grasso M., Hannon B., Limburg K., Naeem S., O'Neill R., Paruelo J., Raskin R., Sutton P. and Van Den Belt M. 1997. The value of the world's ecosystem services and natural capital. *Nature*, vol. 387, pp. 253–260.

Crawford W. 2017. Collaborating. In: *Sustainable Business. A One Planet Approach*, edited by Jeanrenaud S., Jeanrenaud J. P. and Gosling J., United Kingdom, John Wiley and Sons Ltd., p. 150.

Daft R. and Marcic D. 2013. *Management: The New Workplace*. United States, South-Western Cengage Learning, pp. 9, 70, 158–600.

Daft R. L. and Benson A. 2016. *Management*. United States, Cengage Learning, pp. 211, 224, 430, 470, 482.

Dahlen M., Lange F. and Smith T. 2010. *Marketing Communications. A Brand Narrative Approach*, United Kingdom, John Wiley and Sons.

Dam Y. and Apeldoorn P. 2008. Sustainable marketing. In: *Critical Marketing. Contemporary Issues in Marketing*, edited by Tadajewski M. and Brownlie D., United Kingdom, John Wiley & Sons, p. 262.

Daniluk R. 2019. Kierujemy się najwyższymi standardami. *Harvard Business Review Polska*, special issue, p. R15.

Doh J. P. and Luthans F. 2018. *International Management*. New York, McGraw-Hill, pp. 124, 390, 398.

Douglas N. and Wykowski T. 2017. *Rethinking Management*. USA, Palgrave Macmillan, p. 260.

Eccles R. and Serafeim G. 2013. Zrównoważona strategia jako przewaga konkurencyjna przedsiębiorstw. *Przegląd Organizacji*, vol. 2013, no. 4, p. 48.

Eccles R. G. and Klimenko S. 2020. Rewolucja w inwestowaniu. *Harvard Business Review Polska*, February–March 2020, vol. 2/3, pp. 128–132.

Ekstrom K. M. 2015. *Waste Management and Sustainable Consumption. Reflections on Consumer Waste*. New York, Routledge, p. 1.

Elliott G., Rundle-Thiele S. and Waller D. 2012. *Marketing*. Australia, John Wiley and Sons Ltd., pp. 224–225.

Emery B. 2012. *Sustainable Marketing*. New York, Pearson, pp. 11, 80–81.

Epstein M. J. and Buhovac A. R. 2014. *Making Sustainability Work*. United Kingdom, Greenleaf Publishing, pp. 33–95.

Filho W. L., Skouloudis A., Brandli L., Lange A., Veiga S. L. and Rayman-Bacchus A. 2019. Sustainability and procurement practices in higher education institutions: Barriers and drivers. *Journal of Cleaner Production*, vol. 23110, September 2019, pp. 1267–1280.

Flasiński M. 2006. *Zarządzanie Projektami Informatycznymi*, Warsaw, PWN.

Fogel D. 2016. *Strategic Sustainability*. New York, Routledge Taylor & Francis Group, pp. 6–7.

Gareth R. J. and George J. M. 2011. *Essentials of Contemporary Management*, Irwin, New York: McGraw-Hill, pp. 297, 299–315.

Gechev R. 2005. *Sustainable Development. Economic Aspects*. Indianapolis, University of Indianapolis Press, p. 1.

Ghillyer A. 2009. *Management. A Real World Approach*. New York, McGraw-Hill, pp. 4–10, 56, 109–364, 421.

Gosling J., Kaipa P. 2017. In *Sustainable Business, A One Planet Approach*, edited by Jeanrenaud S., Jeanrenaud J. P. and Gosling J., United Kingdom, John Wiley and Sons Ltd., p. 88.

Govindan K., Shankar K. M. and Kannan D. 2020. Achieving sustainable development goals through identifying and analyzing barriers to industrial sharing economy: A framework development. *International Journal of Production Economics*, vol. 227, September 2020, pp. 1–13.

Grądzki R. 2008. Wstęp. In: *Rozwój zrównoważony. Uwarunkowania organizacyjne i techniczne*, edited by Grądzki R., Łódź, Wyd, Media Press, p. 6.

Grądzki R. and Matejun M. 2009. Wprowadzenie. In: *Rozwój Zrównoważony. Zarządzanie Innowacjami Ekologicznymi*, edited by Grądzki R. and Matejun M., Łódź, Wyd, Media Press, p. 4.

Gregor B. 2002. Przedsiębiorstwo i jego otoczenie w globalnym społeczeństwie informacyjnym. In: *e-Commerce*, edited by Gregor B. and Stawiszyński M., Bydgoszcz – ŁódźBydgoszcz – Łódź, Oficyna Wydawnicza Branta, p. 24.

Griffin R. and Pustay M. 2010. *International Business*. New York, Pearson Education Inc., p. 108.

Grove A. 2003. Nie potrafimy dostrzec potencjału. *Business Week*, vol. 2003, no. 9 (138), p. 61.

Hawken P. 1993. *The Ecology of Commerce: A Declaration of Sustainability*. New York, HarperCollins Publisher.

Hawken P., Lovins H. and Lovins A. 1999. *Natural Capitalism: Creating the Next Industrial Revolution*. Boston, Little Brown and Co.

Florek, J. and Klimasara, E. 2003. Techniki informatyczne a procesy transformacji zarządzania organizacją. *Telekomunikacja i Techniki Informacyjne nr*, vol. 3–4, pp. 106–116.

Frączkowski, K. 2003. *Zarządzanie projektem informatycznym. Projekty w środowisku wirtualnym Czynniki sukcesu i niepowodzeń projektów*. Wrocław, Oficyna Wydawnicza Politechniki Wrocławskiej.

Halila F. and Rundquist J. 2011. The development and market success of eco-innovations: A comparative study of eco-innovations in Sweden. *European Journal of Innovation Management*, vol. 14, no. 3, pp. 278–302.

Harrison M., Cupman J., Truman O. and Hague P. 2016. *Market Research in Practice: An Introduction to Gaining Greater Market Insight*, London, Kogan Page Limited.

Hatch M. J. 2002. *Teoria Organizacji*. Warsaw, PWN, p. 136.

Haugan G. 2014. *Sustainable Program Management*. New York, CRC Press, Taylor & Francis Group, pp. 9–19.

Hilty L. M. and Hercheui M. D. 2010. ICT and sustainable development. What kind of information society? In: What Kind of Information Society? Governance, Virtuality, Surveillance, Sustainability, Resilience, Proceedings of 9th IFIP TC 9 International Conference, HCC9, and 1st IFIP TC 11 International Conference, CIP 2010 Held as Part of WCC 2010, IFIP, edited by Berleur J., Hercheui M. D., Hilty L. M., Brisbane 2010, pp. 227–235.

Holden E., Linnerud K., Banister D., Schwanitz V. J. and Wierling A. 2018. *The Imperatives of Sustainable Development*. London and New York, Routledge, Taylor and Francis Group, p. 11, 18, 20, 81–82.

http://jestemnaptak.pl/artykul/utrata-bioroznorodnosci, accessed on 14 March 2020.

http://klasterip.pl/wp-content/uploads/2016/11/aar-2.jpg, accessed on 18 March 2020.

http://laj.pl/transport/5012/grupa-hegelmann-kupuje-pojazdy-ciezarowe-napedzane-skroplonym-gazem-lng/.

http://naukawpolsce.pap.pl/aktualnosci/news%2C30020%2Cnawet-90-proc-powierzchniladowej-ziemi-moze-ulec-degradacji-do-2050-roku, accessed on 14 March 2020.

http://surowce.igo.org.pl/o-surowcach/surowce-na-wyczerpaniu/, accessed on 14 March 2020.

http://surowce.igo.org.pl/o-surowcach/surowce-na-wyczerpaniu/.
http://surowce.igo.org.pl/o-surowcach/zasoby-odnawialne-i-nieodnawialne/, accessed on 14 March 2020.
http://surowce.igo.org.pl/o-surowcach/zasoby-odnawialne-i-nieodnawialne/, accessed on 14 March 2020.
http://www.eere.energy.gov/vehiclesandfuels, accessed on 19 February 2012.
http://www.propertydesign.pl/architektura/104/nowosci_ikea_na_luty_marka_zacheca_do_zrownowazonego_stylu_zycia,27507.html, accessed on 21 March 2020.
http://www.rupprecht-consult.eu/uploads/tx_rupprecht/NICHES_overview_concepts_PL.pdf, accessed on 16 March 2020.
https://businessinsider.com.pl/finanse/raport-unicef-na-temat-ubostwa-wsrod-dzieci/rnrbm9c, accessed on 13 March 2020.
https://businessinsider.com.pl/technologie/nauka/koncza-sie-zasoby-naturalne-ziemi-ostrzega-bank-hsbc/s1w7cxj, accessed on 11 March 2020.
https://ec.europa.eu/eurostat/statistics-explained/pdfscache/14236.pdf, accessed on 14 March 2020.
https://eizba.pl/raport-green-generation-2020-green-e-commerce/.
https://finanse.wp.pl/kawa-w-kapsulkach-niebezpieczna-dla-srodowiska-organizacje-ekologiczne-apeluja-do-nestle-koncern-odpowiada-6111805322053761a, accessed on 19 March 2020.
https://forsal.pl/artykuly/1407981.zatrudnienie-w-gornictwie-rosnie-choc-wydobycie-spada.html, accessed on 6 April 2020.
https://forsal.pl/artykuly/1409732,tempo-wycinki-lasow-deszczowych-na-swiecie-raport.html, accessed on 14 March 2020.
https://greencom.pl/s22-certyfikaty.html, accessed on 24 April 2020.
https://mfiles.pl/pl/index.php/Skutki_bezrobocia, accessed on 13 March 2020.
https://moto.rp.pl/tu-i-teraz/29120-sprzedaz-aut-elektrycznych-na-swiecie-polska-daleko-w-tyle, accessed on 18 March 2020.
https://pim.pl/rewolucja-gazowa-w-transporcie-towarowym/, accessed on 21 March 2020.
https://pl.tradingeconomics.com/country-list/unemployment-rate, accessed on 13 March 2020.
https://polonia.nl/2019/03/07/holandia-sloneczna-droga/, accessed on 14 March 2020.
https://polskatimes.pl/te-wysypiska-smieci-sa-tak-wielkie-ze-zmiescilaby-sie-w-nich-polska-5-razy/ar/c11-13850860.
https://science.sciencemag.org/content/347/6223/1259855, accessed on 10 March 2020.
https://wlaczoszczedzanie.pl/ekolinki/miedzynarodowe-organizacje-ekologiczne/.
https://wlaczoszczedzanie.pl/ekozagrozenia/katastrofy-ekologiczne/najwieksze-katastrofy-ekologiczne-na-swiecie/, accessed on 12 March 2020.
https://wolnemedia.net/samochody-na-sprezone-powietrze/, accessed on 20 March 2020.
https://www.ekologia.pl/styl-zycia/oszczedzaj/5-najbardziej-ekologicznych-laptopow,8209.html, accessed on 21 March 2020.
https://www.europarl.europa.eu/news/pl/headlines/society/20180301STO98928/infografika-emisje-gazow-cieplarnianych-w-unii-europejskiej, accessed on 14 March 2020.
https://www.europarl.europa.eu/news/pl/headlines/society/20190313STO31218/emisje-co2-z-samochodow-fakty-i-liczby-infografika, accessed on 17 March 2020.
https://www.green-projects.pl/najwieksze-zagrozenia-dla-srodowiska-plastik-zmiany-klimatu-bioroznorodnosc/.
https://www.hicopy.gdansk.pl/porfolio-item/redukcja-kosztow-utrzymania/, accessed on 25 March 2020.
https://www.hicopy.gdansk.pl/porfolio-item/redukcja-kosztow-utrzymania/, accessed on 24 March 2020.
https://www.kopalnia.pl/kopalnia-wiedzy/jakosc-powietrza-na-swiecie-i-w-europie-gdzie-znajdziesz-najczystrze-powietrze-fkq3, accessed on 14 March 2020.

https://www.medonet.pl/zdrowie,choroby-cywilizacyjne-przyczyny-i-leczenie,artykul,1735188.html.

https://www.money.pl/gospodarka/mop-25-mln-bezrobotnych-wiecej-na-swiecie-szokujace-6470438699955841a.html, accessed on 13 March 2020.

https://www.motofakty.pl/artykul/liczba-samochodow-na-swiecie.html, accessed on 16 March 2020.

https://www.motofakty.pl/artykul/liczba-samochodow-na-swiecie.html, accessed on 16 March 2020.

https://www.rp.pl/Analizy-Rzeczpospolitej/310099988-Ekologia-to-nie-tylko-redukcja-emisji–z-wielkich-tirow.html, accessed on 16 March 2020.

https://www.rp.pl/Analizy-Rzeczpospolitej/310099988-Ekologia-to-nie-tylko-redukcja-emisji–z-wielkich-tirow.html, accessed on 16 March 2020.

https://www.rp.pl/Handel/191109729-Lavazza-wprowadza-ekologiczne-kapsulki-z-kawa.html, accessed on 20 March 2020.

https://www.trucks.com.pl/2020/03/16/solaris-kolejne-miasta-zamawiaja-wodorowe-autobusy/, accessed on 20 March 2020.

https://www.wfosgw.poznan.pl/kalendarz-ekologiczny/.

https://wyborcza.pl/TylkoZdrowie/1,137474,17025203,Co_jest_bio_a_co_jest_eko_Jak_rozpoznac_zdrowa_zywnosc.html, accessed on 22 March 2020.

https://ziemianarozdrozu.pl/encyklopedia/49/niszczenie-lasow-tropikalnych, accessed on 14 March 2020.

Husted B. 2005. Culture and ecology: A cross-national study of the determinants of environmental sustainability. *Management International Review*, vol. 2005, no. 45, pp. 349–371.

Isenmann, R. and Rautenstrauch, C. 2007. Horizontale und vertikale Integration Betrieblicher Umweltinformationssysteme (BUIS) (in:) Betriebswirtschaftliche Anwendungsszenarien uwf, *uwf UmweltWirtschaftsForum*, vol. 15, pp. 75–81.

Jain S., Gupta P. and Deepa 2019. Analyzing Long-term benefits in the face of higher upfront costs for green affordable housing: A study of Ghaziabad, UP (India). In: *Green Consumerism. Perspectives, Sustainability and Behavior*, edited by Malyan R. S. and Duhan P., USA and Canada, Apple Academic Press, CRC Press Taylor and Francis Group, pp. 200–206.

Janicka K. 2014. Zielone budynki biurowe na rynku nieruchomości w Polsce. *Kwartalnik Nauk o Przedsiębiorstwie*, vol. 2014, no. 1, p. 62.

Jay P. 2000. *Roads to Riches or the Wealth of Man*. London, Weidenfeld and Nicolson, p. 302.

Jaźwińska D. 2016. Efektywność strategii zrównoważonego rozwoju. Zeszyty Naukowe Politechniki Poznańskiej. *Organizacja i Zarządzanie*, vol. 2016, no. 71, pp. 159–161.

Jeanrenaud S., Jeanrenaud J. P. and Gosling J. 2017. Challenging: An overview of our one planet predicament. In: *Sustainable Business. A One Planet Approach*, edited by Jeanrenaud S. and Jeanrenaud J. P., United Kingdom, John Wiley and Sons Ltd., pp. 5–10, 18–19.

Jones G. and George J. 2011. *Essentials of Contemporary Management*. Inwin, New York, McGraw-Hill, pp. 189–247.

Jones M. 2010. *Sustainable Event Management: A Practical Guide*. London, Earthscan, p. V.

Junker, H. 2013. BUIS für den produktionsintegrierten Umwelt-schutz-Wunsch oder Wirklichkeit? (in:) IT-gestütztes Ressourcen- und Energiemanagement. (eds) Gómez J. M., Lang C., Wohlgemuth V. Springer Vieweg, Berlin, Heidelberg , 243-255

Juska J. M. 2018. *Integrated Marketing Communication. Advertising and Promotion in a Digital World*, New York, Taylor and Francis.

Karol A. and Mashood C. 2019. Eco-awareness: Imbibing environmental values in consumers. In: *Green Consumerism. Perspectives, Sustainability and Behavior*, edited by Malyan R. S. and Duhan P., USA and Canada, Apple Academic Press, CRC Press Taylor and Francis Group, pp. 21, 266.

Kerin R., Hartley S. and Redelius W. 2009. *Marketing*. New York, McGraw-Hill, p. 266.

Kinzer K. 2018. How can we help? An exploration of the public's role in overcoming barriers to urban sustainability plan implementation. *Sustainable Cities and Society*, vol. 39, pp. 719–728.

Kolbusz E. 2005. *Inżynieria systemów informatycznych w e-gospodarce*, Warsaw, Polish Economic Society.

Koprowska J. 2019. Zdrowy pracownik, silna firma. *Harvard Business Review Polska*, October 2019, vol. 10, pp. 134–136.

Kotler P., Armstrong G., Saunders J. and Wong V. 2002. *Marketing. Podręcznik europejski*, Warsaw, PWE, p. 59.

Kouchaki M. and Smith I. H. 2020. Etyczny wymiar kariery. *Harvard Business Review Polska*, February-March 2020, vol. 2/3, pp. 138, 141–142.

Kozłowski R. 2010. *Wykorzystanie zaawansowanych technologii w zarządzaniu projektami*. Łódź, Wyd, Uniwersytetu Łódzkiego, pp. 72–74.

Krupanek J. 2004. System informacji o środowisku i zdrowiu. In: *Środowisko a Zdrowie. Polityka, Zarządzanie, Komunikowanie*, edited by Janikowski R. Białystok, Wyd, Ekonomia i Środowisko.

Lenox M. and Chatterji A. 2018. *Can Business Save the Earth? Innovating Our Way to Sustainability*. California, Stanford University Press, p. 4, 61, 76.

Łepko Z. 2017. Wprowadzenie w problematykę konferencji pt. Theoria i praxis idei zrównoważonego rozwoju. In: Materials from Poland-wide Scientific Conference Teoria i praxis zrównoważonego rozwoju. 30 lat od ogłoszenia Raportu Brundtland Warsaw, UKSW – 20 March 2017, edited by Sadowski R. F. and Łepko Z., Warsaw, p. 45.

Lock D. 2009. *Podstawy Zarządzania Projektami*. Warsaw, Polskie Wydawnictwo Ekonomiczne, p. 11.

Longoni A. 2014. *Sustainable Operations Strategies*. Politecnico di Milano, Springer, p. V.

Lussier R. 2009. *Management Fundamentals: Concepts, Applications, Skill Development*, United States, South-Western Cengage Learning, pp. 95–96.

Marcelino-Sadaba S., Gonzalez-Jaen L. F. and Perez-Ezcurdia A. 2015. Using project management as a way to sustainability. From a comprehensive review to a framework definition. *Journal of Cleaner Production*, vol. 99, 15 July 2015, pp. 1–16.

Marnewick C. 2017. Information system project's sustainability capability levels. *International Journal of Project Management*, vol. 35, no. 6, August 2017, pp. 1151–1166.

Martin D. and Schouten J. 2012. *Sustainable Marketing*. New York, Prentice Hall, pp. 10, 171–173, 195.

Martin D. and Schouten J. 2014. *Sustainable Marketing*. United Kingdom, Pearson (First Edition).

McAuley J., Duberley J. and Johnson P. 2007. *Organization Theory: Challenges and Perspectives*. Harlow, Pearson Education, pp. 259–260.

Mirońska D. and Zaborek P. 2014. Polacy wobec marketingu społecznie zaangażowanego, *Marketing I Rynek*, 2014, no. 1, pp. 32–41.

Meister J. C. 2019. Najważniejszy przywilej służbowy. Naturalne światło. *Harvard Business Review Polska*, special issue, spring 2019, pp. 12–13.

Motosalon, November-December 2019, no. 6 (70), p. 31.

Möller A. and Schaltegger S. 2012. *Die Sustainability Balanced Scorecard als Integrationsrahmen für BUIS. (in:) Integriertes Umweltcontrolling*, edited by Tschandl M. and Posch A., Wiesbaden, Gabler Verlag, pp. 293–317.

Nogalski B. and Ronkowski R. 2007. *Współczesne przedsiębiorstwo. Problemy funkcjonowania i zatrudnienia*. Toruń, TNOiK Dom Organizatora, p. 86.

Omar O. 2009. *International Marketing*. New York, Polgrave McMillian, pp. 263–265.

Ottosson M. and Parment A. 2015. *Sustainable Marketing*. Lund, Studentlitteratur, p. 14.

Pabian A. 2008. *Promocja. Nowoczesne środki I Formy*. Warsaw, Difin, p. 29.

Pabian A. 2011. Ecological aspects of sustainability in building industry. In: Proceedings of the 3rd International Conference on Contemporary Problems in Architecture and Construction, Published by Institution of Engineering and Technology, edited by Song G., Liu L., Chen T. and Li F. Beijing, China, pp. 5–25.

Pabian A. 2012a. Działalność edukacyjna ośrodków akademickich w koncepcji sustainability. *Nauka i Szkolnictwo Wyższe*, vol. 2012, no. 1/39, p. 127.

Pabian A. 2012b. Rola Internetu w tworzeniu zrównoważonego społeczeństwa przyszłości. Zeszyty Naukowe nr 703, Szczecin University, Ekonomiczne Problemy Usług, no. 88, Szczecin 2012, p. 798.

Pabian A. 2013a. Zarządzanie przedsiębiorstwem w koncepcji sustainability. In: *Rozwój nauk o zarządzaniu. Kierunki i perspektywy*, edited by Kucęba R., Jędrzejczyk W. and Smoląg K., Częstochowa, Wydawnictwo Politechniki Częstochowskiej, p. 199.

Pabian A. 2013b. Zarządzanie w koncepcji sustainability – Ujęcie funkcjonalne. *Przegląd Organizacji*, vol. 2013, no. 10, p. 5.

Pabian A. 2015a. Koncepcja sustainability w działalności ośrodków edukacyjnych. In: *Edukacja dla zrównoważonego i trwałego rozwoju oraz społecznie odpowiedzialnego biznesu*, edited by Pollok A., Warsaw, Polish Economic Society, p. 185.

Pabian A. 2015b. Rola dyrekcji w promowaniu i wdrażaniu zasad sustainability w przedsiębiorstwie. *Przegląd Organizacji*, vol. 2015, no. 4, p. 7.

Pabian A. 2017a. Planowanie strategiczne z perspektywy sustainability. *Handel Wewnętrzny*, vol. 3, no. 368, p. I.

Pabian A. 2017b. Zrównoważone przedsiębiorstwo jako rezultat zmian organizacyjnych. *Przegląd Organizacji*, vol. 2017, no. 8, p. 12, 15.

Pabian A., Pabian A. and Brzeziński A. 2020. Young people collecting natural souvenirs: A perspective of sustainability and marketing. *Sustainability*, vol. 12, no. 2, pp. 1–12.

Pabian A. and Pabian B. 2012. Perspectives of development of sustainability conception in the aspect of cultural differences. *Ekonomika i Organizacja Przedsiębiorstwa*, vol. 2012, no. 2, p. 7.

Parsons S. 2002. *Game Theory and Decision Theory in Agent-Based Systems*, Dordrecht, Kluwer Academic Publishers.

Pinto J. K. and Patanakul P. 2017. Managing projects. In: *The Oxford Handbook of Management*, edited by Wilkinson A., Armstrong S. J. and Lounsbury M., United Kingdom, Oxford University Press, p. 219.

Płaczek E. 2012. Zrównoważony rozwój – Nowym wyzwaniem dla współczesnych operatorów logistycznych. *Prace Naukowe Politechniki Warszawskiej*, vol. 2012, no. 84, p. 83.

Pride W. and Ferrell O. 2016. *Marketing*. United States, Cengage Learning, p. 358.

Rajasekhar M. V., Challa K. A., Vijaylakshmi D. and Rajyalakshmi N. 2019. Communicating sustainability and green marketing: An emotional appeal. In: *Green Consumerism. Perspectives, Sustainability and Behavior*, edited by Malyan R. S. and Duhan P., USA and Canada, Apple Academic Press, CRC Press Taylor and Francis Group, pp. 229–239.

Rogall H. 2010. *Ekonomia zrównoważonego rozwoju. Teoria i praktyka*. Poznań, Wydawnictwo Zysk i S-ka, pp. 71–134.

Rokita J. 2005. *Zarządzanie Strategiczne. Tworzenie I Utrzymanie Przewagi Konkurencyjnej*. Warsaw, PWE, p. 217.

Rue L. W. and Byars L. L. 2009. *Management. Skills and Application*. Irwin, New York, McGraw-Hill, pp. 443–444.

Sej-Kolaska M. 2002. *Podstawy zarządzania informacją i środowisku*, Wrocław, Wyd, AE we Wrocławiu.

Sharma N. 2019. Innovation in green practices: A tool for environment sustainability and competitive advantage. In: *Green Consumerism: Perspectives, Sustainability and Behavior*, edited by Malyan R. S. and Duhan P., USA and Canada, Apple Academic Press, CRC Press Taylor and Francis Group, p. 212.

Siew R., Balatbat M. and Carmichael D. 2013. A review of building/infrastructure sustainability reporting tools (SRTs). *Smart and Sustainable Built Environment*, vol. 2, no. 2, pp. 106–139.

Silvius G. 2017. Sustainability as a new school of thought in project management. *Journal of Cleaner Production*, vol. 166, pp. 1479–1493.

Silvius G. A. J., Kampinga M., Paniagus S. and Mooi H. 2017. Considering sustainability in project management decision making: An investigation using Q-methodology. *International Journal of Project Management*, vol. 35, no. 6, pp. 1133–1150.

Solomon M. 2006. *Zachowania I Zwyczaje Konsumentów*. Gliwice, Wydawnictwo Helion, p. 605.

Solsbach A., Lipnitskaya S., van Vliet S. 2013. Internetbasierte Nachhaltigkeitsberichterstattung im Kontext des Umwelt-, Energie- und Ressourcenmanagements mit BUIS der nächsten Generation. In: *IT-gestütztes Ressourcen- und Energiemanagement*, edited by Gómez J. M., Lang C. and Wohlgemuth V. Berlin, Heidelberg, Springer Vieweg, pp. 421–431.

Steffen W., Richardson K., Rockstrom J., Cornell S. E., Fetzer I., Bennett E. M., Biggs R., Carpenter S. R., de Vries W., de Wit C. A., Folke C., Gerten D., Heinke J., Mace G. M., Persson L. M., Ramanathan V., Reyers B. and Sorlin S. 2015. Planetary boundaries: Guiding human development on a changing planet. *Science*, vol. 347, p. 736–746.

Szkudlarek P. and Milczarek A. 2014. Rola społeczeństwa informacyjnego w kreowaniu zrównoważonego rozwoju. *Ekonomia i Środowisko*, vol. 2014, no. 3, pp. 232, 235.

Szmith D. 2019. Jeśli opakowania to tylko zrównoważone. *Harvard Business Review Polska*, vol. 2019, special issue, p. R10.

Sieńkowska E. 2013. Zielony marketing na zielonym świetle. *Marketing w Praktyce*, no. 2, pp. 38–40.

Sustainable Manufacturing. 2017. *Challenges, Solutions and Implementation Perspectives*, edited by Stark R., Seliger G. and Bonvoisin J., Berlin, Springer.

Sustainable Design and Manufacturing. 2017. *Selected Papers on Sustainable Design and Manufacturing*, edited by Campana G., Howlett R. J., Setchi R. and Cimatti B., Berlin, Springer International Publishing AG.

Templar R. 2015. *The Rules of Management: A Definitive Code for Managerial Success*. New York, Pearson, pp. 32–33, 116, 208.

Thiele L. P. 2016. *Sustainability*. Cambridge, UK, Polity Press, pp. 200–201, 204.

van der Waal J. and Thijssens T. 2020. Corporate involvement in sustainable development goals: Exploring the territory. *Journal of Cleaner Production*, vol. 252, April 2020, pp. 1–11.

Varghese G. and Viswanathan L. 2019. Green practices for greener living: The road ahead. In: *Green Consumerism: Perspectives, Sustainability and Behavior*, edited by Malyan R. S. and Duhan P., USA and Canada, Apple Academic Press, CRC Press Taylor and Francis Group, p. 83.

Wajer J. 2019. Elektromobilność bez zasilania. *Harvard Business Review Polska*, December 2018–January 2019, vol. 12/1, p. 36.

Weick K. E. 1990. Technology as equivoque: Sensemaking in new technologies. In: *Technology and Organizations*, edited by Goodman P. S. and Sproull L. S., San Francisco, Jossey–Bass, pp. 1–44.

Werewka J. 2013. *Wybrane zagadnienia zarządzania projektami w przedsiębiorstwach informatycznych*, Cracow, AGH in Cracow.

Wilkinson A., Armstrong S. J. and Lounsbury M. 2017. Introduction and theoretical overview. In: *The Oxford Handbook of Management*, edited by Wilkinson A., Armstrong S. J. and Lounsbury M., United Kingdom, Oxford University Press, p. 1.

Witzel M., Organizing. 2017. In: *Sustainable Business: A One Planet Approach*, edited by: Jeanrenaud S., Jeanrenaud J.P. and Gosling J. United Kingdom, John Wiley and Sons Ltd., pp. 205–210.

Wright C. and Nyberg D. 2019. An inconvenient truth: How organizations translate climate change into business as usual. Academy of management journal, *2017*. In: Harvard Business Review Polska, February 2019, p. 20.

WWF International. 2016. Living Planet Report, 2016: Risk and Resilience in a New Era. Switzerland, pp. 6, 10, 13, 18.

WWF International. 2018. Living Planet Report, 2018: Aiming Higher. Grooten, M and Almond, R. E. A., Gland, Switzerland, WWF.

Yu T., Shi Q., Zuo J. and Chen R. 2018. Critical factors for implementing sustainable construction practice in HOPSCA projects: A case study in China. *Sustainable Cities and Society*, vol. 37, February 2018, pp. 93–103.

Ziemba E. 2013. Ku zrównoważonemu społeczeństwu informacyjnemu. *Roczniki Kolegium Analiz Ekonomicznych*, vol. 2013, no. 29, p. 401.

Index

T

U

V

W